Liberty Hyde Bailey

The Forcing Book

A manual of the cultivation of vegetables in glass houses. Vol. 1

Liberty Hyde Bailey

The Forcing Book
A manual of the cultivation of vegetables in glass houses. Vol. 1

ISBN/EAN: 9783337373702

Printed in Europe, USA, Canada, Australia, Japan

Cover: Foto ©Lupo / pixelio.de

More available books at **www.hansebooks.com**

THE
FORCING-BOOK

*A MANUAL
OF THE CULTIVATION OF VEGETABLES
IN GLASS HOUSES*

BY

L. H. BAILEY

New York
THE MACMILLAN COMPANY
LONDON: MACMILLAN & CO., Ltd.
1896

All rights reserved

COPYRIGHT 1896
BY L. H. BAILEY

Mt. Pleasant Printery
J. Horace McFarland Company
Harrisburg, Pa.

THE FORCING-BOOK

The Garden-Craft Series

THE HORTICULTURIST'S RULE-BOOK
PLANT-BREEDING
THE NURSERY-BOOK
THE FORCING-BOOK

Others in preparation

PREFACE.

ONE of the most interesting and significant evidences of the abiding expansion of horticultural business is the evolution of the glass house within the present century. It is only within the last one or two generations that the growing of plants in glass houses for the purpose of selling the product of bloom or of fruit has come to be important and widespread. The most recent part of the expansion, at least in this country, is the commercial growing of winter vegetables. It speaks well for the prosperity and refinement of our people when they are willing and able to purchase freely of the delicacies of the winter garden. This is one of those branches of agriculture which demands the nicest skill and the closest fellowship with plants. It is, therefore, one in which comparatively few people are fitted to engage, but it must, from the very force of civilization, be one of those occupations which shall gain impetus with time. If it is a business which demands much care and pains, then its promoters must be students. They will need helps. It is this thought which has produced this book.

The writer must hasten to say — what the attentive reader will soon discover — that he cannot consider himself to be an authority upon the subject. It has happened that he has been associated with considerable experimental work in the forcing of vegetables during the past few years, and he has endeavored to see much of the forcing industry of the country. In this time there has been a great accumulation of information and of notes which, since there is no adequate literature upon the subject, he has now set down in these pages. The book has been written for the commercial grower of winter vegetables, but the writer will be glad if it shall lead anyone to make the effort to grow the vegetables for his own table. The very obstacles which one must overcome make the effort all the more worth the while; and the satisfaction of growing a garden when the snow lies deep against the house is of the keenest and most unselfish kind.

The American writing upon vegetable-forcing is very recent. I have referred to most of it at various places in the text. It only remains to say that the basis of much of this book is the series of publications from the Cornell Experiment Station; and it is justice that I add a list of these papers. This list will also aid the student in tracing the bibliography of the literature of the forcing of plants. The Cornell bulletins upon the forcing of vegetables in glass houses (some of which are permanently out of print) are these: No. 28, Experiments in the Forcing of Tomatoes, June, 1891; No. 30, Some Preliminary Studies of the Influence of the Electric Arc Light upon Greenhouse Plants, August, 1891; No. 31, Forcing of English Cucumbers, September, 1891; No. 41, On the Comparative Merits of Steam and Hot Water for Greenhouse Heating, August, 1892; No. 42, Second Report upon Electro-Horticulture, September, 1892; No. 43, Some Troubles of Winter Tomatoes, September, 1892; No. 53, Œdema of the Tomato, May, 1893; No. 55, Greenhouse Notes (Third Report upon Electro-Horticulture, Winter Cauliflowers, Second Report upon Steam and Hot Water Heating), July, 1893; No. 94, Damping-Off, May, 1895; No. 95, Winter Muskmelons, June, 1895; No. 96, Forcing-House Miscellanies (Remarks upon the Heating of Forcing-Houses, Lettuce, Celery Under Glass, Cress in Winter, Forcing Eggplants, Winter Peas, Bees in Greenhouses, Methods of Controlling Greenhouse Pests by Fumigation, Treatment of Carnation Rust), June, 1895.

Whilst this manual discusses only the forcing of kitchen-garden vegetables, the essential principles which are set forth apply with almost equal directness to the forcing of plants for their bloom. It should be added, also, that it is the purpose of the book to treat only those crops which are raised to maturity in glass houses, so that the starting of plants for setting in the open, and all questions of hotbeds and coldframes, are omitted.

L. H. BAILEY.

ITHACA, N. Y., January 1, 1897.

CONTENTS.

CHAPTER I.

	PAGE
INTRODUCTORY SUGGESTIONS	1 to 15
General Remarks	1
Specific Remarks	4
The Category of Forcing Crops	4
Locations for Vegetable Forcing	8
Cost of Heat and Labor	9

CHAPTER II.

CONSTRUCTION OF THE FORCING-HOUSE	16 to 48
Types and Forms of Houses	16
Some of the Structural Details	24
The Frame	24
The Sash-bar	29
The Plate	30
The Gutter	33
Walls	33
Ventilators	35
The Glass and Glazing	36
Beds and Benches.	40
Heating	40
Steam and Hot Water	40
Piping	43
Flues and Stoves	46
Cost of Forcing-houses	46

CHAPTER III.

	PAGE
MANAGEMENT OF THE FORCING-HOUSE	49 to 92
Temperatures for the Various Crops	49
Soils for Forced Vegetables	50
The Question of Fertilizers	52
The Connecticut Experiments with Tomatoes	53
The Connecticut Experiments with Lettuce	61
On the Use of Fresh Stable Manure	62
Watering	65
Watering by Sub-irrigation	68
Construction of Beds and Benches for Sub-irrigation	69
Experiments with Lettuce and Other Plants	72
Conclusions	77
Ventilating and Shading	78
The Electric Light for Forcing-houses	80
Pollination	81
Insects and Diseases	83
Methods of Controlling Greenhouse Pests by Fumigation	86 to 92

CHAPTER IV.

LETTUCE	93 to 107
Temperature	94
Light	94
Beds and Benches	94
Soils	96
Growing in Pots	99
Sowing and Transplanting	101
A Grower's Remarks	102
Varieties	104
Enemies and Diseases	104

CHAPTER V.

	PAGE
CAULIFLOWER	108 to 114
Unsuccessful Experiments	108
The Successful Crops	109
Subsequent Experience	114

CHAPTER VI.

RADISH	115 to 126
Cornell Experience	115
Sowing	115
Soil	116
General Management	117
Varieties	120
Washington Experience	121
Houses Adapted to Growing Radishes	121
The Soil	122
Planting the Seed	122
Varieties to Plant	124
Preparing the Crop for Market	124
Approximate Yields per Square Foot	125
Temperature, Moisture, Insects and Diseases	125
Summary	126

CHAPTER VII.

ASPARAGUS AND RHUBARB	127 to 134
Asparagus	130
John Gardner's Method	132
Forcing in Hotbeds	132
Rhubarb	134

CHAPTER VIII.

MISCELLANEOUS COOL PLANTS	135 to 152
Pea	135
Experiments at Cornell	135

	PAGE
Celery	139
Salads, Pot-herbs, and Mints	141
Water-cress	141
Garden Cress	142
Parsley	142
Spinach	142
Dandelion	143
Mustard	143
Mints	143
Onion	144
Beets, Carrots and Turnips	145
Potato	145
Pepino	146
History and Description of the Pepino	147

CHAPTER IX.

TOMATO	153 to 183
The House	153
Soil and Fertilizers	154
Raising the Plants, and Bearing Age	155
Beds, Benches and Boxes	157
Training	160
Watering	161
Pollination	162
Second Crop	166
Yields and Prices	169
Varieties	172
Marketing	174
Animal Parasites	175
Diseases	177

CHAPTER X.

CUCUMBER	184 to 203
The English Forcing Type of Cucumber	184
General Requirements	186

CUCUMBER—

	PAGE
Training	188
Bearing Age	189
Varieties	190
Origin of this Type of Cucumber	192
Pollination—Ill-shaped Fruits	195
Crosses	199
Enemies	200
The White Spine Type of Cucumber	201

CHAPTER XI.

MUSKMELON . . . . 204 to 224
    The House 205
    The Soil 207
    Sowing and Transplanting 210
    Training 211
    Pollinating 214
    Varieties 215
    Yields and Markets 220
    Insects and Diseases 221

CHAPTER XII.

MISCELLANEOUS WARM PLANTS . . . . 225 to 244
    Bean 225
    Eggplant 228
    Pepper, or Capsicum 238
    Cyphomandra 241

CHAPTER XIII.

SUMMARIES OF THE MANAGEMENT OF THE VARIOUS CROPS . . . . 245 to 259

INDEX 260

THE FORCING-BOOK.

CHAPTER I.

INTRODUCTORY SUGGESTIONS.

GENERAL REMARKS.

THE growing of vegetables under glass for the winter market is one of the most special and difficult of all horticultural operations. It is a more uncertain and perplexing business than the growing of cut-flowers, because it is newer, less understood, there are comparatively few varieties of vegetables particularly adapted to winter forcing, and the markets are less extensive and more unstable. To succeed with forced vegetables requires great skill in the management of glass houses, close attention to every detail, and the complete control of all the conditions of plant growth. To these requirements must be added a thorough knowledge of the markets, and the ability to have the crop ready at any given time.

No amount of reading or study can make one a successful grower of plants under glass. He must first of all possess a love for the business, a determination to surmount all difficulties, and especially the ability and desire to give personal attention to all the details day by day. Having these requisites, reading and study will afford him most efficient aid by way of direction and suggestion. One who reads horticultural literature should bear in mind the fact that its value depends very much upon the reader. Instructions should suggest lines of work, and should explain and enforce the fundamental reasons for the various operations; but the directions are not to be rigidly and perfunctorily applied to the particular work in hand. The reader must check up the printed instructions with his own experiences.

Persons who succeed in the growing of fruits and vegetables in the field do not necessarily succeed with crops under glass. Success out of doors is often the result of favorable conditions of soil and weather; but under glass the grower must not only know the conditions which the plants require, but he must actually create those conditions. The skill of the horticulturist lies in his ability to override difficulties. Leonard Coates, a well-known horticulturist of California, has recently put this truth into an aphorism: "Let the conditions be adverse, and his measure of success will prove the man."

The person who desires to grow vegetables under glass for market must, first of all, count up the costs and the risks. Glass houses are expensive, and they demand constant attention to repairs. They are short-lived. The humid atmosphere and the high temperature engender decay. The heating is the largest single item of outlay in maintaining the establishment. Moreover, it is an item upon which it is impossible to economize by means of reducing the temperature, for a reduction of temperature means delayed maturity of the crop and, in the case of warmth-loving plants — like cucumbers, melons and tomatoes — it invites debility and disease. Labor is the second great item of expense in maintaining a forcing establishment. This, however, may be economized if the proprietor is willing to lengthen his own hours; but economy which proceeds so far that each one of the plants does not receive the very best of care, is ruinous in the end.

The risks in the forcing of vegetables are great. In the first place, there are risks of accidents, as fire, frosts and hail. There are risks of serious insect and fungous invasions. But, above all, there are risks arising from lack of experience and knowledge. One must discover the knack of ventilating, watering, heating and training adapted to every crop, and this can be learned only by patient work and study. Every failure should stimulate inquiry, and the operator should not rest until he has ascertained its cause.

It is imperative that the person who desires to grow vegetables under glass should begin in a small way. Let him begin with a small house — say 20 by 60 feet — and gradually feel his way, both in the growing of the plants and in the marketing of the product. If he is successful in a small house, he need have no hesitation in extending his area, for it is easier to control the conditions of temperature and moisture in a large establishment than in a small one.

As a rule, in all those industries in which a very superior product is to be obtained, and in which the risks are great, the rewards are good to those who succeed. Good winter vegetables, placed attractively upon the market at timely occasions, are sure of ready sales. Quite as many persons fail to market their products successfully as to grow them well. A forced vegetable is a luxury. It is a special product. Its sale depends, therefore, very much upon its beauty and attractiveness. Every tomato and melon should be neatly wrapped in clean, thin paper, and if each wrapper bear the name and address of the grower, so much the better. Great care must be taken to pack the product so that it shall not wilt, nor be touched by frost, nor bruised or soiled in transit. In short, the product must be dainty.

In general, it may be said that the common open market is rarely profitable for winter-forced vegetables, unless they are grown upon such a large scale that the grower controls the market, rather than the market the grower. The person who desires to make money from these crops should secure special markets for them, either by placing them directly in the families of the consumers, or consigning them to dealers who have a particular or fancy trade in such products. The choicer and rarer the product, the greater should be the care in finding a market for it. Common things are not worth great effort in the marketing, but uncommon things are worth nothing less than such effort.

A dealer in hothouse vegetables in New York writes that "most all forced vegetables bring good prices in winter, but they must be packed and shipped in first-class order. A good many people raise fine vegetables in winter, but they do not understand the packing, and the products are spoiled in shipping." The average prices of forced vegetables in the New York market for the winter of 1895-6 are given me by this dealer, as follows:

	Dec.	Jan.	Feb.
Lettuce . . . . per doz. .	$0 63	$0 50	$0 50
Cucumbers (forcing type) . . . . per doz. .	1 50	2 00	2 50
Peppers . . . per crate (1 bus.) .	$2 00 to 3 00	3 50	2 50
Beans . . . . per crate (1 bus.) .		2 00 $3 00 to 5 00	4 50
Tomatoes . . . . per lb. .	15 to 20	25	20 to 30
Beans, in bundles of 40	10 to	20 through the winter.	

"Chicory, escarole and romain salads generally bring good prices in winter."*

SPECIFIC REMARKS.

The category of forcing crops.—The vegetables which are forced to edible maturity under glass are conveniently distributed into two groups,—the "cool" plants, and the "warm" plants.

The cool plants are such as thrive best in a night tem-

---

* These three plants are not properly forced vegetables in the sense of being grown in glass houses, and are, therefore, not included in this book. They are grown in late fall, and are bleached in cellars or in frames; or, in the case of chicory, the roots (raised from spring-sown seeds) are dug in the fall and stored in a dark cellar, where the leaves soon start. The chicory may also be grown under benches much like asparagus, if it is kept dark in order to bleach it. Escarole is bleached endive. Romain salad is winter Cos lettuce. Sea-kale is often forced in frames after the manner of asparagus, and it might be managed in the forcing-house if necessary.

perature of 55° or below, and a day temperature of 65° to 70°. The plants of this category are:

Lettuce,
Asparagus,
Rhubarb,
Cauliflower,
Pea,
Carrot,
Beet,
Radish,
Cress, mustard, mints, parsley,
Onion,
Spinach,
Celery,
Pepino.

The warm plants demand a night temperature above 55°, and the day temperature may run above 75° when the weather is clear and bright. They are:

Tomato,
Eggplant,
Pepper,
Cucumber,
Muskmelon,
Bean,
Cyphomandra.

The above categories comprise about all the species of vegetables which are actually forced for market in this country, and even of this short list there are a number for which the market is so limited, or the methods of growing them so little understood, that they really have no place in the staple demands of the market. Vegetables of very minor importance as a forced crop are peas, carrots, beets, cress, celery, eggplant, and pepper. In fact, there are only three staple commercial forced vegetables, and these, in the order of their commercial importance, are lettuce, tomatoes, and cucumbers.

It is possible to grow any vegetable under glass, but it is only those products of a perishable nature which can be expected to yield any degree of profit. Those, also, which require a very long season in which to mature, and which yield a small amount of product — such as beets, carrots, spinach, peas — are of little importance for forcing. The Lima beans require a too long season, and they are chiefly consumed in the dry state; but the common "string" beans are a good forcing crop. There are special reasons why some other vegetables are not forced with profit. Cauliflower, for example, is a most satisfactory crop to grow under glass, but the best heads of the late fall crop are so easily kept through the winter in cold storage as to almost despoil the market for the forced product. Spinach was once forced in cheap houses and in hotbeds and coldframes, but the southern-grown spinach now reaches the market in perfect condition from the holidays until spring. Radishes are more popular in spring than in midwinter but the demand for them in early spring is met more by hotbed-grown roots than by a house-grown product. The forcing of celery is practically unknown, having been made a success, apparently, only in an experimental way. Eggplants require a long season and much heat and care, and the demand for them is slight in winter. The regular season of the vegetable is long, beginning with those from the Gulf states and ending with the October and even November fruits of the north. The pepino is little known, either to growers or to the market. Winter peppers — used for the making of "stuffed peppers" — are in limited demand, and they are readily shipped in from the south. Winter muskmelons are an exceedingly fancy product, and very difficult to grow with good flavor, so the price must be very high to enable them to yield a profit. Squashes and marrows can be grown in glass houses, but the plants require much room, and the product has small commercial value.

The near future will no doubt see many new departures

in the forcing of vegetables. The demand for forced beans is already fairly good, and is undoubtedly destined to increase. The other minor forcing crops which are probably destined to receive greater attention are celery, asparagus, rhubarb, muskmelon; and there may be others which we do not now conceive of as forcing crops. With the increase of population and the augmentation of the appetite for luxuries in the dietary, the forcing of vegetables is bound to become an industry of great importance. It is yet in its merest infancy. It has practically all arisen, in this country, in twenty years, yet the demand for information respecting it, in the Eastern states, is even now very earnest and widespread. There is a constant tendency for consumers to prefer a forced home-grown product to a transported and exotic one. The forced tomatoes generally sell well in the very presence of the cheaper product shipped in from Florida. The best consumers desire the product at first hand from the plant, and they enjoy the sentiment which is attached to the forcing of a plant into the pink of perfection in the very teeth of blizzards. Whilst the author does not desire to urge anyone into the forcing of vegetables, he is nevertheless convinced that the business is bound to open up great possibilities in the future.

It is generally best to devote an entire house to one kind of crop, for every crop demands a particular treatment to insure the most profitable results. Yet it is often advisable to grow an alternation or rotation of crops, in order to employ the house to best advantage, and to meet the requirements of the markets. Houses which are too cold for winter crops of tomatoes or cucumbers may be devoted to lettuce or other cool crops during the cold months, and to the warm crops in early spring and summer. Two crops of lettuce during the winter may be followed by the White Spine type of cucumber for spring and early summer. Winter tomatoes may often be followed advantageously by cucumbers or preceded by late fall melons. Vegetables are often alternated with flowers or with plant stock. In the famous "carnation belt" of Chester county, Pennsylvania, tomatoes are largely grown as an early spring crop, following the crops of carnation cuttings.

Locations for vegetable forcing. — The items which chiefly enter into the choice of an ideal location for the forcing of vegetables are the transportation facilities and the price of fuel. The operator makes his climate, and mixes his soils to order. Yet a sunny climate is always to be preferred, for it is essential to quick and sure results in midwinter that there be an abundance of direct sunlight. The severity of the climate as respects cold is a very minor factor, for the operator is able, in the construction and protection of his house, to make himself very largely independent of the outside temperature without great additional consumption of fuel. Whilst the gardener manufactures his soil, so to speak, yet in certain crops (as in heading lettuce) it is very important that the soil of the neighborhood should be free of hard clay.

The transportation facilities are all-important. The product must reach the market expeditiously, and there should be direct access to several good markets. The product is not bulky, and the expense of shipping it is not heavy. Distance from market, therefore, is a less important factor than frequent and expeditious means of shipping. If one has a large product to ship, the actual distance from market is of still less moment, for the gardener can secure concessions on transportation rates; but it is nevertheless important that the market be directly accessible. Many of the large vegetable forcers ship their products two and three hundred miles. All winter products are shipped by express.

The vegetable forcing establishments are widely scattered. The larger part of them are in the environs of the large cities of the east, but many of them are in small cities or villages several hours removed from the markets. They can often be established with profit upon farms which are near one or more good railway stations, and when the farmer desires employment for the winter months. Many of the smaller cities — even of twenty thousand and less — afford a ready market for a considerable quantity of lettuce, tomatoes and cucumbers, making it necessary to ship only a comparatively small surplus to distant markets. A home and personal market is always to be preferred to a distant or metropolitan one.

Cost of heat and labor.—The two important items of expense in the management of a forcing structure, as already said, are the heating and the labor. It is impossible to give any exact estimates of the necessary outlay for these items, because these expenses are most intimately associated with the exposure, tightness, efficiency of the heating apparatus, and handiness of each particular house. A single glass house, standing alone, is more expensive to heat than the same house in a range or nest of houses. In central New York, where the winters are long and severe, a detached house, 20 x 100 ft. in ground area, will generally require, for a tomato-forcing temperature, from 15 to 20 tons of coal for the year, whether heated by steam or hot water. For a lettuce-forcing temperature, one-third less coal is usually sufficient.

A good workman, who is acquainted with the business, should be able to do all the work of growing tomatoes, except the firing, in two houses 20 x 100 ft. of ground surface. In lettuce-forcing, one man will handle four times as great an area after the plants are transplanted. These estimates assume that the houses are convenient, with facilities for watering with a hose. The larger the establishment, the less proportionate help does it require, if the houses are so arranged that the workmen are not required to walk more than 50 or 60 feet from any given point to reach an opening into another house, and if they are not obliged to pass back and forth out of doors while at their work. It is, therefore, evident that for economy in both heating and labor, a range of two or more parallel houses is more satisfactory than a single house or than several detached houses. When, however, each house is large enough to completely employ the labor of one or two men, the advantages of the nesting of the houses is not so great; and it may even be better, in such cases, to have the houses entirely separate, in order to facilitate the hauling of earth and other supplies into them.

Aside from the labor required to grow the plants, the operator must figure on the cost of the heating. It is imperative that the temperatures be kept fairly uniform during the night. In fact, variations of temperature are usually more hurtful at night than at day. For the best results, every forcing establishment should have a night man; but such a man can not be afforded for a small house. In this case, the gardener must place his dependence upon the self-regulating devices of the modern heaters; but even then he will need to give some attention to his house on very severe nights. Very much depends upon the faithfulness and efficiency of the night man. Very often the owner will find the temperature of the houses to be ideal at bed-time and at 6 in the morning, while, if he had been astir at 4 o'clock, he would have found it ten degrees too low. He would, if he knew the circumstances, cease to wonder why his crops were slow in growth and always attacked by mildew.

In order to arrive at actual expenditures for heat and labor, I have asked a few of my friends and correspondents—all wide-awake commercial growers—to give me their judgment upon the quantity of coal required to heat for one year a rose house of modern construction, 20 x 100 feet ground surface, even span, 10 ft. high at the ridge. I also asked, "About how large an establishment does it require, in roses or winter tomatoes, to keep one good workman busy during the forcing season, in watering, ventilating, training, picking the product, etc. (not attending to the firing)?" The answers to these questions are given below. Where the size of the house is not specified, it is understood to be 20 x 100 ft., as stated in the problem.

ONTARIO—

1. I have two tomato houses, each 20 x 200 ft., 13 ft. high at the ridge, heated with steam. I used last year 110 tons of anthracite coal.

One good man will attend to one house 20 x 200 ft., in the spring. In the winter, the man and a boy can thoroughly care for two such houses.

MASSACHUSETTS—

2. For roses, using hot water, it takes about 18 tons of coal for the year.

One man will care for two to three houses, if he is active and thorough, and keeps them clean and in first-class order.

NEW YORK—

3. I am heating 500 lineal feet of rose house, 20 ft. wide and 11 ft. high, at a cost (last year) of $333. This is about 65 cents per lineal foot. The system is hot water in small pipes.

For roses, a good man should manage 400 lineal feet of a house 20 ft. wide.

4. I should estimate 12 tons of coal. This is about my actual outlay in the winter of 1895-6.

A man should handle 8,000 or 10,000 sq. ft. of glass, in roses.

5. I have about 15,000 square feet of glass, in ten houses. I grow roses, carnations, violets, plants, etc. Four of my own family, including myself, work in the houses, and I usually keep one man besides. Outside of my own family, it costs me about $2,000 a year to run my place,—for coal, help, repairs, water rent, taxes, bulbs, insurance, lumber for boxes, and all other incidentals. My houses are in good condition, and I keep the place in first-class order.

6. I judge that a single rose house 20 x 100 ft., in this climate (Mohawk Valley), kept at rose-forcing temperature, would take about 25 tons of anthracite coal a year.

In a nest or block of several houses, the heating could probably be done with 20 tons.

In rose-forcing, a careful and industrious man can take care of about 10,000 sq. ft. of glass. With a smart boy for weeding and cleaning up, he could handle 5,000 ft. more.

7. To keep an average temperature of 60°, for roses, by steam, would require about 18 tons of hard coal. Much will depend upon the boiler, the placing of the radiating surface, and the carefulness of the fireman.

With things conveniently arranged, one smart man could care for a rose house 20 ft. wide and 250 to 300 ft. long.

8. I grow violets, and heat with water. I use 60 to 70 tons of hard coal for 15,000 sq. ft. of glass.

MICHIGAN—

9. With coal at $2.75 per ton, and including fireman's wages, it will cost anywhere from $75 to $125 per year, depending upon the efficiency of the boiler and the severity of the season.

Much depends upon the handiness of the place, and how neat the proprietor wants to keep his house. For the most thorough care, one man can manage, of roses, 5,000 to 6,000 sq. ft. of glass.

10. Last season, I used 8½ tons of Hocking Valley lump coal per 1,000 sq. ft. of glass for roses, and 6½ tons for carnations and violets mixed. I use steam.

If a man is not bothered by visitors he can care for two rose houses 20 x 125 ft. If this amount of glass were in four houses, he could not care for it well.

11. If built in a range of say ten houses, heated with steam, it would require for each house about 18 tons of soft (lump) coal. In a smaller range, the heating would cost more.

One good man can care for two such houses; or if help is furnished occasionally and no propagating is done, more glass can be cared for.

MINNESOTA —

12. In one season I used 470 tons of Illinois coal (costing $1,424) in four houses 16 x 200 ft., four houses 16 x 100 ft., and nine houses 20 x 90 ft. The next season I added two houses 35 x 200 ft. each, and then used 850 tons, costing $3,238. By rearranging the steam pipes, I heated these same houses the following two winters with 649 tons and 608 tons respectively.

INDIANA —

13. I use natural gas, and cannot give figures.

One good man should attend to four such houses, if he has help for four weeks in planting, etc.

14. A three-fourths span house, 20 ft. wide and 11 ft. high, in an exposed place, cost us in 1895-6 at the rate of $89.04 for a house 100 ft. long (coal $2 per ton). We can reduce this figure somewhat by careful management. An equal span, 20 ft. wide and 10 ft. high, cost us about $35.20 per 100 ft. This house is on the sheltered side of the range. (This correspondent is on the Ohio river.)

One good workman should attend to about five such houses, in roses.

ILLINOIS —

15. It cost me last winter (1895-6) for coal, for rose house 20 x 100 ft., — as nearly as I can figure the proportion, — $50, with soft coal at $2.30 per ton, and the use of some slack at 75 cents and $1 per ton. This house is three-fourths span and 12 ft. high.

In my place, where cut flowers and pot plants are both handled, and with a retail trade to wait on, it requires about one man to a house 20 x 100 ft. If I were growing only roses, I should not need so much help.

PENNSYLVANIA —

16. Such a house in roses here (Philadelphia) would require about 12 tons of pea coal at $3.25, or 9 tons of larger size at $5.50.

An experienced rose grower ought to manage 5,000

sq. ft. of glass. If a variety of stuff is grown, twice the help is necessary.

17. With hot water, 15 tons egg hard coal.

One good man should give good results in two houses 20 x 100 ft.

18. I burn on an average 200 tons of hard coal per year to heat ten houses 9 x 100 ft., 8 ft. to ridge, and four houses 21 x 140 ft., 10 ft. to ridge. Temperature at night, 50° to 60°.

I want one man to each 5,000 sq. ft., if there is little potting to do.

19. In tomato growing, it costs me about $50 per year for such a house, with coal at $3.30 per ton.

One spry workman should do the work in two tomato houses 20 x 100 ft.

20. Two houses 20 x 100 ft. of tomatoes will keep one man occupied. As usually heated hereabouts ["Carnation belt," Chester county], the firing could be done by the same person if he is an interested participant in the crop returns. The tomato ranges are usually two or four houses heated with hot water circulation, and seldom require re-coaling during the night.

21. I have had no experience with growing roses. With carnations I find that it takes about 5 tons (long) coal for 1,000 feet of glass. Some winters rather more, but mostly less. I find it takes about this, no matter what system of heating is used (flue or hot water), if used with all care in both cases. But by using pea coal in our horizontal tubular boiler we effect a saving in cost, as it takes little or no more pea coal than it does broken or egg.

In our business it takes about one man to 5,000 sq. ft. of glass, during the forcing season.

NEW JERSEY—

22. My rose house, 20 x 80 ft., consumes about 9 or 10 tons of coal yearly.

Two houses, 20 x 100 ft., are enough for one man in rose growing, and he should have a boy to assist him in busy times. In large establishments, two men working together can turn off as much as three men working alone in small establishments.

KENTUCKY—

23. For ordinary winters (southwestern Kentucky), 250 bus. coal at 10 cents. For severe winters, 350 bus.

One man will care for three such houses.

WASHINGTON—

24. To heat a 20 x 150 ft. house, three-fourths span, 10 ft. high, for tomatoes, will cost here (Seattle) about $50 per year with 4-ft. fire wood at $1 per cord. I use steam.

Two men will take care of the crops and do the firing for two houses 20 x 112 ft., one house 52 x 150 ft., one house 20 x 150 ft., and three houses 20 x 80 ft.

NOTE.—The reader will find tables for computing the radiating and grate surfaces in the heating of glasshouses, and other greenhouse matter, in the last edition of The Horticulturist's Rule-Book.

CHAPTER II.

THE CONSTRUCTION OF THE FORCING-HOUSE.

It is of the greatest importance that the most particular attention be given to the construction of the forcing-house, for it is by means of this structure that the gardener is to make and maintain the climate in which his crops are to be grown. It is not the purpose of this book, however, to give a manual of instructions for the building of glass houses, but it may be advisable to make a few summary statements respecting some of the features which are particularly useful to forcing-houses, and then refer the reader to other treatises for more detailed instruction.*

TYPES AND FORMS OF HOUSES.

Forcing-houses should be of the simplest possible construction. Every feature in their make-up should be characterized by directness. The walks and benches should be straight and of uniform width. The greatest possible amount of space should be reserved for the actual growing of the plants, by making the walks narrow (not more than two feet in most commercial houses) and by carrying the heating pipes and construction timbers out of the reach of the plants to be grown. The side walls of forcing-houses

---

*The best current American text upon the subject is Taft's "Greenhouse Construction," published by the Orange Judd Co. The reader may also find some suggestions upon these and similar topics in Winkler's "Vegetable Forcing," Columbus, O., 1896; and also in Dreer's "Vegetables Under Glass," which comes to hand just as these pages are going through the press.

are only high enough to allow of room for the plants to be grown under the glass, or, in the case of shed-houses, to give a proper slope to the roof. It is a common practice to secure head room in the forcing-house by sinking the walks below the ground level. In this way, the house is kept low, thus saving in cost of construction and in exposure to winds. Such sunken walks are shown in Figs. 1 and 3 (pages 17 and 18). It is always handier, however, to have the main walks on a level with the surface, thus avoiding steps in passing to and from the establishment. In wet or springy ground it is

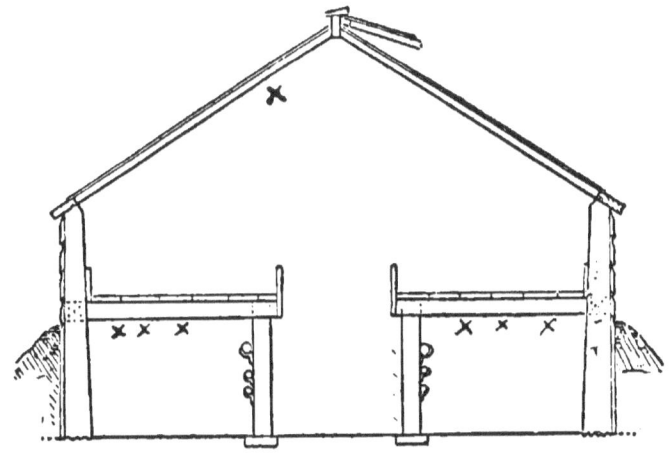

1. A simple even-span, 10 feet wide.

important to avoid sinking the house. The roof of the forcing-house should be as flat as is consistent with the ready shedding of rain and snow, in order that all the plants may grow close under the roof; for it should be said that plants are usually more stocky and productive and healthy when grown near the glass. The house should be of the lightest possible construction in order to gain sunlight, particularly if tomatoes, melons, cauliflowers and other sun-loving plants are to be grown.

There are three general types or shapes of houses in common use for the forcing of vegetables. These are: The roof with an even span, those with a lean-to or true shed roof, and those with an uneven or broken roof. These various types of houses are illustrated in the accompanying diagrams. Figs. 1 and 2 show the ordinary types of an even-span house, Figs. 3 and 4 (page 19) forms of an uneven or broken span, and Figs. 5, 6 and 7 (pages 20, 21 and 22), of a lean-to or shed house. The older type of forcing-house was rather narrow in proportion to its width; that is, it was rarely more than 20 feet wide, whilst the length might vary from 50 to 300 feet. A house of this width is proportionately more difficult to heat and to manage than one of greater width, and the tendency at the present time is towards much wider houses, especially in establishments where a large product is expected to be grown. The wide house, however, when built with a gable roof, becomes too

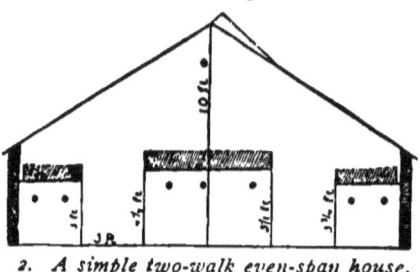

2. *A simple two-walk even-span house, 20 feet wide.*

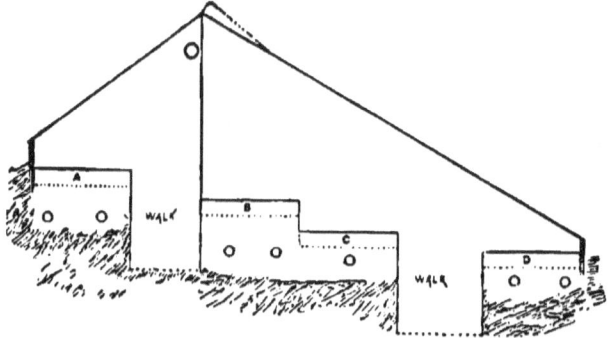

3. *A broken or uneven span, 20 feet wide, on a side hill.*

high to admit of economical construction and heating, and the plants are also too far removed from the glass for best results. It is necessary, therefore, in these very wide houses, to treat the building as a shed, and to take extra care in making the roof strong and tight.

A single house, standing by itself, is always more difficult and expensive to heat and to manage than a range of houses. It is, therefore, very important that houses should not only be heated, so far as possible, from one central system, but also that the houses should lie alongside of each other so that the interior walls may answer for two houses, and that one house may protect another from sweeping winds. For

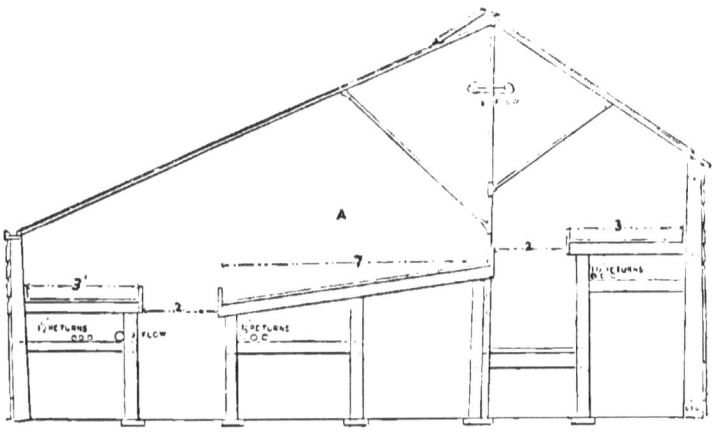

4. *A broken roof on the level, 18 feet wide, with sloping center bench.*

purposes of convenience in repairing the roof, and to avoid injury by snow, it is better to have these parallel houses separated from each other by a space or alley of two or three feet; but inasmuch as this doubles the number of walls and exposes every wall to the weather, this method of construction is rarely used for small houses in this country. Two contiguous houses are allowed to rest upon a common wall, but the gutter between the two is made deep and wide so that the water may be carried off quickly, and a workman may walk through it when repairing or painting the roof. In the case of very large houses, however (say those 35 ft. or more wide and 200 ft. or more

5. *A shed house 60 feet wide and 300 feet long.*

long), which are large enough to make and control their own temperature and to employ all the time of a man, it is probably better, for the sake of the convenience of hauling to and from them and the ease of repairing the roofs, to have them separated from other houses by a space two or three rods, or more, wide.

It is probably true that the best direction or exposure for an even-span house is from north to south, because both sides of the structure then receive an equal amount of sunlight during the twenty-four hours. It is not always practicable, however, to run the houses north and south, and when it is not, it is better to run them directly east and west, and to break the roof into uneven spans. Just which span should face the south, whether the long one or the short one, is a matter of dispute. It probably depends very largely upon the kind of plants to be grown, and the slope of the land, and upon the exact exposure; but it is, no doubt, true that, for general conditions, the

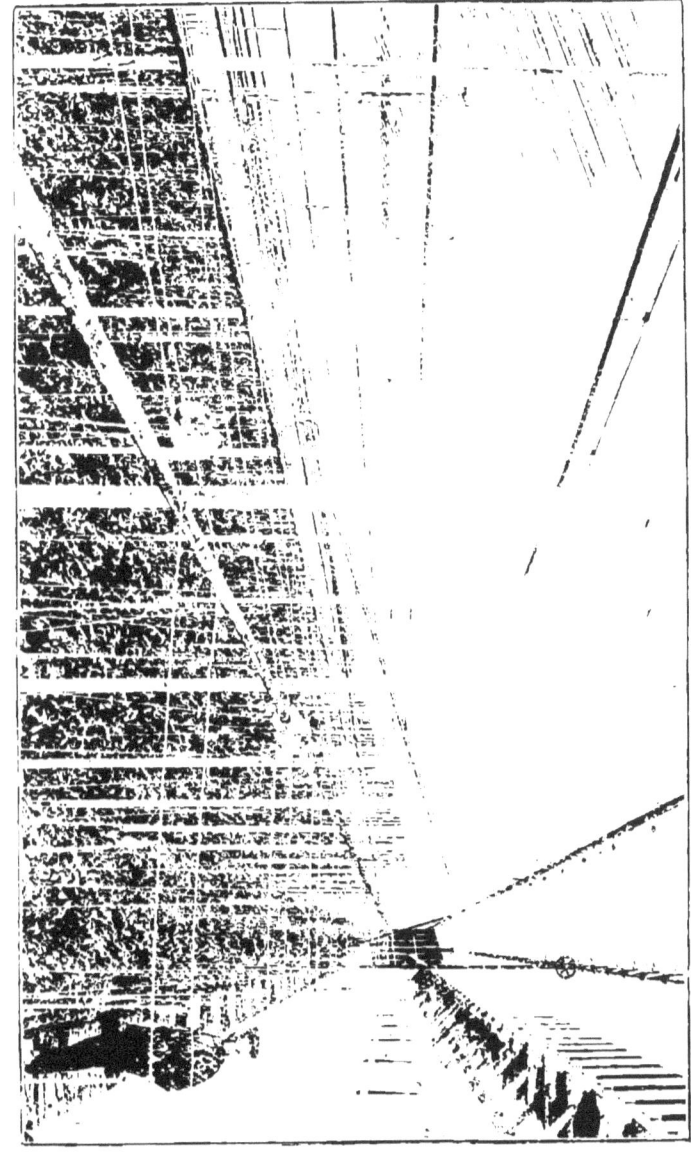

22 THE CONSTRUCTION OF THE FORCING-HOUSE.

7. *A shed roof covering a city back yard.*

HOUSES TO BE RECOMMENDED.

long span should face the sun. The short-span-to-the-south greenhouse, of which much has been said in recent years, is built with a very steep, short south roof, with the purpose of intercepting nearly all the sun's rays and carrying them directly back into the farthermost corners of the house. Where high plants are to be grown near the front of the house, however, so much shade is cast upon the rear plants as to seriously interfere with their growth. These houses have not yet come into general use for vegetable forcing, and they need not be further considered in this summary account.

Of the various houses which are represented in the accompanying illustrations, Fig. 1 is the least satisfactory for forcing purposes, because of its narrowness. In such slim houses there is not a sufficient body of air to guard against rapid fluctuations of temperature. They cool off quickly; and with variations in temperature there arise serious difficulties with insects and fungi. Fig. 2 is an excellent

8. *A range of thirteen even-span houses and two shed houses.*

house for a small or ordinary establishment, and is a good type for the beginner. The same remarks may be made for Fig. 3, except that the unequal elevations of the walks and beds make it unhandy. Such a side-hill house, however, brings the glass very close to the greatest number of plants,—a result which is sometimes sought by elevating the benches in the center of even-span houses, but this raises the beds so high as to make them awkward. Fig. 4 is an excellent type of house. Figs. 5, 6 and 7 are probably the best types for very large establishments. Fig. 7 (page 22) covers the entire back yard of a city lot. These shed roofs are most easy to build and to keep in repair. The absence of gutters is a most important feature, for the gutter is the part of the frame which is most difficult to properly construct and which generally soonest gives out.

It is advisable, in cases where an entire range or nest of houses is to be permanently used for one given crop, to omit entirely the side walls, and to simply place the plates and gutters on the tops of posts or pillars, allowing the spaces between the posts to remain open. This construction results in throwing the whole range into practically a single house, keeping the structure low, with considerable economy of heat and labor. Such a construction is never admissible, however, when it is expected that the different houses of the range are to be used for the growing of plants requiring different degrees of heat and moisture. The range of nine houses shown at the left in Fig. 8 (page 23) are open beneath the gutters in this way, and Fig. 9 (page 25) is a crosswise view in them. The reader sees a gutter near the top of the picture, with a steam pipe running along the plate, and the man is sitting under the second gutter.

SOME OF THE STRUCTURAL DETAILS.

The frame.—The framing of a forcing-house is well explained by Figs. 10 and 11 (pages 26 and 27). These pictures represent the common rafter-and-sash-bar house.

THE PARTITION WALLS OMITTED.

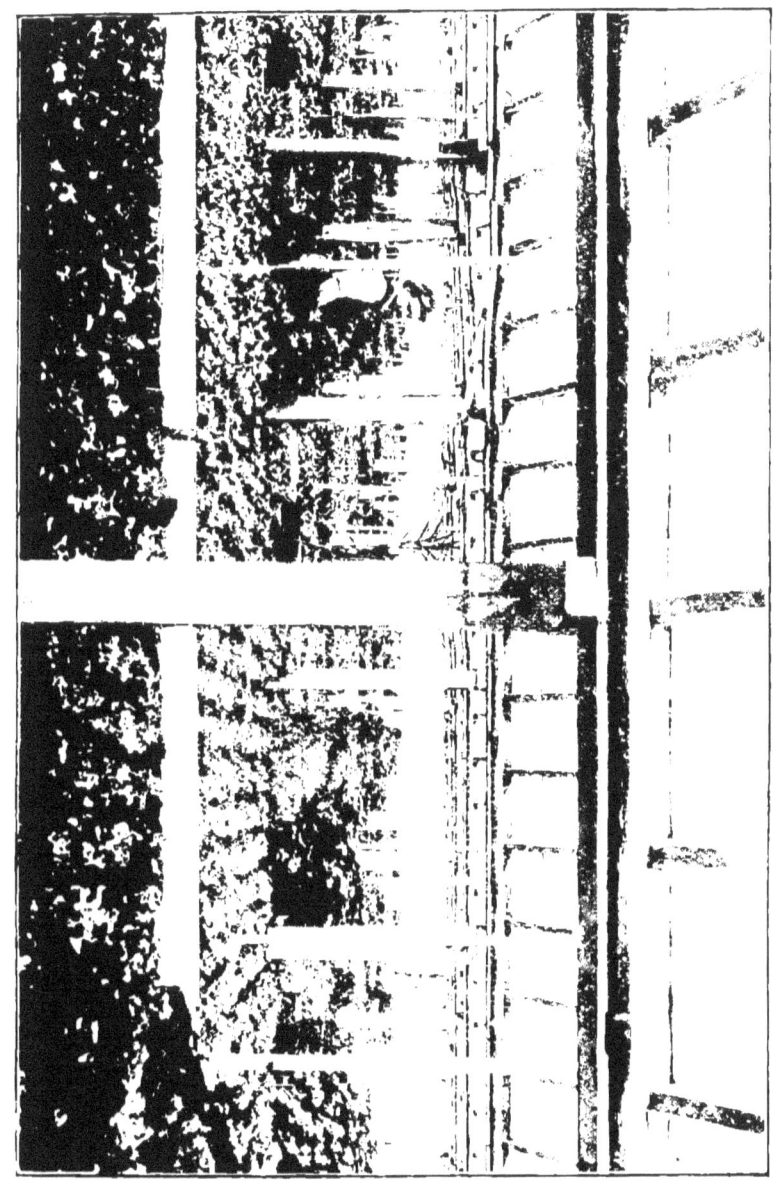

9. *Interior cross-wise view in the nine houses shown at the left in Fig. 8.*

In Fig. 10 the rafters are in place, and on the further half the sash-bars have been put in between them, being toe-nailed at the upper end to headers cut in between the rafters. The space above these headers is to be covered by the ventilator sash.

It is very doubtful, however, if it is ever necessary to use

10. *Putting up a rafter-and-sash-bar house.*

rafters in the construction of a forcing-house. The entire roof should be built wholly of sash-bars, which run from the sill or the plate to the peak, as shown in Figs. 12 and 13 (pages 28 and 29). This construction admits the greatest amount of light to the house, and is also less expensive. If purlines of steam pipe are freely used upon which to rest the sash-bars, each bar being secured to the purline by a loop of strap iron, the house may be made as stiff as the old-time rafter-built frame. Fig. 14 (page 31) shows the interior of Figs. 12 and 13. The house (used for tomatoes) is 24 feet wide, 11 feet high at the ridge and 4 feet at the eaves, with sash-bars 13 feet long. These bars have a body measure of 1¼ x 1½ inches, and carry glass 14 x 24 inches. They are supported in the center by a 1¼-inch pipe. A

11. *Construction of a rafter-and-sash bar frame.*

row of these pipe supports upon either side of the house is the only intermediate support which the roof receives; yet this house stands in an exposed place and has withstood several severe gales without the slightest injury. A similar sash-bar construction is shown in Fig. 15 (page 32). Another is seen in Fig. 16 (page 34), but in this case the bars are nailed to wooden plates which rest upon pipe supports.

THE CONSTRUCTION OF THE FORCING-HOUSE.

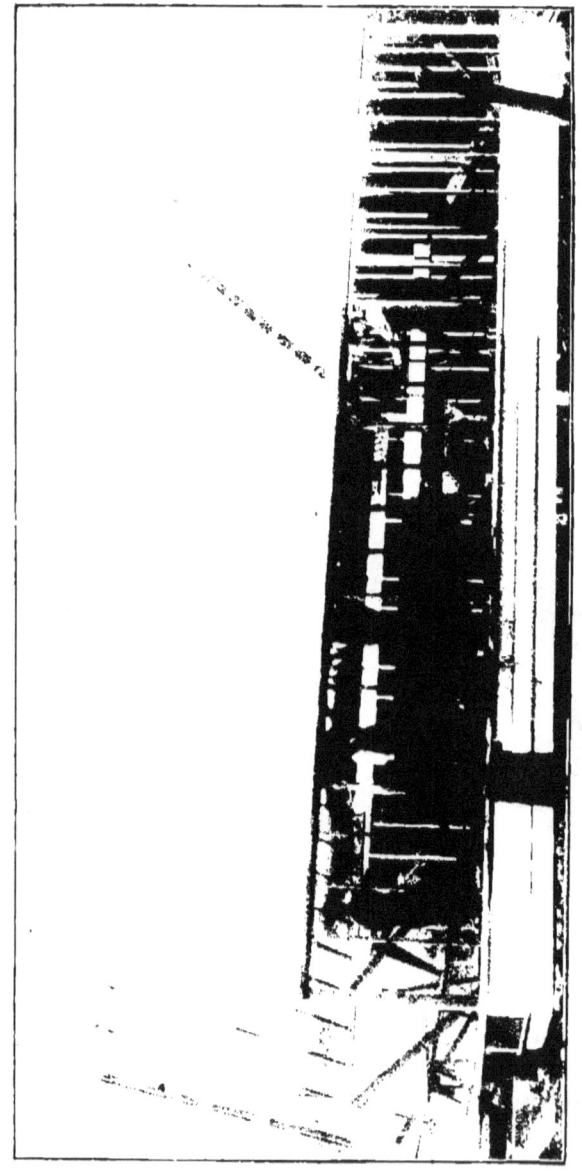

12. *Construction of a sash-bar frame forcing-house*

THE DETAILS OF THE SASH-BAR.

The sash-bar.—There is much diversity of opinion respecting the best form of sash-bar. Common types are shown, half natural size, in Fig. 17 (page 35). The shoulders at the top are to receive the edges of the panes of glass. The cap upon the sample at the right is to hold the glass in place when the panes are butted, a matter to be explained shortly. The grooves in the sides of the bars are designed to catch the water which condenses on the glass, carrying it down to the plate, and thereby preventing the "drip."

For myself, after long study of glass houses, I am convinced that this groove has little if any value. It weaken the bar and adds to its cost. It rarely catches all or even most of the water, for the condensation flows downwards off the pane, and not sidewise. It is said that the condensation may be carried into the grooves by taking care to lay

13. Houses with sash-bar frames.

the crowning side of the pane up, thereby having the hollow side underneath; but good glass should have very little or no crown, and it is rarely possible to make sufficient slant towards the bar to carry the water to it. But I should consider the draining of the water into the groove to be the very thing to be avoided, for it is then discharged at the bottom of the bar into the joint with the plate, and hastens decay in one of the very weakest points in the frame. I now use entirely a perfectly plain sash-bar, which is "run" from white pine at the home mill. Its form is shown in Fig. 18 (page 35). For ordinary roofs, and glass not more than 12 inches wide, these bars may be 1 x 1½ or 1¼ x 1¾ inches in body measure. The illustration shows a cross-section of a heavy bar, at one-half natural size. In lots of 1,000 lineal feet, this bar costs us the price of the lumber plus $4 for "running." If the grooves were added, the cost of "running" would be about $6. In large quantities, these prices could be much reduced. In very wide roofs of little slope, and especially when very large glass (18 to 20 inches wide) is used, a bar 2 x 3 inches is safest and best. Such bars will hold a man's weight. If the house is properly glazed, there will be no "drip" of consequence.

The plate.—Perhaps the shortest lived part of the frame of the ordinary glass house is the plate at the eaves. Much of the condensation upon the glass finds its way to the plate, and if the glass is butted, all the condensation strikes it which does not fall in "drip." In the very wide shed roof or broken-roof houses, the front plate (upon the lower wall) receives nearly all the roof drainage, and this is the one, therefore, to be chiefly protected. The plate, therefore, soon decays unless the greatest care is taken to give it a bold slant, and to keep it well painted. Fig. 19 (page 36) shows an excellent plate, half-size, cut from a pine or cypress stick. A plate with half the slope of the side A B will still hold the water in globules and miniature pools, particularly after the paint has begun to blister. In order to prevent the water from following back on the plate and keeping the wall wet, a groove like that at a, a, in Figs. 20 and 25 (pages 37 and 39), is useful. A similar one on the outside of the plate will keep the rain from following down the wall. If the drip from the inner edge of the plate

FRAMEWORK OF A TOMATO HOUSE.

32   THE CONSTRUCTION OF THE FORCING-HOUSE.

15. *A broken-span sash-bar frame house adapted to lettuce and chrysanthemums. The upper bench not yet built.*

is annoying, it may be caught in a little trough and carried away. The best trough for this purpose is made from a pine strip 1¼ inches thick and 2 inches deep, with a V-shaped groove sawed in the top. This trough, freshly painted on the back, is nailed to the wall in such position that the bottom of the groove lies directly beneath the corner of the plate.

All tenons or mortises should be avoided upon the plate, or in any other place where the wood is likely to remain moist. The simplest and most efficient union of sash-bar and plate is shown in Fig. 20 (page 37), in which the bar is nailed on top of the outward slope of the plate. Figs. 24 and 25 (page 39) show a similar construction, except that the rafter is used and is toe-nailed to the inward slope of the plate. If much water is likely to follow down the sash-bar, it is a good practice to place a tin shoe or trough underneath the foot of the bar (between it and the plate) to carry off the water, as illustrated in Fig. 21 (page 37). Where the sash-bar strikes the ridge-pole, a notch or half-mortise may be used, as in Fig. 22 (page 38), but even here it is usually preferable to simply toe-nail the bars on, as in Fig. 23 (page 38).

The gutter is ordinarily built of lumber, a heavy plank forming its bottom, as in Figs. 24 and 25 (page 39). In order to keep this plank from warping, it is advisable to saw a slit across each end and to drive a bar of iron into it, as seen in Fig. 26 (page 40). The life of the gutter may be much prolonged by tinning it. A sharp fall will also add to its life and to the ease of keeping it clean. In some cases, the entire house is built upon a pitch in order to give a proper fall to the gutter, but in general it is best to build the house level and to give the gutter an independent slope. Upon masonry walls, a good gutter is made by leaving a trough on top and plastering it thoroughly with Portland cement.

Walls.—The best side walls, in point of durability, are

34 THE CONSTRUCTION OF THE FORCING-HOUSE.

16. Interior of a sash bar frame shed roof house, containing cucumbers and lettuce.

WALLS AND VENTILATORS.

made of brick or stone, but unless they are very thick or are hollow they are likely to be colder than a well built board wall upon posts. The space represented by the thickness of the posts affords an admirable dead air space. Nearly all commercial forcing-houses are upon posts, and it is commonly said that such walls will last as long as the plate will. This is probably true, but the plates, as usually made, are unnecessarily short lived. A forcing-house should stand fifteen or twenty years without extensive repairs, if well built; and if the side walls are of masonry (stone or cement), the plates well made, the roof so well supported that it cannot sag, and the whole freshly painted every year or two, the structure should stand nearly a life time. Good board walls are shown in Figs. 20 and 25. In each, there is an airspace between the posts. In Fig. 20, there are two air-spaces. The sheathings covering the posts are shown at b b, the post at p, and the siding at c. This wall, if well built, is no doubt as warm as a 12-inch solid brick wall.*

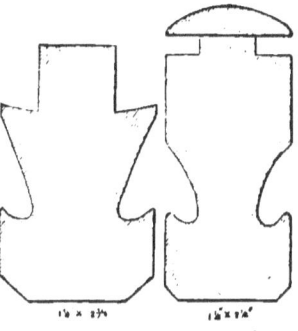

17. *Two types of sash-bars.*

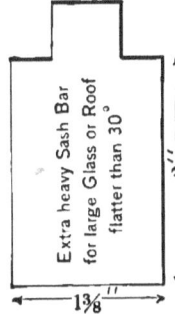

18. *A plain sash-bar.*

Ventilators.—The house should have ample provision for ventilating it, yet it is easy to get the openings so large that the temperature of the interior may be lowered too suddenly and too far when the sash are lifted. In windy days, it is impossible to open very large sash at all without letting in too much cold air to the plants immediately underneath. Many small sash are pref-

---

* Experiments with greenhouse walls have been made at the Minnesota Station (Bull. 7) and the Massachusetts Station (Bull. 4).

4 FORC.

erable to a few very large ones. The house shown in Figs. 12 and 13, which is unusually light and fully exposed to the sun, is ventilated by a continuous double row of sash a foot wide, and this width is sufficient for all narrow even-span houses. Uneven spans may require ventilators a foot and a half in width, and I should think that two feet would be the utmost desirable width for any ordinary purpose. It is generally unnecessary to have side ventilators in forcing-houses whose side walls are under four feet in height. In general, it is best to hang the ventilators at the bottom, thereby allowing the heated air to pass out at the very peak. If a row of sash is placed upon either side, and each row is operated by a separate mech-

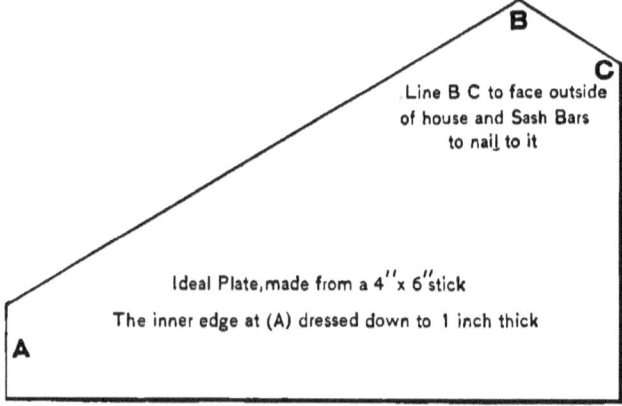

19. *A good forcing-house plate.*

anism, the most perfect means of ventilation will be secured. In the very wide shed houses, ventilators upon the sides may be necessary.

The glass and glazing.—Glass for forcing-houses should always be double-thick, not single-thick. The double-thick glass may be expected to save its extra cost within a year or two in the less breakage, and it makes better joints and a warmer house than the single-thick. The difference in cost between the two grades may be indicated by stating that when the price per box (of 22 lights) of single-thick glass, 14 x 24, was $2.25, the cost of double-thick was $2.85.

There are two styles or methods of laying glass,—the old-time or common method of lapping it, and the butting it end to end. The advantages of the butting method are supposed to be the greater ease and speed of laying the roof, a tighter roof, one which admits more light because of the absence of laps, and economy of glass. The style of bar to be used for butting is one with a very shallow muntin or projection on top, as in that shown on the right in Fig. 17. The glass is not laid in putty*, but it is advisable to have the bar freshly painted in order to close the joint with the glass. The panes are laid end to end, and are held in place, when an entire run has been laid, by screwing down a cap, as shown in the illustration. It is often advised to cover the ends of the panes with a thin film of white lead, in order to cement the panes together and thus close the joints. All the lead which is squeezed out of the joint is afterwards scraped off, so as to make a clean and

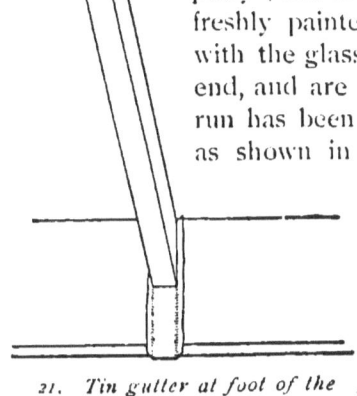

20. *Wall, plate, and sash-bar.*

21. *Tin gutter at foot of the sash-bar.*

---

*A durable putty for glazing purposes is made by mixing pure whiting in oil, and then using about three parts of this, by weight, to one of pure white lead, mixing the ingredients thoroughly.

smooth job. After considerable experience with butted glass, the writer has abandoned it. It is practically impossible, with any ordinary grade of glass, to make a perfectly smooth joint between the panes, and at every irregularity or roughness at the joints the water will collect and drip off. This difficulty is particularly liable to occur if panes are used which are over twelve or fourteen inches wide. It is rare, also, that the panes are squarely enough cut to make perfectly tight joints possible. Another serious objection to butted glass is the fact that all the water of condensation which does not fall as drip is carried down upon the plate, keeping it constantly wet and tending to make it decay. The drip from the plate is often a serious nuisance, particularly if there are heating pipes directly beneath from which a constant shower of vapor arises. In lapped glass, the condensed water follows down the pane and passes out through the lap onto the roof. If glass is to be butted, only the double-thick should be used. The single-thick grade is too irregular and uneven in thickness and curvature to allow of making good joints; and its very thinness makes it impossible to secure sufficient contact to make a tight job.

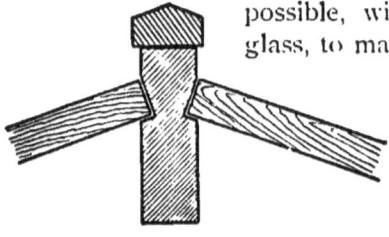

22. *Mortice-joint at the ridge*

In the lapping of glass, the panes are bedded in soft putty, and are then held from slipping down by a straight shoe-nail at each lower

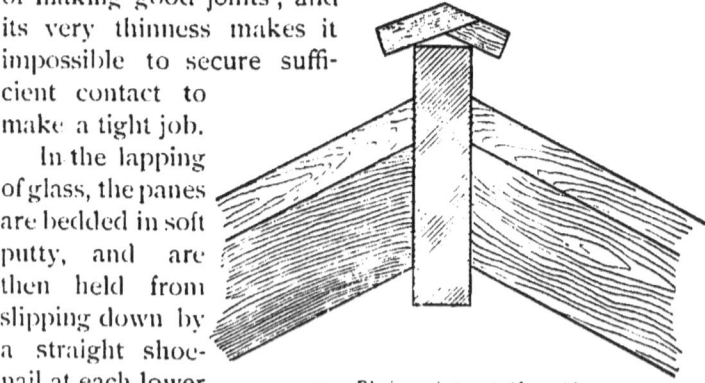

23. *Plain joints at the ridge.*

GLASS AND GLAZING. 39

corner (a a, Fig. 27, page 41), and are held firmly to the bar by glaziers' points (e e, Fig. 27). The panes are seen edgwise, in cross-section, at B in Fig. 27. It is important, to avoid breakage, that no nail or point be placed on the middle of the pane. No putty is placed over the glass, for, in the nearly horizontal or inclined position in which the panes lie, the water would collect underneath any such putty and would crack it off by freezing. If the panes are well bedded, and if the bars and the edges of the glass are given a coat of paint, the job will be perfectly tight. It is imperative that the lap on the panes should be very short. A long lap collects dirt and thereby obstructs the light, and it also holds so much water that the freezing of it snaps the corners of the panes. A lap of a quarter of an inch, or at most of three-eighths inch, is ample. In this narrow lap the water of condensation collects and makes a warm joint.

24. *Wall, gutter, and rafter and sash-bar.*

There has been a tendency in recent years towards the use of very large glass. Panes as large as 20 x 36 inches have been used. These seem to be too wide for economy, and they impose severe strains upon the sash-bars, and weaken the rigidity of the house. The glass bears too great a proportion to the structural frame of the roof. It is doubtful if it is wise to use glass above 14 or 16 inches wide, and, through inquiry and experience, the writer has now settled upon 14 x 18 inches as about the best size

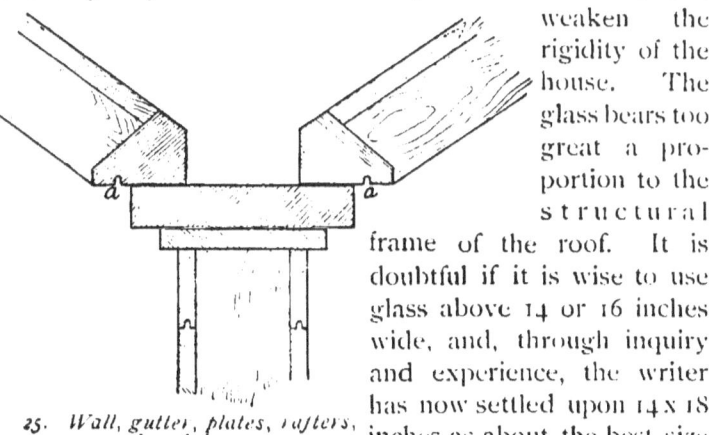

25. *Wall, gutter, plates, rafters, and sash-bars.*

for all purposes. Indeed, I should prefer glass 12 inches wide to that which is 18 inches wide.

Beds and benches.—Those plants which thrive best without bottom heat, as lettuce generally does, are most commonly grown in solid beds,—that is, on the earth. Those crops requiring bottom heat must be grown on benches. The height of these benches above the ground must be determined wholly by circumstances.

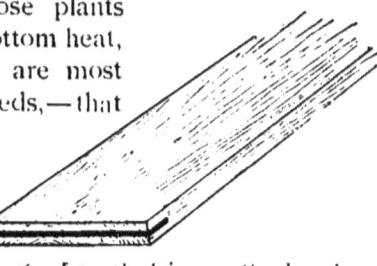

26. *Iron cleat in a gutter-board.*

The first thing to consider is to secure sufficient head room for the plants, or, in the instance of low plants, to get them near to the glass. Benches will run from a foot to three feet above the ground. They are handiest when the extreme height is about two feet and the width not over three and a half or four feet. The depth of the bed (that is, of the soil) varies with different operators from 5 to 10 inches. As a rule, with good soil, 6 or 7 inches of earth is sufficient. A greater body of earth is likely to make a too continuous growth, with consequent loss of earliness, and it requires more care in the watering if it should become hard or somewhat impervious to water. Benches are ordinarily built of common lumber. One-inch hemlock boards, in single thickness, will last about three winters if the soil is removed in the summer. Cracks of a half inch or a little more should be left between the boards, and it is then not necessary to place drainage material—as broken crocks or clinkers—on the bottoms of the beds. With shiftless watering, however, no amount of drainage material can insure safe results.

HEATING.

Steam and hot water.—Modern forcing-houses are heated by either steam or hot water in wrought-iron pipes.

The old method of heating by means of the large cast iron pipes is not adapted to the forcing business. The comparative merits of steam and water as media for conveying heat have been much discussed in recent years, with the result that neither system has gained a complete victory. In other words, each system has peculiar merits. Our own experience emphasizes the greater value of steam, but we do not condemn hot water. We believe that steam is superior for very large houses where the fall is slight, for

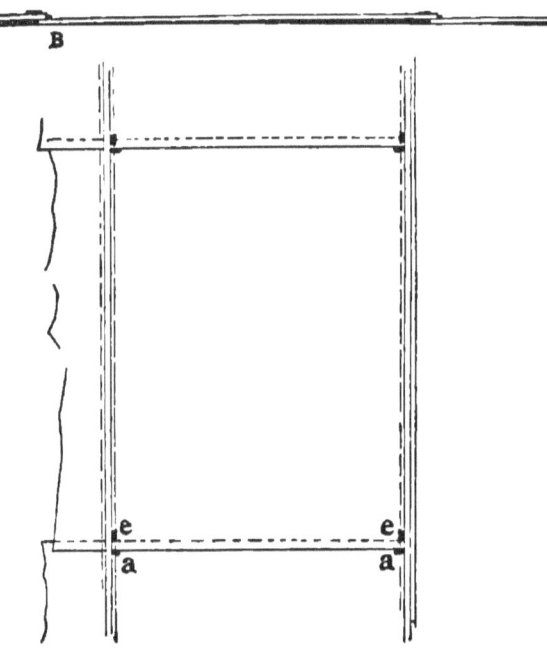

27. *The laying of lapped glass.*

most forcing-houses, and for all establishments which are likely to be often modified and extended. It is particularly desirable in the forcing of such "warm" plants as tomatoes and melons. For conservatory purposes, for straight runs and small and cool houses, it is equaled—probably surpassed in many instances—by water. Steam overcomes obstacles, as elbows and angles and obstructions, better than hot water. It travels faster and farther. Crooked runs with little fall are great difficulties in hot water heating. Steam can be varied more quickly than hot water. On the other hand, steam is as steady as hot water under proper management, and it requires but little more attention. Practically the same treatment is required by both water and steam heaters. Plants thrive as well under steam heat as under hot water heat. The opinion that steam heat is a "dry heat" is erroneous. Hot water heating demands from a half to twice more piping than steam heating, and the original cost is, therefore, greater. This additional piping has a certain advantage, however, inasmuch as each pipe is less hot than in steam systems and is less likely to injure plants which stand close to it. This advantage is not great, however, especially in forcing establishments, where no injury need ever come from hot steam pipes. There is no uniform advantage in consumption of fuel in either system. Theoretically, hot water is probably more economical than steam, but in practice the cost is determined largely by the particular pattern of heater and the general efficiency of the system. Some tests show water to be the more economical, and other tests give the advantage to steam. In other words, the fuel consumption is largely a local question.

The summary results of various experiments upon the comparative merits of steam and water for heating plant houses, made at Cornell University (and reported in Bulletins 41, 55 and 96), are as follows:*

1. The temperatures of steam pipes average higher than those of hot water pipes, under common conditions.

2. When the risers or flow pipes are overhead, the steam spends relatively more of its heat in the returns, as bottom heat, than the water does.

---

*Other studies in glass house heating will be found in Bulletins 4, 6, 8 and 15 of the Massachusetts Hatch Station (by S. T. Maynard), and in Bulletin 63 of the Michigan Station (by L. R. Taft). In these experiments, water gave the better results.

3. The heat from steam distributes itself over a great length of pipe more readily than that from hot water, and steam, therefore has a distinct advantage for heating long runs.

4. Steam is preferable to hot water for irregular and crooked circuits.

5. Unfavorable conditions of piping can be more readily overcome with steam than with water.

6. The addition of crooks and angles in pipes is decidedly disadvantageous to the circulation of hot water, and of steam without pressure; but the effect is scarcely perceptible with steam under low pressure.

7. In starting a new fire with cold water, circulation begins with hot water sooner than with steam, but, in ordinarily long runs, it requires a longer time for the water to reach a point where the temperature of the house is materially affected than for the steam to do so.

8. The length of pipe to be traversed is a much more important consideration with water than with steam, for the friction of the water upon the pipe is much greater than the friction of steam, and a long run warms slowly with water.

9. It is necessary to exercise greater care in grading pipes for water heating than for steam heating. With steam, a satisfactory fall towards the boiler is much more important than the exact manner of laying the pipes.

10. In heating by water in closed circuits, a high expansion tank may increase the efficiency by allowing the water to become hotter throughout the system, and probably by giving a better circulation.

Piping.—The arrangement of the pipes must be adjusted by the shape and size of the house and the crop to be grown. The "cool" plants, like lettuce and cauliflower (see page 5), do best without bottom heat, and for these crops the pipes should be above the soil or bed. The "warm" plants, like tomato, melon and cucumber, require bottom heat, and for these the return pipes, or some of them, should be underneath the bed. The steam or hot water is carried into the house by means of one or two pipes,—called risers when steam is used, and flow-pipes when water is used,—and is returned to the heater through from two to six times as many returns. The risers or flows are usually carried into the house overhead, and the returns are carried underneath the benches, along the walls, or the sides of the walks. Aside from the greater number of pipes required in water heating, there is little difference in the methods of piping for the two systems. The highest point in the steam riser should be directly over the heater, or, when this is not practicable, it should be at the near end of the house or system, and the riser should gradually fall from this point to the far end of the house. This gives a down-hill system. It is generally considered that the highest point in the water flow-pipe should be at the far end of the house or system. This is an up-hill system. Flow-pipes should not be less than 2 inches in diameter for runs of 60 ft., while steam may be carried in a 1½-inch riser under similar circumstances. In water runs of this length, there should be two risers for houses 16 to 20 feet wide, particulary if warm plants are to be grown.

The amount of pipe required for special cases may be determined by examining some of the plans and illustrations. Fig. 1 illustrates two methods of piping. It may be piped by running a water flow-pipe underneath the bench on either side and carrying back two returns under each flow. This type of heating is not common. In such cases, it would no doubt be necessary to keep the space under the benches open next the walk in order to heat the house. A commoner method is to carry a riser or flow overhead at X, and to bring back six returns from it. In Fig. 2, a 2-inch steam riser is carried overhead in the center, and it breaks into seven 1¼-inch risers underneath the benches. There is a similar arrangement in Fig. 3. These two houses would grow tomatoes in New York state. In Fig. 4, two 3-inch water flows near the peak supply six 1½-inch returns under

28. *Piping with hot water for tomato growing.*

the two upper benches, and another 3-inch flow and three 1½-inch returns heat the lower bed. This same house could be heated with steam by one 2-inch riser and six to eight 1¼-inch returns. An exposed tomato house (Fig. 14, page 31), is heated by a 1½-inch steam riser which feeds a 1-inch loop running around the house just under the plate, and four 1¼-inch loops just above the soil. Another loop and a half (from an independent riser) runs about the center walk. In this house, the bottom heat is supplied by the heaters themselves, which stand just beneath the floor. The floor is made of two layers of inch boards, with tar between the layers.

Fig. 15 (page 32), showing a house used for lettuce, cauliflowers, carnations and chrysanthemums, 20 ft. wide and 60 ft. long, is heated by one 2-inch steam riser and two 1½-inch returns under each side bench. The middle bench is solid, and has no bottom heat. Fig. 28 (page 45) shows the water returns in a tomato house near Philadelphia. There are eight returns under each bench, the coil standing edgewise under the left-hand bench, and lying flat-wise under the other.

Flues and stoves.—Beginners with little capital can make a very good forcing-house with old sash, and can heat the same with flues from a home-made furnace. Lettuce houses can even be heated with a coal stove. The novice will always do well to begin with a small and simple establishment, although it rarely pays to erect a very cheap house if it can be avoided.

COST OF FORCING-HOUSES.

Only the most general remarks can be made respecting the cost of forcing-houses, for so much depends upon the finish, the expense put in foundations, and the experience and efficiency of the workmen. Taft estimates the expense of building a three-quarter span rose house, 20 x 100 ft., including heating apparatus, to average about $1,100 to

$1,200. A forcing-house 20 x 60 ft., uneven-span, on posts, with heavy rafters and glazed with large sash, heated by steam, cost complete as follows, including a rough shed in which to place the heater:

Lumber	$99 61
Carpenter work	72 75
General labor	63 63
Iron supports and plates	9 16
39 sash	39 00
Glass, 12 x 16	62 37
Glazing	18 13
Paint, oil, etc.	14 52
Hardware and miscellaneous	20 36
	$379 63
Heating apparatus and piping	375 00
	$754 53

The labor of building the benches was done by the gardener after the house was completed.

Seven years later, this house was wholly rebuilt, an entire new roof being put on and comprising only sash-bars and double-thick glass. This rebuilt house, with the upper bench not yet made, is shown in Fig. 15. The total cost of the new roof, new plates, one new bench, and general repairs, was as follows:

52 sash-bars, 16 ft. long	$18 78
52 " 12 ft. long	14 08
Work upon bars	14 33
Sills	19 42
Glass, 14 x 18	96 00
150 ft. pine for ventilators	7 40
50 panes glass for ventilators	10 00
Putty and points	5 75
Tinning 80 ft. gutter, and labor	13 08
Painting, 2 coats	6 50
Labor	80 48
250 ft. pine for jambs and repairs, and hardware and incidentals	14 20
	$300 02

In general, it may be said that a house 20 x 100 ft., 12

feet high at the ridge, with no glass on the sides, on post wall, can be built for $1,000 to $1,200, steam heating plant complete, if the workmen about the place assist in the construction.

A forcing-house 50 x 400 ft., broken span, with the rear roof 20 ft. wide and the front one 32 ft. wide, with the front wall 4 ft. high and the rear one 8 ft. high, 17 ft. high at the ridge, on post walls, glass 20 x 30 inches, sash-bars 2 x 3 inches, was built, and fitted with steam, for $6,000.

The house shown in Figs. 5 and 6 (the property of Fred. Busch, Minneapolis) is 60 x 300 ft., with a mushroom shed 16 x 300 ft. on the back. The total direct cash expense of this structure was $3,300. To this has to be added the work of the regular hired men in doing all the grading, the setting of the pipe posts for purlines, half of all the glazing work, all the work of steam fitting, and half of the painting; also 4,000 ft. of old pipe which had been used in hot-beds, and all the glass used in the gables and which had been taken from an old house which was torn down. The estimated expense of all this extra work and second-hand material is $700, making the total cost of the house, shed and all, $4,000.

The range of nine houses shown at the left in Fig. 8, and again in Fig. 9 (also the property of Mr. Busch), each house 20 x 90 ft., cost, complete, as I am informed by the owner, $3,600. This is an unusually low cost, being only $400 per house.

CHAPTER III.

MANAGEMENT OF THE FORCING-HOUSE.

PROBABLY there is no horticultural industry in which experience counts for so much as in the management of plants in glass houses. Yet it is not essential that one "serve his time" in the business in order to learn it. Many of our best greenhouse men have taken up the occupation late in life, or have come to it from widely different vocations. Even then, they have come to their success by actually doing the work, but they shorten their period of manual experience by bringing to bear upon their work all the helps of reading, observation, and reflection. Whilst it is impossible to teach a person how to run a greenhouse, it is nevertheless profitable to give certain hints and suggestions to direct the course of his effort.

TEMPERATURES FOR THE VARIOUS CROPS.

The following figures represent the approximate average temperatures at which winter vegetables are forced. The night temperatures are supposed to represent the lowest or minimum averages, and the day temperatures are taken in the shade in days of average sunshine :

Cool Plants—

	Day	Night
Lettuce	55° to 60°	40° to 45°
Radish	55° to 60°	45° to 50°
Asparagus and rhubarb (when forced from established plants)	60° to 65°	55°
Celery	60° to 65°	55°
Cauliflower	60° to 70°	55°

Warm Plants—

	Day	Night
Tomato	75°	65°
Cucumber	75° to 80°	65° to 70°
Melon	75° to 85°	65° to 70°
Eggplant	75° to 80°	65°
Pepper	75°	65°
Asparagus and rhubarb (when forced from temporary roots)	75° to 85°	65° to 70°

In bright days the temperature may run much higher than these figures, but if plenty of fresh air is given on such occasions no ill results should follow.

SOILS FOR FORCED VEGETABLES.

Forcing-house soils should not only be rich in available plant food, but they should be of a mellow and friable texture, so that the water soaks through them uniformly, leaving them dryish and loose on top. A soil with much clay tends to run together, or to cement itself, especially if watered from a hose, and the plants tend to make a spindling and unwilling growth. On the other hand, a soil with very much manure or litter is so loose as not to hold sufficient water to keep the plant in health; or if it does hold the requisite moisture, it tends to produce a robust and over-willing growth at the expense of fruit. Yet, despite all this, the skill of the gardener is much more important than the character of the soil, for a skillful man will handle even hard clay soils in such manner as to give good results. The chief single factor of manipulation in determining the productivity of soil in forcing-houses is the watering, to which we shall presently advert.

The best forcing-house soils are those which have a foundation of good garden loam, and are lightened up with sharp sand and some kind of fiber. This fiber is usually very well rotted manure, or rotted sods. Thin sods cut from an old pasture—especially from one which has a clay loam soil—and allowed to stand in a low flat pile for a year or so, being turned or forked over once or twice in the meantime, make a most excellent foundation for a greenhouse soil. A satisfactory mixture may be made by using one-third of these rotted sods, one-third of mellow garden loam, and one-third of fine old horse manure which has not been leached. If the garden soil has itself been well enriched with stable manures, it will not be necessary to add so much in the mixture. If the completed soil contains so much clay as to be sticky, the addition of sand will correct it. Leaf mold (not leaves) in limited quantity is a most excellent substitute for manure. Broken and pulverized peat may also be used. It is always important that the materials used in the forcing-house soil should be fine and well broken down by the processes of decay. Fresh and undecomposed materials give variable and unpredictable results; they are the "raw" soils of gardeners. Heavy clays are to be avoided in the making of forcing-house soils, particularly if one desires to grow the heading lettuces.

The forcing-house soil is mixed by shoveling the ingredients from piles into a central common pile, a given number of shovelfuls from each, and then shoveling the mixture over once or twice. It is a good practice to cover the bottom of the bench — especially for melons and cucumbers — with inverted sods, and then to put on the prepared soil. Many gardeners do not take this trouble of mixing the soil, and it is not necessary if one is able to find a natural soil to his liking; but unless the right soil is at hand, it is always safer to take this extra pains rather than to rely upon an indifferent soil. One cannot afford to take any unnecessary risks in the forcing of vegetables.

When the crops are grown on benches — as those must be which require bottom-heat — it is necessary to change the soil every year. This is because the soil loses texture or fiber and becomes partially exhausted of available plant food, and it is likely to contain the spores of fungi or the eggs of insects. Houses in which the soil remains unchanged rarely long remain free of serious insect or fungous invasions; and in selecting soils for houses, it is of the utmost importance to avoid bringing in grubs, cutworms, wire-worms, tomato rust, and the like. It is perfectly possible to add plant food to the old soil, but it is impossible to restore its texture by that means, and the physical texture is usually more important than its actual store of food. In the forcing of lettuce upon ground beds, it is not always essential to remove the earth every year, although an inch or two of the top must be removed if the mildew has been serious, and the soil should always be fertilized before another season of forcing is begun. The best growers prefer, however, to replace four or five inches of the top soil every summer.

THE QUESTION OF FERTILIZERS.

Most forcing-house crops need to be fertilized as they grow. This is particularly important for tomatoes, cucumbers and melons. The fertilizer most liked by gardeners is liquid manure. This is made from old unleached cow manure (such as has been lying for some months in a barn basement). A bushel of it is placed in a half-barrel or tub and the receptacle is filled with water. After standing two or three days, being stirred occasionally in the meantime, the liquid is ready for use. This liquid must be reduced before it is applied to soil in which plants are growing, and the amount of reduction to give it can be determined only by experience. Ordinarily, one quart of liquid made as here directed will be sufficient for a gallon of the diluted material; that is, one quart of the manure water is added to three quarts of clear water. If the manure is strong, the tub may be filled with water three or four times before the strength of the material is dissolved out. A tub of this manure liquid should always be accessible in forcing-house work. How often the liquid shall be applied to the crops must be determined for each particular case. If the soil is rich, the plants will not be likely to need the liquid manure in their young or maiden stage, but as soon as the melons or tomatoes are set the fertilizing will usually be appreciated. It is then sometimes profitable to apply it freely once or twice a week.

There is very little exact knowledge respecting the use of chemical fertilizers for forcing-house crops. The best gardeners generally like to add bone flour or some commercial fertilizer to soils which have not already been well fertilized, and it is a common practice to work a dressing of bone into the soil after the plants become well established.

The Connecticut experiments with tomatoes.—The best experiments which have been made in this country upon fertilizers for forced vegetables were conducted at the Connecticut Experiment Station.* These experiments were concerned with tomatoes and lettuce under glass. A full abstract of these studies, so far as they give direct horticultural results, will be useful and suggestive to the gardener and the student.

"To those who are raising or contemplate raising winter crops under glass, the question of substituting fertilizers for manure, in part at least, is a very important one. Forcing-house soil, as it is usually prepared, consists of rich garden soil or rotted turf, composted with from one-fourth to one-half its bulk of horse manure. Aside from the labor of hauling and of repeatedly working over this material to secure the fine mellow condition which is desired, the cost formerly was not great. But the general introduction of electric cars has cut down enormously the production of horse manure in cities, which has been the main dependence of our market gardeners. In consequence, the preparation of suitable

---

* E. H. Jenkins and W. E. Britton in Nineteenth Rep. Conn. Agr. Exp. Sta. (for 1895), pp. 75-98. The reader may also find experiments upon forcing-house fertilizers in Bull. 10 (1890) and 15 (1891) of the Mass. Hatch Exp. Sta., and in Bull. 43 (1892) of the Ohio Station.

soil for forcing-houses is increasingly expensive. Besides this, it is found that even a rich natural soil cannot carry forcing-house tomatoes to their highest productiveness, and therefore liquid manure is often used to water the soil after the plants have come into bearing.

"The admirable work on the use of commercial fertilizers on field tomatoes done at the New Jersey Station has proved that the ripening of the crop may be very materially hastened by the proper use of fertilizer chemicals, especially of nitrate of soda.* To hasten the ripening of crops under glass, where the expense of growing them is so much greater than in the field, must greatly increase the profits of the business.

"These considerations have led us to endeavor to determine with all possible accuracy how much plant food various forcing-house crops take from the soil during their growth, and whether commercial fertilizers can be used instead of stable manure, wholly or in part, to supply this plant food. A further question also connected with these is, whether the humus of rotted manure, generally regarded as necessary to regulate the storage and circulation of moisture in the soil under natural conditions, can be replaced by some cheap substitute, or dispensed with altogether in forcing-house culture, where the supply of soil moisture can be well regulated by artificial means."

"Our first endeavor was to find out how much nitrogen tomato plants raised under glass take from the soil, in their fruit and vines, and how much nitrogen needs to be in the soil to meet fully this demand of the plants. These questions we studied by raising tomatoes in plots on the forcing-house benches which were filled with a soil known to be practically free from available nitrogen, but believed to contain all other ingredients necessary

---

*[Similar, though less specific, results have been obtained by the Cornell Station. See its Bulletins X., XXI., 32, 45.]

for a maximum tomato crop. To these plots were added known quantities of nitrogen in form of nitrate of soda."

Five plots (numbered from 4 to 8) were set aside in the center bed of a forcing-house, each plot containing about 14 square feet. The benches were 9 inches deep, and the artificial soils were filled in to the depth of 8 inches. " The soil for each plot was separately mixed as follows : 300 pounds of anthracite coal ashes, sifted to pass a wire screen with four meshes to the inch, were spread on a cement floor, and 9 pounds of peat moss, such as is sold in the cities for stable bedding, screened like the ashes, were scattered over them. To these were added three and one-half ounces of precipitated carbonate of lime, to neutralize a slight acidity of the peat and give to the whole a mild alkaline reaction. These materials were shoveled over twice carefully and then spread as before.

"The fertilizers designed for the plot — [nitrate of soda, dissolved bone black, and muriate of potash] — were sprinkled over this mixture and the whole was carefully shoveled over twice again to secure as perfect a mixture as possible of fertilizers and soil, and then carried in a hand-barrow to the designated plot in the forcing-house.

"The north bench in the same house was filled with a rich soil prepared by composting good thick turf with one-third its bulk of stable manure. Plants were set in this bench mainly to make a rough comparison between crops grown on the two radically different soils. The exposure of the two benches was slightly different, that of the north bench being, perhaps, somewhat less favorable as regards light. The plants set in the north bench were also much closer together.

"Three varieties of tomatoes were used : Ignotum, Acme, and Dwarf Champion, two plants of each variety being set in each plot, and all receiving the same treatment."

The tabular results of these experiments are as follows :

MANAGEMENT OF THE FORCING-HOUSE.

Fertilizers applied.	Plot 4.				Plot 5.				Plot 6.				Plot 7.				Plot 8.			
	Ignotum.	Acme.	Dwarf Champion.		Ignotum.	Acme.	Dwarf Champion.		Ignotum.	Acme.	Dwarf Champion.		Ignotum.	Acme.	Dwarf Champion.		Ignotum.	Acme.	Dwarf Champion.	
Nitrate of soda	none.				68.1 grams.				113.5 grams.				158.9 grams.				204.2* grams.			
Equivalent nitrogen					10.9				18.?				25.4				32.7			
Dissolved bone black	none.				47.9				47.0				47.9				47.9			
Equivalent phosphoric acid					8.1				8.1				8.1				8.1			
Muriate of potash	none.				58.6				58.6				58.6				58.6			
Equivalent potash					29.3				29.3				29.3				29.3			
Total yield of fruit	316 grams.				4,840 grams.				8,331 grams.				10,595 grams.				12,522 grams.			
Variety	Ignotum.	Acme.	Dwarf Champion.		Ignotum.	Acme.	Dwarf Champion.		Ignotum.	Acme.	Dwarf Champion.		Ignotum.	Acme.	Dwarf Champion.		Ignotum.	Acme.	Dwarf Champion.	
Yield of each variety, 2 plants, grams	120	155	41		1934	1853	1053		2285	3870	2176		3081	4421	3003		4194	5205	3123	
Average yield per plant, grams	60	77.5	20.5		967	926.5	526.5		1142.5	1935	1088		1540.5	2210.5	1501.5		2097	2602.5	1561.5	
" " " pound	.13	.17	.04		2.13	2.04	1.16		2.52	4.27	2.40		3.40	4.88	3.31		4.63	5.74	3.44	
Average number fruits per plant	1	1.5	.5		8	12.5	6		4.27	18.5	11.5		12	19.5	19.5		23.5	23.5	16	
Average weight per fruit, grams	60	51.6	41		120.8	74.1	87.7		142.8	104.6	94.6		124.2	113.3	77		89.2	110.7	97.5	
Average number of double fruits	0	0	0		0	0	0		.5	1	0		3	.5	5		0	1.5	.5	
" " perfect shaped fruits	0	1.5	.5		0	4.5	2		4	3.5	3.5		3	10.5	7.5		3	11.5	4	
Per cent of perfect shaped fruits	0	100	100		0	36	33		50	19	30		25	51	38		13	48	25	
Average yield per square foot of bench area, grams	25.95	32.52	8.86		418.34	400.82	227.77		494.26	837.11	470.69		666.45	956.30	649.58		907.20	1125.89	675.52	
Average yield per square foot of bench area, pounds	.057	.074	.012		.92	.88	.50		1.09	1.84	1.03		1.47	2.11	1.21		2.00	2.48	1.48	

* One-half mixed with the soil at setting time, the rest spread on the surface Feb. 11.

Some of the horticultural statistics of these results are as follows:

"1. The highest average weight per fruit of the Ignotum variety was on plot 6, of the Acme on plot 7, and of the Dwarf Champion on plot 8.

"2. The tendency to bear double flowers, which produced irregular-shaped fruit, seemed to bear no relation to the quantity of nitrogen applied, nor to the variety. The same plant produced both single and double blossoms.

"3. The number of perfect fruits was absolutely larger on the plots receiving most nitrogen, but there was no very marked relative increase in number.

"4. Comparison of the three varieties shows that Acme gave the largest yield in artificial soil, but the yield of Ignotum was considerably the largest of the three when grown in rich garden soil.

"Acme gave the greatest average number of tomatoes per plant, while the average weight per fruit of Ignotum was considerably greater than that of the other varieties.

"5. The Dwarf Champion proved to be an unprofitable variety in this test.

"6. Tomatoes from the unfertilized plot (Plot 4) were small, smooth, and of good shape, but the color was not normal. They were too light in color and slightly rusty-looking,—having a faded appearance. The flesh of the tomato was very dry, and sweet to the taste—much sweeter than tomatoes from other plots.

"Tomatoes of best form, size and color grew upon plots 6 and 7. Those from plot 8 (and a few from plot 7) ripened very unevenly, and were green about the stem when the other side of the fruit was of good color and apparently ripe. These tomatoes had a decided tendency towards softness while still green; the form and size were very good."

We come now to a comparison of plants grown in natural soil with those grown in artificial soil. "These were set much closer in the bench than those grown in artificial soil. The latter had a bench space of 2.31 square feet per plant, the former about 1.15 square feet. The plants in soil had three weeks the start of those in ashes and peat, being set in the beds on December 7th, while the plants were not set in the ashes and peat until December 31st. These facts render any very strict comparison of the two impossible, nor was strict comparison intended when the experiment was begun. The following facts, however, deserve notice. In what follows we refer only to the crops grown on plots 7 and 8. The others, 4, 5, and 6, had no adequate supply of nitrogen, and it must also be borne in mind that plots 7 and 8 in all probabilty did not have a full supply of either nitrogen, phosphoric acid, or potash.

"The tomatoes grown in ashes and peat grew and fruited much more rapidly than those in natural soil, and then suddenly stopped their growth and bearing, the leaves turned brown and the plants appeared to be dead. They were not dead, however, by any means, and after cutting back to near the roots and supplying more fertilizers, they made a new and vigorous growth and fruited again. The plants grown in natural soil, however, kept bearing a little fruit till the following July, when they were thrown out to make room for other experiments.

"We believe the plants in peat and ashes fruited more quickly and abundantly, because they had at first a larger supply of soluble plant food than those in natural soil:— that when that was exhausted, they had no resource, and died back in consequence:— that if they had been sufficiently fertilized, they would have proved far more prolific and profitable than those in natural soil. To decide this will be one point in further experiments.

"The following statement gives the average yield per plant of the three varieties (4 plants of each) on plot 8 in artificial soil with commercial fertilizers, also the average yield per plant (an equal number of each of the three varieties was used to calculate this) of the three varieties grown in rich natural soil up to April 17th, the date when, as already described, the plants in artificial soil died back for lack of nourishment. Up to this date the plants had been growing in the natural soil three weeks longer than in the artificial soil. The total yield of the plants in natural soil, up to July 16th, is also given, though after the middle of April there is little or no profit in forcing-house tomatoes." The tabular results are as follows:

	Peat and ashes with fertilizers.	Natural soil.	
	To April 17th	To April 17th	To July 16th
Yield per plant (grams)	2087	976	1820
Yield per plant (pounds)	4.59	2.15	4.00
Number of fruits per plant	21	10.4	22.7
Weight of fruits (grams)	99.1	91.7	82.4
Yield per square foot (grams)	904	847.0	1583
Yield per square foot (pounds)	1.99	1.86	3.5

"The table shows that up to the time when the fertilizers in the artificial soil were proved (by the chemical analyses) to be exhausted, the plants in artificial soil had produced, per square foot of bench space, 7 per cent more tomatoes than those in the natural soil, while the latter had, up to that time, three weeks more of growing season. It is possible that the plants in natural soil, if they had been set further apart, would have, in the same time, made a larger crop per foot of bench space. It is possible, too, that with an increased supply of fertilizers the plants in artificial soil would have given a largely increased yield. We cite these figures only to show that the tomato crop can be successfully grown in a soil made of ashes and peat, such as we have described, with the aid of commercial fertilizers."

While these experiments were inaugurated "solely to determine how much nitrogen in the soil was necessary for the full development of the tomato plant," the experimenters nevertheless " feel justified in calling attention to certain apparent advantages in using the artificial soil." In this artificial soil there is less liability to fungous troubles and insects, and the cost is less than for natural soils. "For every 100 square feet of bench space, about 2,200 pounds of sifted coal ashes and 63 pounds of dried peat or leaf mold is required to fill the bench 8 inches deep with soil. Experiments are now in progress to determine whether the use of peat is necessary. About 10 pounds of commercial fertilizers are needed for this bench space, costing, at present ruling ton rates, less than 21 cents. The cost of these things is to be compared with the cost of providing a considerably greater weight of rich compost containing a large relative amount of stable manure. In very many cases, the cost of filling the benches with the artificial soil must be very much less than the cost of filling them with rich garden soil.

"The greatest expense in running a forcing-house is the artificial heat required, and for this reason, quick growth and early maturity are extremely desirable. Regarding the relative availability of the potash and phosphates in compost and in commercial fertilizers, we know little, but it is very certain that the nitrogen of composts is slowly available as compared with the nitrogen of nitrates. Our tomato tests showed, too, very clearly, that plants in natural soil made much slower growth and were slower in fruiting than those in artificial soil supplied with nitrates. Though the former were set fully three weeks earlier, both began fruiting at the same time."

The general summary of all the results of fertilizing the tomatoes is as follows:

"1. A forcing-house tomato crop yielding about two pounds of fruit for each square foot of bench room, takes, in the vines and fruit, for every hundred square feet of bench space, not less than:

	Grams.			Lbs	Ozs.
Nitrogen	168	Equivalent to	Nitrate of soda	2	5
Phosphoric acid	65	"	" Dissolved bone black	0	13
Potash	362	"	" Muriate of potash	1	9

"Of this from a fourth to a fifth only is in the vines.

"2. To enable the plants to get these fertilizer elements as required, there should be a large excess of them in the soil, perhaps double the quantity given above.

"3. Every 100 pounds of tomato fruit takes from the soil approximately:

	Ounces.		Ounces.
Nitrogen	2.2	Equivalent to Nitrate of soda	14
Phosphoric acid	0.9	" " Dissolved bone black	5
Potash	4.5	" " Muriate of potash	10

"4. It is possible to grow a crop of forcing-house tomatoes, amounting to two or more pounds per square foot of bench space, perfectly normal in size, color, taste and chemical composition, by the aid of commercial fertilizers alone, and in soil composed of coal ashes and peat."

The Connecticut experiments with lettuce. — Experiments like those detailed for the tomatoes were also made upon lettuce. Four plots (numbered from 38 to 41) of Simpson White-seeded and Tennisball varieties, each containing about 11½ square feet, received each 200 pounds of the peat and ashes mixture (containing 5 per cent of peat). The bed was filled to a depth of 6 inches. Some of the details of the test are as follows:

Fertilizers applied.	Plot 38.	Plot 39.	Plot 40.	Plot 41.
Nitrogen	7.11 grams	11.80 grams	16.59 grams	21.34 grams
Equivalent nitrate of soda	44.4 "	74.0 "	103.7 "	133.4 "
Phosphoric acid	6.80 "	6.80 "	6.80 "	6.80 "
Equivalent dissolved bone black	40.0 "	40.0 "	40.0 "	40.0 "
Potash	24.24 "	24.24 "	24.24 "	24.24 "
Equivalent muriate of potash	48.5 "	48.5 "	48.5 "	48.5 "
Crops harvested.				
Lettuce Heads	1232.8 "	2217.6 "	2720.6 "	3083.1 "
Lettuce Roots (with much adhering soil)	219.6	361.3 "	368.4 "	368.5 "
Total	1452.4 "	2578.9 "	3089.0 "	3451.6 "
Dry substance of crop	205.5 "	346.2 "	349.56 "	355.83 "

"The facts which this experiment has developed may be summarized as follows:

"1. Lettuce of good quality can be grown under glass in an artificial soil such as we have described, with the use of commercial fertilizers. We are not prepared to say at present that its quality is as good as the best lettuce grown in rich, natural soil.

"2. A crop of forcing-house lettuce, raised as above described, takes from the soil in roots and heads, per 1,000 heads, not less than:

	Grams.		Pounds.	Ounces.	
Nitrogen	282.6	Equivalent to	3	15	Nitrate of soda
Phosphoric acid	87.7	"	1	2	Dissolved bone black.
Potash	621.0	"		2	10	Muriate of potash.

"3. To supply this plant food to the soil under the conditions of our experiment, it was necessary to add to the soil the following quantities of fertilizers per 1,000 plants, or per 387 square feet, the area used in our experiment for 1,000 plants:

	Pounds.	Ounces.	Costing, cents.
Nitrate of soda	9	13	25
Dissolved bone black	2	15	4
Muriate of potash	3	8	7
			36 "

On the use of fresh stable manure.—All experienced gardeners place the greatest faith in old well-rotted stable manure, and uniformly avoid fresh manure. A discussion of the behavior of fresh manure in its relation to nitrification is made in the Connecticut report which is quoted above, and it seems to throw much light upon the craft of gardeners. A somewhat full abstract of the article is here given. It is known that when nitrogen compounds, either in the form of nitrates or occurring in organic matter in manures, are fully exposed to the air, the nitrogen may be lost as gas by the action of certain denitrifying microbes. It now seems probable that similar losses, though much less in amount, may be occasioned in the soil by the use of fresh stable manure. Wagner has found that the nitrogen of well-rotted stable manure is much less readily available to plants than has been generally supposed. If the availability of the nitrogen of nitrates be taken as 100, that of the nitrogen of well-rotted manure was only 45 per cent. Kühn has found, on the other hand, that the nitrogen of fresh cattle dung is very readily available. If the availability of the nitrogen of sulphate of ammonia be taken as 100, that of fresh manure was 92 per cent. Wagner further observed that fresh manure has a decided tendency to liberate the nitrogen of nitrates or of green manures, so "that the increase of crops secured by the horse dung and nitrates, etc., together, may be less than is produced by the nitrates, etc., alone."

"It appears that soils, to which were added three grams of nitrogen; viz., two grams in form of fresh horse dung and one gram in form of nitrate of soda, yielded a very considerably smaller crop than the same soil to which one gram of nitrate nitrogen was added without dung. This, according to Wagner, is explained by the fact that the microbes in the fresh dung expelled nitrogen in the gaseous form, both from the dung itself and from the nitrate, before vegetation could assimilate it.

"While the horse dung applied in Wagner's trials was fresh and the quantities were much larger than are ordinarily used in farm practice, yet the facts above cited have a very important bearing on the use of fresh stable manure and possibly on the value of composts, such as are used for forcing-house soil, in which the proportion of stable manure is approximately near to that which was used in Wagner's tests, where a large loss of nitrogen was observed. It might, therefore, happen that applications of nitrates or other nitrogenous fertilizers to the soil of the forcing-house would have no marked effect on the crop, while nevertheless available nitrogen was deficient and the crop suffering in consequence. This result might at least be expected to follow the use of fresh manure water."

Tests made at the Connecticut Station itself confirmed these general results. The investigation was carried to mixtures of nitrates with garden loam and to potting soil, as well as to mixtures with fresh manure. The garden soil had very little effect in reducing the nitrates.

In another experiment, fresh horse dung and potting soil were used. The potting soil "was made of pasture sod and the soil just beneath, composted with about one-third their bulk of mixed horse and cow manures. The mixture, made in the summer of 1894, had stood in a conical, compact pile, exposed till the fall of 1895. The soil for this experiment was taken from the interior of this pile at a depth of 2-3 feet." * * * "While the surface soil of the garden, although heavily dressed each year with stable manure, had little or no effect in destroying nitrates, the potting earth (made by composting contiguous pasture sod and a few inches of underlying soil with stable manure), reduced nitrates to about half the extent caused by fresh horse dung.

"This result is in accord with familiar facts. The surface soil of tilled ground is commonly or always charged with oxidizing and nitrifying organisms. Fresh and damp compost heaps where vegetable or animal matters are abundant and the soil of forests, low meadows and bogs, contain little or no nitrates, and their bacterial growths are of the deoxidizing or reducing kinds. It is probable that, near the surface of the heap of potting earth, nitrifying organisms were abundant at the very time when the sample taken from the interior was found to have a denitrifying effect. Accordingly, the use of potting earth from the exterior of a compost heap may occasion no loss of nitrate-nitrogen, while earth from the interior of the heap may reduce nitrates and cause serious waste of any nitrate that is applied as a fertilizer. It is therefore advisable, some time before using potting compost, to place it under cover away from rain, and to intermix it thoroughly and frequently, and to keep it in rather shallow heaps."

WATERING.

Of all the operations which fall to the lot of the gardener, there is perhaps none which requires the exercise of so much judgment as the watering of plants growing under glass. The frequency of the watering, the amounts to apply, and how to apply it, must all be determined by the immediate conditions. There can be no rules for the practice. The best single statement to make, perhaps, is to say that plants should be watered when they need it; but this means little. Plants may need water and yet be ruined by the giving of it. Watering is performed primarily to supply the plant with food, yet there are certain secondary effects of the practice which should be thoroughly understood.

It must first be said that the application of water radically changes, for the time being, both the temperature and physical condition of the soil, and these features are the very ones which bear most intimate relations to plant growth. Watering modifies the temperature of the soil, both because the water itself absorbs heat and because the evaporation of it is a cooling process. Plants which love a high temperature receive a serious check the moment the soil is drenched with cold water. The grower of winter melons, for example, must never hope for the best success if he soaks his benches with hydrant water. As a rule, water must be given at such times that it will change the temperature of the soil the least and will allow the quickest return to its normal warmth. In the middle of the day, the change produced by watering may be too violent. Water is then supplied indirectly by wetting down the walks; and when the temperature of the air has been somewhat reduced the plants may be syringed and the soil may be watered, if it needs. It is generally better to water forced vegetables early in the day in order that the soil may become thoroughly warmed up again before night. Watering towards night is likely to carry the plants too cool through the night, for the body of warm earth is a powerful factor in regulating and conserving the night temperature of the house. While it is generally not advisable to thoroughly water the soil from a hose in the middle of the day, it is, nevertheless, very essential that the most profuse waterings be given on sunny days. This is because, as already stated, the sun soon warms up the house, and also because the house and foliage soon dry off. Houses which have a continually damp air breed soft plants and fungous diseases. The plants should go into the night dry—never wet. It is always best to withhold water on dull days, unless the plants are actually suffering for it. Perhaps these remarks cannot be better summed up than by saying that glass houses should be watered on a rising temperature, not on a falling temperature.

The next most important secondary effect of watering, as already indicated, is the modification of the physical texture of the soil. The application of water tends to run the soil particles together, thus solidifying or compacting the earth. In the instance of clay soils, this cementing action of the water may proceed so far that the surface of the bed may become actually hard and almost non-absorbent of water. When soils arrive at this condition, they are incapable of producing good plants, no matter how much plant food they may contain. There is greater danger of compacting the soil when watering from a hose than from a pot. A good forcing-house soil remains open and porous to the last. The water quickly settles away into it and leaves the surface friable and open. When the surface remains wet and sticky, good plants are grown only with much difficulty. The physical condition of the surface soil may also be greatly improved by frequent tillage, for stirring the soil (an inch or so deep) as often as it becomes hard is quite as necessary in the forcing-house as out of doors.

The entire body of soil should be wetted when water

is applied, and the normal condition of the surface should be simply moistness, not wetness. Of the two extremes, an habitually dry surface soil is much better than an habitually wet one. The fungi of damping-off breed profusely upon wet surfaces; and these soils are the ones, too, upon which the green "moss" (which is really an alga) thrives. All this means that when water is used on the soil, it should be applied thoroughly, and that the under soil should remain moister than the surface soil. Frequent and slight waterings produce just the opposite conditions of distribution of moisture, and thereby invite fungous disorders at the same time that they withhold water from the roots of the plants.

Benches usually require closer attention than beds do, especially (as in the case of tomatoes and melons) when they are subjected to strong bottom heat. The earth then dries out both on top and bottom. It is the commonest thing to find the soil in such benches as dry as powder at the bottom whilst it is abundantly moist on top; and the gardener is generally found to be wondering why his plants ripen up prematurely and bear no crops of consequence. The thorough watering which has been advised above — applying the water until the moisture can be seen or felt along some of the cracks on the bottom of the bench — will remedy this common difficulty; but the operator must be warned that if he allows any water to drip through his bench he may be leaching away valuable plant food. Beds upon the ground dry out from only one surface, and they usually replenish their store of water from the earth by means of capillary action. It is, therefore, necessary to exercise care not to water such beds too heavily. With profuse watering, they soon become soggy, cold and "sour." In the fall and spring months, it is generally necessary to water forcing-house soils every day, but in winter the operation may not be necessary oftener than once or twice a week. There is particular danger of keeping the soil too wet and cold in the long, dull spells of midwinter. In such weather, plants tend to grow soft and succulent, a tendency which is aided by over-watering. If there is a sudden rise in temperature and a spell of bright weather, such flabby plants are likely to flag, scorch, curl, or otherwise suffer. It is, therefore, extremely important that the gardener should aim to keep his plants "hard" in these cloudy days.

In cold weather, the chill should always be taken off the water before it is applied to soil in which "warm" plants — like cucumbers, melons, tomatoes and egg-plants — are growing; and it should also be done with lettuce if the hose water is colder than 60°. There are devices (of which the so-called Kinney pump is a good example) for drawing hot water from a tank or pail into the hose in just the right proportion to temper the water; or, if the establishment is not too large, a watering-pot may be used. In large establishments, where steam power is used, an arrangement can be perfected for ejecting steam into the water. Rain water is undoubtedly the best water for plants, but ordinary spring or reservoir water is not injurious, and is generally used.

WATERING BY SUB-IRRIGATION.

Recent experiments have shown that water may be economically and efficiently applied to forced plants by means of pipes laid in the bottom of the bench. The writer's attention was first called to this line of investigation in 1890, when certain studies were proposed to determine what relation the supply of soil water has to the transpiration of water from the foliage and to the consequent rate of growth of the plant. Experiments were begun at Cornell in 1891, but facilities were not at hand to continue them. In this same year, Mr. W. J. Green published preliminary results of somewhat similar and more important experiments at the Ohio Experiment Station, and his investigations were begun in 1890, in advance of those of any other Station. He has continued these studies until the present time, and he and his colleagues have published various reports of them. Professor F. W. Rane has also made similar investigations at the West Virginia Experiment Station, the results of which are published in Bulletin 33 of that Station.* The entire subject is so important in its relation to the forcing-house industries that I shall make copious extracts from Mr. Green's last bulletin (No. 61, September, 1895) upon the subject.

Construction of beds and benches for sub-irrigation.— "A water-tight bed, or bench bottom, is necessary in sub-irrigation, and there are several methods by which this may be secured. Our first attempt was made with matched lumber or flooring, the joints being filled with white lead. The objection to this method of construction is partly on account of the cost, but more particularly because of the fact that when the boards swell the bottom bulges upward, displacing the irrigating tile and causing leakage. It has been found that common barn boards, or any rough lumber, answers better, if the cracks are battened with lath, and a layer of cement is spread over the entire bottom, deep enough to almost cover the lath. About one-third of good cement and two-thirds sand, made quite thin with water, spread on to the depth of about half an inch, and not allowed to dry too quickly, answers the purpose very well. The bottom boards will last longer than when the soil is placed directly upon them, but the supports underneath need to be somewhat nearer together than in the ordinary method of construction, so as to prevent springing of the boards, which cracks the cement. The greatest difficulty is found in making the sides of the benches water-tight, as no matter how well the side boards are nailed to the bottom boards,

---

*Rane has also published an account of sub-irrigation in the open in Bulletin 34 of the New Hampshire Experiment Station.

they will spring away and cause leakage. To obviate this the cement needs to be put on more thickly at the sides, bringing it up against the side boards two or three inches high, and from one to two inches thick. In fact the office of the cement is to hold the water, while the side boards protect the cement and retain the soil.

"In case it is desired to make a bed on the ground, the bottom may be constructed in the same manner as an ordinary cellar bottom, except that the cement need not be as thick. Sometimes the bottom may be made directly on the clay sub-soil, or clay may be brought in for the purpose and no cement used. There may be some leakage in a clay bottom, but not sufficient to do any harm. In all cases there must be a level bottom, or at least the slope must be slight, and all in one direction. Inequalities in the bottom will prevent the proper working of the irrigating tile and result in unequal distribution of the water, hence a perfect grade is essential. In case benches are constructed, the best plan is to use indestructible material altogether.

"The irrigating tiles [common drain tile] may be laid lengthwise or crosswise the beds, but about fifty feet is the greatest length of tile that will work satisfactorily on a level, and if the runs are to be longer than this, there should be one or two inches fall to each fifty feet. It will be necessary, however, in case there is a fall, to check the water at intervals in order to prevent a too rapid flow towards the lower end. This may be easily done by inserting strips of tin into the joints as often as need be, so as to partially intercept the flow, and to cause the water to run out at the joints wherever needed. When properly laid, rows of tile several hundred feet in length could be made to work satisfactorily, but we have had the best success with short runs of tile, laid crosswise the benches. Instead of using elbows of sewer pipe, a cheaper plan is to employ common tile altogether. In this case, the end of the outer tile is raised so as to come above the top of the bench, in order to admit of inserting the hose in watering. When the tiles are laid crosswise the benches, several may be watered at once by means of a piece of gas pipe with holes bored at suitable distances. When the tiles are laid, they are simply placed end to end, and no cement is needed, although it is sometimes used to prevent the tiles becoming displaced in filling the benches with soil.

"Gas pipe, with holes bored at intervals, has been used with success; also a pipe, called 'structural iron pipe.' This differs from ordinary iron pipe in having a slot along one side. Where the slot is nearly closed, so as to not allow the water to flow too freely, this pipe answers very well, but 2½-inch drain tiles are cheaper than anything else, and are perfectly satisfactory. These tiles are, of course, removed and put in place again each time the soil in the benches is renewed. Another thing in favor of 2¼ or 3-inch tiles, is that the capacity is sufficient, so that it may be filled quickly and the operator may go on to another tile, allowing the water to soak out into the soil, knowing that enough has been given to last several days; but if iron pipes are used, the size must be small because of the cost, and the watering must be more frequent in consequence."

Rane speaks as follows (Bull. 33, W. Virginia Station) of the equipment of the sub-irrigation bench: "The question of economy, when considering the advisability of using sub-irrigated beds, is justly a worthy and important one. There must be a water-tight bed to retain all the water in the soil, the construction of which is necessarily more expensive than in the ordinary method of making beds, provided boards are used. The pipe or tiles are likewise an extra expense. Now, will this expenditure be realized from the advantages gained? The cost of raw material, for example, in two houses, each 50 ft. long and 20 ft. wide, one being arranged for surface and the other for under-surface watering, would be about as follows:

SURFACE.		UNDER-SURFACE.	
Center bed 40 x 8 ft. @ $12 per M	$3 84	Center bed 40 x 8 ft. @ $25 per M	$8 00
2 Side benches 50 x 4 ft. @ $12 per M	4 80	2 Side benches 50 x 4 ft. @ $25 per M	10 00
182 ft. Sideboards @ $20	3 64	182 ft. Sideboards @ $20	3 64
		150 ft. Quarter round @ 1 ct.	1 50
		320 ft. Tile @ $18 per M	5 76
		White lead	1 10
Total	$12 28	Total	$30 00

"The difference between the first cost of the beds in the two houses is, therefore, $17.72. Dividing this amount by two, since the beds will certainly last two years, we have $8.86 as the actual yearly expense of the one house over the other. The fact of this small expenditure in comparison with the great advantages derived from it, establishes its economic importance and thorough practicability.

"Lead or iron pipe may be used in place of the tiles, but are not as practicable when a quantity is to be used. They are more expensive, and better adapted to smaller areas. Lead pipe costs 6 cents per pound, the number of pounds to the foot varying according to the quality. It gives very satisfactory results, and can be used indefinitely. The cost of iron pipe varies according to the size. Although it is less expensive than the lead, it rusts easily, and can not be relied upon after one or two seasons' use. That used the past season, after having been cleaned, is in fair condition for use this year."

Experiments with lettuce and other plants. — After various preliminary tests at the Ohio Station, "three houses, each 20 x 100 ft., have been devoted almost wholly to lettuce, nearly all of which has been sub-irrigated. A middle section in each house has been reserved for surface watering, and the end benches are divided, half being watered by one method and half by the other. Incidentally, this arrangement may be referred to as affording an opportunity to note the behavior of plants in houses where the moisture in the air, in addition to the normal quantity, comes almost wholly from plant transpiration.

"In the following table, the results with a number of varieties are given. This was not intended as a variety experiment, as those in the list are not comparable in the manner presented, since some are varieties which form heads while others do not. All that it is intended to show is the relative development of each variety by the two methods of watering. In this experiment each lot is carried through the entire season of growth by the method indicated. That is, the sub-irrigated plants were treated in that manner from the time the seed was sown until the crop was harvested. The surface-watered plants, on the other hand, were surface-watered during their entire season of growth. This is referred to particularly because it is not the plan which has been followed in the greater number of our experiments. It will be seen that the average gain in favor of the sub-irrigated plots was about 100 per cent.—

THE RESULTS OF SURFACE- AND SUB-IRRIGATION WITH TEN VARIETIES OF LETTUCE.

Variety.	Surface-watered.		Sub-irrigated.	
	Number of plants.	Weight, ounces.	Number of plants.	Weight, ounces.
Chicago Forcing	5	11	5	22
Denver Market	5	8	5	12
Tilton's White Star	5	11	5	32
Henderson's N. Y.	10	22	10	40
Hanson	10	18	10	48
Grand Rapids	25	80	25	208
Iceberg	15	32	15	47
Big Boston	15	21	15	51
Large Boston	10	14	10	31
Rawson's Hot-House	15	23	15	41

"In the next table, the separate results of 15 experiments are given. * * * No effort has been made to select examples, further than to secure a fair average, rather than to present the highest or the lowest. The average gain of the sub-irrigated over the surface-watered in the above cases was a little more than 40 per cent. This increase in weight was made in a little more than six weeks, or from the time the plants were set in the benches to the end of the experiments. That is, all of the plants were sub-irrigated while growing in the flats, or during about half of their period of growth, and not until they were planted in the benches was surface-watering commenced. This is a less favorable showing for sub-irrigation than is made in the last table, by the plan above described, of carrying the plants through the entire period of growth by the respective methods of watering.—

RESULTS IN FIFTEEN SUB-IRRIGATION EXPERIMENTS WITH GRAND RAPIDS LETTUCE.

Experiment.	Surface-watered.		Sub-irrigated.	
	Number of plants.	Weight, ounces.	Number of plants.	Weight, ounces.
I	140	474	140	637
II	100	374	100	512
III	75	287	75	383
IV	100	299	100	453
V	55	297	55	340
VI	100	545	100	602
VII	25	132	25	176
VIII	25	121	25	130
IX	35	212	35	242
X	150	477	150	572
XI	107	554	107	644
XII	144	262	144	337
XIII	32	107	32	147
XIV	96	280	96	380
XV	160	156	160	452

"In the above examples, the surface- and sub-irrigated plots were side by side, but a more satisfactory plan is to alternate the plots. This, however, cannot be extended very far, as the difference in heat in the two ends of a house is considerable. A very good plan is to take a section of a bed in the middle of a house and treat by one method of watering, while two sections of the same size on either side are treated according to the other method. This has been done in several cases, and some examples are given in the third table. In these experiments, the plants were treated in the same manner as those in the experiments above mentioned, $i.$ $e.$, all were sub-irrigated until they were planted in the benches. After that time sections A and C were sub-irrigated, and section B was surface-watered. The average gain of the sub-irrigated plots over the surface-watered was about 38 per cent, or very nearly the same as the average of the 15 experiments in the second table.—

COMPARISON OF SURFACE-WATERED SECTIONS WITH SUB-IRRIGATED SECTIONS ON EITHER SIDE, 75 GRAND RAPIDS PLANTS IN EACH SECTION.

	Section A, sub-irrigated.	Section B, surface-watered.	Section C, sub-irrigated.
Experiment I	Weight, 385 ozs.	Weight, 325 ozs.	Weight, 420 ozs.
Experiment II	" 487 "	" 329 "	" 496 "
Experiment III	" 308 "	" 229 "	" 345 "

"In all of the experiments thus far referred to, but one point has been considered, and that is the increase in weight by sub-irrigation. Aside from the relative prevalency of disease in plants treated by the two methods, there are but few practical questions.

"Although not a matter of much practical importance, some interest attaches to the fact that sub-irrigated lettuce is earlier than that grown in the ordinary manner. It does not really come to maturity any earlier if by that is meant the stage at which the plants cease to increase in weight, caused by the dying of the lower leaves, but it does reach a marketable size sooner. It is customary to allow the plants to stand as long as they continue to improve, but in case it is desirable to cut before that time it will be found that the sub-irrigated lettuce will be a week to ten days ahead of the other. Should the size to which surface-watered lettuce can be grown be set as a standard, and the sub-irrigated cut when it reaches that size, it will be found that the latter will be ready four to six weeks from the time of planting in the beds, and the surface-watered must be allowed to remain from six to eight weeks to attain the same size. Whether we reckon in this manner, or by the actual weight of the crops harvested during the season, there is a gain in one season of about one crop by sub-irrigation. Both the yield and price vary, of course ; but for a house 20 x 100 feet the difference in a single season between surface- and sub-irrigation might safely be estimated at from $50 to $100. The latter figure might not be reached, except on very heavy clay soil, and on soil specially adapted to lettuce the difference might be even less than the lowest, but experience has shown that it is more likely to exceed than to fall below $50. The difference is likely to be greater with new beginners than with those of experience, as more skill is required to manage a crop by surface- than by sub-irrigation. It is an established fact that good head lettuce cannot be grown on heavy soil by surface watering, and the same is, in a measure, true of all varieties. It is evident, therefore, that sub-irrigation greatly enlarges the possibilities of lettuce culture under glass. It not only makes the work easier for new beginners, but it makes it possible to use soil that would otherwise be precluded. More than that, it solves the problem of meeting competition from the south, which competition bids fair to ruin the business of vegetable forcing at the north, unless improved methods are adopted by northern gardeners."

Very similar results with lettuce have been secured by Rane, who also found much less trouble with rot in sub-irrigated beds. "The lettuce rot, which appeared to a marked extent in the surface-watered beds," he writes, "was apparently absent in the sub-irrigated beds. The disease was first noticed at time of marketing, at which time it could not be detected in the other beds. During the growth of the second crop it became very troublesome, and some of the varieties in the surface-watered beds required marketing before they were fully grown, while in the under-surface-watered beds the disease was completely held in check."

Rane also found "marked superiority" in sub-irrigation for tomatoes, "no marked difference" in turnip-rooted radishes, "very beneficial" effects in long-rooted radishes, "a slight difference" in earliness in spinach, "no marked difference" in turnip-rooted beets, and "very marked" gain in maturity of parsley from seed but "no perceptible difference in its growth" after the plants in the surface-irrigated soil "once reached maturity."

Conclusions.—Green makes the following points of advantage of sub-irrigation in glass houses:

"Watering by sub-irrigation in the greenhouse is more cheaply done than by the ordinary method.

"Watering by sub-irrigation in the greenhouse is more efficiently done than by the ordinary method.

"Where sub-irrigation is practiced in the greenhouse, the soil does not become compacted as by surface waterings, but retains its original loose, friable condition, even without frequent stirring, nor does it become mossy, water-logged and sour.

"Plants are less liable to suffer from over watering and diseases by sub-irrigation than where the water is applied to the surface.

"All classes of plants which may be grown upon greenhouse benches thrive better by sub-irrigation than by the ordinary method of watering."

Rane writes as follows: "The saving of labor through sub-irrigation is almost inestimable. The expenditure of time in watering was as follows: In the case of under-surface irrigation, the water was dipped out of a tank and poured into a funnel, through which it entered the various portions of the bed. On the other hand, in surface irrigation, the water was dipped out and applied by a sprinkling can, containing either a rose spray or a spout long enough to reach all sections of the bed. In the former case, the size of the plants did not matter, while in the latter, the more mature the crop, the more time it required for watering. Again, the sub-irrigated beds did not require watering over once or, at the outside, twice a week; while, generally speaking, the other beds were watered daily.

"The idea that a water-tight bed is detrimental to plant growth on account of lack of drainage is overcome, we believe, in the fact that the pipe or tiles receive the excess of water, which, in a bed not water-tight, would leak out at the bottom, thus making it serve a double purpose. If the soil contains too much moisture, it serves as a reservoir; if not enough, it imparts the amount necessary for good conditions. In either case, the pipe or tiles act as a safety-valve. These openings underneath the soil allow free access of air, render plant food digestible, and act as a drain to water-soaked soil. In view of these results, we feel safe in saying that under-surface watering is a pronounced success."

VENTILATING AND SHADING.

The one imperative thing to be borne in mind in ventilating glass houses is to avoid draughts. This means that ventilators should be many and small rather than few and large, for thereby the warm air can be discharged from houses without much danger of an in-rush of cold air, because the ventilator sash need be lifted only very little. Houses should be cooled by letting out heated air rather than by letting in cold air, although it is impossible to wholly exclude the outside air when ventilators are opened. In forcing-houses of ordinary size, sufficient ventilation can be secured by means of sash at the peak alone, thus obviating the danger of currents of cold air which arises when there are ventilating sashes in both the sides and top. In very large houses, particularly in those of the shed roof pattern, it may be necessary to place ventilating openings in the walls, more especially on the back or high side of the house. Ventilating openings should be removed as far as possible from the plants in order to reduce the danger of cold draughts to the utmost.

Particular care should be taken with the ventilating during dull, cold weather, when the plants become soft and are very quickly injured by draughts. It is not necessary to ventilate primarily for the purpose of securing fresh air, but to regulate the temperature of the house. When the house becomes over wet and close, it is often necessary to ventilate for the purpose of drying it out. The larger the house, the less, as a rule, is the necessity of ventilating.

Houses are shaded to prevent the sun from scorching the plants. The shading is supplied by coating the glass with some white covering, like whitewash. The necessity for shading may be largely obviated by not allowing the plants to become over-vigorous, sappy, and soft. The greatest danger from sun-scald occurs after a spell of dark and wet weather. It is then essential to keep the house rather cool when the weather brightens, and it may be necessary to shade it. Plants which are suffering from root-galls or other disease of the roots, or those which are growing in very leachy soils or on very shallow benches, may have to be shaded in order to check the evaporation from their tops and thereby prevent them from wilting. Many plants thrive best under shaded roofs, but amongst the forced vegetables there is only the English or frame cucumber which appears to thrive best under a tempered light. This plant was developed in the humid and soft climate of England, and it seeems to be impatient of our violent suns; yet it may be made to withstand the sun if grown rather slowly.

For plants which require permanent shading, a paint

made of naphtha and white lead may be put upon the glass. This is removed with difficulty. For forcing-houses, which only infrequently need shading, an ordinarily slaked-lime-and-water whitewash, which can be both applied and washed off by means of a spray pump, is the best covering. A still less durable wash is made of flour and water.

THE ELECTRIC LIGHT FOR FORCING-HOUSES.

Can the electric light stand for sunlight? Can it be profitably used at night and in dull weather to hasten the growth of plants? These questions have received greater attention in the United States than elsewhere in the world. Experiments have been made at the Cornell Experiment Station,* the West Virginia Station,† and by W. W. Rawson, an extensive vegetable forcer at Boston. It is found that the electric light, both the arc and the incandescent, can be advantageously used upon lettuce to piece out the sunlight in midwinter. In various florists' plants it also produces earlier bloom. It is usually injurious, or has only negative results, upon radishes, peas, carrots, beets, spinach and cauliflowers.

Upon lettuce, the value of the electric light in hastening maturity is emphatic. Mr. Rawson saves about a week upon each of his three winter crops by the use of three ordinary street lamps hung over a house 370 ft. long and 33 ft. wide.

At Cornell, the results upon lettuce have been marked in many tests, and the gains in maturity have been as much as two weeks. It is found in every instance that the naked arc light—that is, a light without a globe—hung

---

*Bailey, Bulletins 30 (Aug. 1891), 42 (Sept. 1892), 55 (July 1893); also, "Electricity and Plant-Growing," in Trans. Mass. Hort. Soc'y, 1894. Experiments with electric currents upon plants, by Clarence D. Walker, will be found in Bulletins 16 (1892) and 23 (1893) of the Mass. Hatch Exp. Sta.

†Rane, "Electro-Horticulture with the Incandescent Lamp," Bulletin 37 (July, 1894).

inside the house, injures the plants which are within a few feet of it, and tends to make all plants within reach of its rays run too quickly to seed. The use of a clear glass globe, however, overcomes all injury. The best results are to be obtained by placing the light — either naked or surrounded by a clear globe — a few feet above the roof. An ordinary 2,000-candle-power arc light — such as is commonly used for street lighting — will exert a marked effect upon lettuce for a radius of 75 to 100 feet, if the roof is clean and the framework of the house is light. The light may be allowed to burn all night. Incandescent lamps have the same influence as arc lights, but to a less degree. It will be found profitable to use the electric light for plant-growing, if at all, only in the three or four months of midwinter.

POLLINATION.

It is generally necessary to transfer the pollen by hand in fruit-bearing forced vegetables. The methods are fully explained under the discussions of the various vegetables. In order to secure the pollen, the house should be dry and warm. Upon a bright morning, when the flowers need pollinating, the gardener should withhold water and let the foliage and walks become thoroughly dried off, and before midday the pollen will usually discharge readily.

Bees may sometimes be utilized as pollen-carriers in spring and fall, when they can forage in and out of the house as they choose, but they are impracticable in the winter time in houses of ordinary size. In very large houses, in which there is abundant room for the bees to work, and where ventilators do not need to be opened so much, bees may sometimes be used to advantage. Three or four swarms should pollinate a house 40 x 400 ft. The bees will have to be fed. In general, however, bees are found to be unsatisfactory. The following account of an experiment in this direction at Cornell (Lodeman, Bulletin 96) will indicate some of the perverseness of these insects:

"Much has been written regarding the value of bees in greenhouses. It is said that all hand-pollinations may be dispensed with if desired, as the bees will work among the blossoms, and thus cause the fruit to set.

"During November, 1893, a hive of bees was received, and on the 23rd day of the month they were set free in the brightest of all the station houses. The hive was placed at the south end of the house, and the bees were kept constantly supplied with proper food. At this time the house was filled with tomato plants in full bloom, and it was hoped the bees would work among them so that the tedious but very necessary hand-pollination of the flowers need no longer be practiced. The bees evidently did not catch the idea, however, for if there was one place in the house which they did not visit it was the tomato blossom. They spent most of their time in bumping their heads against the glass sides and roof of the house, and at every opportunity, when the ventilators were raised a little, they took pains to pass through them, even though the mercury stood far below the freezing point out of doors. The bees which did not succeed in finding the ventilators continued to fly against the glass, leaving it only for the purpose of withdrawing far enough to get a start for a fresh attack. In this way the busy bee finally wore herself out, and, in the course of three weeks, those less ambitious individuals which did not fly heavenward in the friendless atmosphere of December, were scattered as corpses along the sides of the house close to the glass; and thus ended the attempt to make these little creatures useful in midwinter. It may be said that bees do not like tomato flowers, but our specimens took no pains to find out whether they liked them or not. It is probable that every bee in the swarm went to his honeyless bourne without ever having discovered whether the plants were tomatoes or buckwheat, or, in fact, if there were any plants at all in the house."

INSECTS AND DISEASES.

Insects and fungi are amongst the best of all educators. They force the gardener to learn, whether he will or not. They are always the curse of poor gardeners. It occasionally happens that the very best gardeners are overtaken by some dire pest, but it is the exception, not the rule. The gardener boasts that the glass house affords him the means of keeping plants directly under control. By the same means, he should also keep the pests under control. There is a constant struggle for mastery between the plant, the bug, the fungus, and the man, and it often happens that the combatant which is the biggest, oldest and knows the most turns out to be the slave of all the others.

The one universal and invariable precaution against insect and fungous attack is this: Keep the plants in a constant and uniform state of normal and healthy development. Avoid all extremes of temperature and moisture, and be particularly careful in this regard in the dark weather of winter. One is growing cucumbers, for example. He is in a hurry for the crop. The season is advancing. A dull spell comes on. He keeps his house close and waters freely. The plants respond quickly. The stems lengthen and thicken and the leaves expand to enormous size. Presently the sun appears. He must have air. He swings open the ventilators. The cold air rushes in and stirs the foliage. Two or three days later, he may look for a well-established case of mildew!

If he is growing lettuce in the same fashion, his plants appear to suddenly begin to collapse. The lower leaves rot, and presently the crop is worthless. In less than a week, one January, the writer lost an entire house of most beautiful lettuce by just such management. If he is growing tomatoes, the plants become sappy and congested under such treatment, and may actually contract the dropsy, as is shown in the chapter upon tomato forcing. In a spell of dull weather in winter, the gardener must be particularly careful to keep his houses dry and sweet, for then the mildews develop rapidly.

The houses should be kept sweet and clean. All trimmings from the plants should be carried out of the establishment. The soil should be changed every year, particularly on benches (as explained on page 51). If there have been serious infections of fungi or insects, the framework of the house should be painted during summer, or else sprayed or washed with kerosene. Care should be taken to avoid filling the benches with infested soil. It is always safest not to select soil from fields which have recently grown the same kind of crops which it is desired to grow in the house; and if the forced plants have been badly infected, the soil in which they are grown should not be used again for forcing purposes.

All possible precautions having been taken, the gardener may next exercise himself to devise means of killing the pests. For aphis and the like, he will fumigate with some tobacco preparation; for mealy-bugs he will use a fine hard stream of water from a hose, a proceeding which will greatly upset their domestic affairs; for red spiders and mites he will syringe the foliage thoroughly with water above and below on all bright days; for mildews he will evaporate sulphur or dust it on the plants; for rusts he will spray with Bordeaux mixture; for damping-off (and "canker" at the root) he will dry off the surface of the soil and mix a little sulphur or charcoal into it;* for the nematode or root-gall (the work of which

---

*See Atkinson's monograph of damping-off, Bulletin 94, Cornell Exp. Sta. (now out of print), for an account of the various fungi concerned in the trouble. The advice which Atkinson gives for the treatment of

is shown in Fig. 29, page 87), which is one of the most serious of all greenhouse pests, he will remove the soil, paint the benches with lye or kerosene, and thereafter use only soil which has been very thoroughly frozen since a crop was grown in it (a proceeding which is practically impossible in solid beds).

---

damping-off is here reprinted because the disorder is a very common and serious one, although it is not particularly germane to the subject of the forcing of vegetables:

"In the treatment of this trouble, especial attention must be given to the environment of the plants and those conditions which favor the rapid development of the parasites. These conditions are known in most cases to be high temperature accompanied by a large moisture content of the soil, humid atmosphere, insufficient light, and close apartments, and soil which has become thoroughly infested with the fungi by the development of the disease in plants growing in the same. Some excellent notes on the treatment of the disease by gardeners and horticulturists are given in the American Garden for 1890, by Meehan, Massey, Maynard, Watson, Lonsdale, Gardiner, and Bailey, and a short description of the potting-bed fungus (*Artotrogus Debaryanus*) by Seymour. The principal lines of treatment suggested there from the practical experience of the writers are as follows:

"When cuttings are badly diseased, they should be taken out, the soil removed, benches cleaned and fresh sand introduced, when only the sound cuttings should be reset. For cuttings is recommended a fairly cool house, and confined air should be avoided in all cases. As much sunlight as possible should be given as the plants will stand without wilting. When close atmosphere is necessary, guard against too much moisture, and keep an even temperature. The soil should be kept as free as possible from decaying vegetable matter. This is a very important matter, for several of the most troublesome of the parasites grow readily on such decaying vegetable matter, and in many cases obtain such vigorous growth that they can readily attack a perfectly healthy plant which could resist the fungus if the vegetable matter had not been there to give it such a start. Soil which is dry beneath and wet on top, as results from insufficient watering by a sprinkler, favors the disease more than uniformity of moisture throughout the soil.

"In seed beds, use fresh sandy soil free from decaying matter. Avoid over-watering, especially in dull weather, shade in the middle part of the day only, and keep temperature as low as the plants will stand.

"If the seedlings are badly diseased it will be wise to discard them and start the bed anew. In the early stages, however, they can frequently be saved by loosening the soil to dry it, and placing the pots in sunny places at such times as they will not wilt. Some advocate sprinkling sulphur on the soil, and in some cases sulphur at the rate of 1 to 30 is mixed in the soil before sowing, with good effect. When the beds are badly infested, Humphrey (Rept. Mass. State Agr. Exp. Sta. 1890) advocates the entire removal of the soil, whitewashing the beds, and the introduction of fresh soil.

"In houses heated by steam if it were possible to have, without too great expense, a steam chest, where the pots and seed pans which are used could be placed and the soil thoroughly steamed for

Methods of controlling greenhouse pests by fumigation.*—The insects and the fungi which seriously injure greenhouse plants are comparatively few in number, but if allowed to develop unchecked they are capable of entirely ruining every susceptible plant in the houses. There are some plants which are almost entirely free from such attacks, but they form isolated exceptions to a very general rule. All who have had any experience in growing plants under glass know that diseases are sure to appear, and that insects will originate apparently from nothing. Indeed, so certain are these pests to appear that every thorough gardener is at all times prepared for them, or even takes steps towards their destruction before they have been seen. Fortunately, he has at his command abundant means of protecting his plants, and houses in which insects or fungi are found in large numbers are silent but convincing witnesses of bad management and neglect. When a greenhouse has once become thoroughly infested, it is almost impossible to rid the plants of their parasites, and it requires constant and prolonged attention to bring about this result; and even when this has been done, the plants will in many cases have become so weakened that they will scarcely repay the time and labor employed in saving them. The care of plants should begin before they are attacked, and this care should be given uninterruptedly. By treating apparently uninfested plants many invisible enemies may be de-

---

several hours, it could be sterilized, and the finer and more delicate seedlings be grown then with little danger if subsequent care was used to not introduce soil from the beds. In testing the virulence of the *Artotrogus Debaryanus*, and of the sterile fungus, several experiments have been made by steaming pots of earth, growing seedlings in them and then inoculating some of the seedlings with the fungus while other pots were kept as checks, and all were under like conditions with respect to moisture, temperature, etc. The seedlings which were not supplied with the fungus remained healthy, while those supplied with the fungus were diseased and many were killed outright."

*Lodeman, Bulletin 96, Cornell Exp. Sta.

stroyed, and such treatments are by far the most valuable ones.

Tobacco.— Several of the most common and often very serious organisms may be overcome by vapors with which a house may be filled, and the best known and the most valuable remedy of this nature is undoubtedly

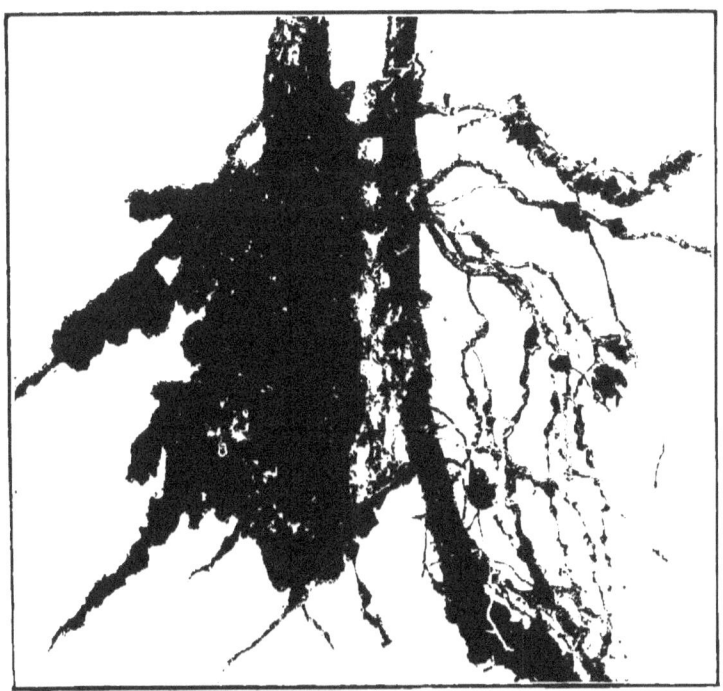

29. *Galls of a nematode worm on the roots of two tomato plants. The root on the left is unusually severely affected.*

tobacco. The poisonous alkaloids found in the tobacco plant are fatal to many insects. The waste parts of the plants, particularly the "stems," are utilized by florists and others for purposes of fumigation.

These stems, which are almost invariably the dried mid-veins of the leaves, may be obtained for almost nothing at any cigar factory. When wanted for fumigating purposes they should not be too dry, else they will blaze, instead of slowly smouldering and forming a dense smoke. In case the stems are too dry, they may be moistened by sprinkling water upon them; a better way, however, is to store the stems in a moderately damp place, and then they are always in good condition for burning. If they blaze while the house is being fumigated, much of their value is lost, and it is also said that plants are positively injured in such cases, although our experience has not supported this view.

Tobacco stems may be burned in a variety of ways. Some gardeners merely pile the required quantity upon a brick or stone floor in the house and set fire to it by means of paper or shavings. An old coal scuttle answers the purpose very well. Fig. 30 represents a home-made tobacco-stem burner which we have designed, and which is perhaps as simple, serviceable, and easily managed as any in use. The body of the burner is made of heavy, galvanized sheet-iron. It closely resembles a stove pipe in form, but is about 7 inches in diameter and 2 feet in length. The bottom is made of the same material, and is perforated by about a dozen holes, each ⅜-inch in diameter. Four legs support the burner and keep the bottom 3 inches from the floor. A handle at the top completes the device. When filled, the stems being packed sufficiently close to insure their burning, it contains an amount that will answer for a house of 4,000 to 6,000 cubic feet. Much, of course, depends upon the tightness of the house, and considerable variation will also be found in the strength of the stems. Occasionally some will be had which are much weaker than those last used, and hence larger quantities must be employed. It has been our practice to test each new lot of stems to determine their strength before they

30. *A home-made fumigator.*

are freely used in all the houses. The quantity must also be varied in accordance with the plants growing in the house. Some plants are much more easily injured by the smoke than others, and the amount used must be insufficient to hurt the most tender plants. Less injury is apt to result if the houses and plants are dry; wet foliage is quite easily scorched by the smoke. Our method of starting a "smudge" is to place a single sheet of newspaper, previously lighted, in the bottom of the burner, and upon this the stems are immediately placed. If properly dampened, they will take fire readily and smoulder without blazing.

The frequency with which a house should be smoked cannot be definitely stated. Some conservatories will require the operation scarely more than two or three times during the winter, while others may need that many treatments each week. In the latter case, it is well to have the smudges upon consecutive days, as in this manner insects receive a second treatment before they have recovered from the first. The evening is perhaps the best time for fumigating, as most of the disagreeable odor is thus escaped. But it may be advisable, in badly infested houses, to follow the evening treatment by another the next morning. In such cases, care should be exercised that the houses do not become overheated by the morning sun.

Tobacco smoke may be used successfully in the destruction of the various aphides which are found upon greenhouse plants, and of a small white fly, a species of aleyrodes. Other insects cannot be practically treated by its use.

The rose-leaf extract of tobacco we find to be one of the best of all insecticides for glass houses. It is a liquid, which we reduce one-half with water, then drop a large piece of hot iron into it. The fumes are fatal to aphis, but have proved to be harmless to plants with us.

Bisulphide of carbon.—This material has recently assumed a prominent position as an effective insecticide. It is a clear, transparent liquid, which evaporates rapidly, even at a low temperature. These fumes are fatal to insect as well as animal life, and may be used to a limited extent in the greenhouse. The vapor is of greatest value in destroying a small mite (*Tetranychus bimaculatus*), that closely resembles the red spider. This mite is not as easily overcome by water as the red spider is, and in certain cases it may be advisable to resort to the bisulphide of carbon treatment. This treatment is adapted to plants which are growing in pots, or to low-growing plants in beds. Whole houses could scarcely be treated in this manner, as the vapor is heavy, and an uneven distribution would probably result. But for small, confined spaces, as bell-jars, tubs, or barrels, the remedy can be used with success. I have had no difficulty in destroying mites and red spider by the use of 60 minims or drops of the liquid to a space containing about 7 cubic feet. The liquid was poured on cotton batting, which was spread over a small rose from a watering can, the stem of the funnel being set in the soil. The plants remained covered with enamel cloth nearly two hours, which sufficed to kill all the insects, and did not injure the violets, these being the plants treated.

Hydrocyanic gas.—The success which has followed the use of hydrocyanic gas in the treatment of scale insects infesting the orange groves of California has suggested the idea of its possible value in destroying greenhouse pests. The common method of making the gas is as follows: One fluidounce of sulphuric acid is slowly added to 3 ounces of water. To this diluted acid there is then added 1 ounce of 60 per cent cyanide of potassium (very poisonous). Effervescence immediately takes place, and the gas is freely given off. The quantities here given are sufficient for a space containing 150 cubic feet, the plants being exposed to the gas for one hour. When trees are perfectly dormant, such treatment is not followed by any evil effects.

During the past spring several growing plants were exposed to the action of the gas when used according to the above directions. Tomatoes, eggplants, oranges, and roses were used. The day following the treatment showed that all the plants were injured, but to what extent could not be well determined. After two weeks had passed, however, the effect of the treatment was plainly seen. The tomato plant died; the eggplant and the rose lost all their foliage, but fresh leaves were appearing on the stems; the orange suffered the least, since only the young leaves were affected. The mites had all been killed, so that in this respect at least the experiment was successful.

Other trials were made with the gas, using the same kinds of plants, but it was found to be impossible to destroy the mites without injuring at least some of the plants. The use of hydrocyanic gas for the destruction of greenhouse pests can therefore scarcely be recommended. It should also be remembered that this gas is exceedingly poisonous, and must not be inhaled.

Sulphur.—This element is of the greatest service in greenhouse work. It is an invaluable agent for the destruction of mildews, and is also of great assistance in overcoming red spider. As commonly used, it is mixed with an equal bulk of air-slaked lime or some similar material, and then water, oil, milk or some other liquid is added until a thick, creamy paste is obtained. This is then painted upon the heating surfaces in the house, and the sulphur fumes are given off. The same result can be obtained much more rapidly and energetically by heating the flowers of sulphur until it melts; the fumes are then given off in great abundance. Our practice has been to put the sulphur in a shallow pan and then set it over an oil-stove, having the flame turned just high enough to keep the sulphur in a melted condition. Almost continuous watching was necessary to prevent the material from taking fire, for if this should occur it would prove almost instantly fatal to all the plants which might be reached by the gas. The difficulty was in a great measure overcome by L. C. Corbett, at that time an assistant at Cornell, who suggested the use of a sand-bath as a means of modifying the intensity of the heat. Our present outfit is shown in Fig. 31. It consists of two pans placed on an ordinary hand oil-stove. The lower pan is half filled with clean, coarse sand, and the upper one contains the sulphur. By its proper use our houses have been kept remarkably free from mildew, even under very adverse circumstances. But there is constant danger that the sulphur will become heated to the burning point, and then the entire stock of plants in the house is lost. This use of sulphur is often very convenient, but the work should be placed in the hands of a most trustworthy person. If a house should be thoroughly treated in this manner every week or two, scarcely any mildew could develop.

31. Sulphur bath.

CHAPTER IV.

LETTUCE.*

LETTUCE is the most popular and the most uniformly profitable of all vegetable crops grown under glass in this country. It grows rapidly, so that three crops can be taken from a house between September and April, and the demand for a choice product is always good. Lettuce is generally considered to be an easy crop to grow under glass, and yet it is a fact that few gardeners are entirely successful with the crop, year by year, particularly if the heading varieties are grown. It thrives best in late winter, but if careful attention is given to watering and ventilating, it thrives well in midwinter. Good head lettuces should bring 50 cents or 60 cents a dozen heads at wholesale, and they often bring more. The loose types generally bring somewhat less.

Lettuce varies greatly in quality, and this variation is due in very great measure to the immediate conditions under which it is grown. If the plant is very rank, and has dark green, thick leaves, the quality is low. A good

---

*As stated in the preface, much of the discussion upon methods of forcing of vegetables which is presented in this book is founded upon bulletins of the Cornell Experiment Station. Some of these bulletins are now out of print, and new notes and experiences are constantly accumulating, so that it seems to be necessary to revise the advice and to extend it with the observations and experiences of others, and thereby to present a consecutive manual. It should be added that these same bulletins formed the basis of much of Winkler's "Vegetable Forcing," and this fact may account for some similarities of language in the two books.

lettuce plant is yellowish green in color upon delivery, and the leaves are thin and brittle. The product should be wholly free from lice, or green-fly, and the tips of the leaves should show no tendency to wither or to turn brown. If heading lettuce is grown, the leaves should roll inward like cabbage leaves, and the heads should be compact and nearly globular and yellowish white towards the core (see Fig. 34, page 103).

Temperature.—Lettuce must have a low temperature. The night temperature should not rise much above 45°, while it may go as low as 40°. The day temperature, in the shade, should be 55° to 65°. Lettuce which is kept too warm grows too tall, and the leaves are thin and flabby, and there is generally more danger of injury from aphis, rot and leaf-burn. In midwinter particular attention must be given to ventilation, for if the air becomes damp and close, mildew or rot is almost sure to develop. In raising head lettuce, it is common to do the watering with tepid water just before heading, in order to accelerate the growth.

Light.—Whilst a lettuce house must have an abundance of light, the plants do not suffer if they are some distance from the glass, and even if they receive little direct sunlight. The house should have an exposure towards the sun, and the framework ought to be as light as possible, if the best results are to be obtained; but diffused light is often as good as the direct burning rays of the sun. It should be said, however, that good lettuce may often be grown in heavy, rather dark houses, but more care is required (particularly in watering), the results are less certain, and there is difficulty in growing the heading varieties to perfection. The electric light may also be used to advantage (see pages 80 and 101).

Beds and benches.—Most of the commercial lettuce forcers prefer to grow the crop in solid or ground beds, where the temperature is cool and the conditions of moisture are uniform. This is more especially true of the heading varieties. Our own experience has fully demonstrated the superiority of solid earth beds over benches, for lettuce. We have had good crops in benches, but they have required special attention to heating and watering, and even then the results are generally

32. A ground bed, with Grand Rapids lettuce.

precarious. If, however, the benches have no bottom heat — that is, if there are no heating pipes close under them and if the sides are open below — very good results, particularly with the loose or non-heading sorts, may be had from year to year. The benches, when used, should contain about six inches of earth. Fig. 32 shows an earth bed, about 9 inches deep, in which we have had excellent success with lettuce.

Soils. — Probably no forced vegetable is so much influenced by soil as the lettuce, and no doubt more failures are to be ascribed to uncongenial soil than to any other single cause. Fortunately this matter has been made the subject of a most admirable study by Galloway,[*] who finds that the famous heading lettuce of the Boston gardeners can be grown to perfection only in soils which contain much sand and very little clay and silt. These soils allow the water to settle deeply into them, and yet hold it without percolation; the surface is dry, preventing the occurrence of rot; the roots forage far and wide, and the plant food is quickly available. The full characters of the soil used by the Boston growers are set forth as follows by Galloway: "Loose at all times, regardless of treatment, it being possible to push the arm into it to a depth of 20 inches or more. Never 'puddles' when worked, no matter how wet. Clods or lumps never form. A 4-inch dressing of fresh manure, when spaded in to a depth of 15 to 20 inches, will be completely disintegrated in six or eight weeks. Sufficient water may be added the first of September, when the first crop is started, to carry through two crops and a part of a third without additional applications, except very light ones merely to keep the leaves moist and to induce a movement of the moisture at the bottom of the bed toward the top, where it will come in contact with most of the roots. The surface to a depth of an inch dries out quickly, and this has an important bearing on the prevention of wet rot of the lower leaves. The active working roots of the plants are found in abundance throughout the entire depth of soil, even if this exceeds 30 inches."

Galloway was able to prepare soil which "gave practically the same results" as that which he imported from Boston. This soil was made as follows: "Mixture of

---

[*] B. T. Galloway, "The Growth of Lettuce as Affected by the Physical Properties of the Soil," Agric. Science, viii. 302 (1894).

two parts of drift sand and one part of greenhouse soil. The sand was obtained from the valley of a stream near by, which frequently overflowed its banks, flooding the spot where the material was found. The greenhouse soil was a mixture consisting of one part of the ordinary clay, gneiss soil of the region, and two parts of well-rotted manure. Such soil will grow 20 bushels of wheat to the acre without fertilization."

Whilst all these remarks about the great importance of the selection of a proper soil are certainly true, it should nevertheless be said that a good gardener can get good results from a very uncongenial soil, chiefly by giving skillful attention to watering. It is always essential to the best lettuce growing, however, to avoid "heavy" soils. These soils usually lose their water quickly, necessitating frequent watering, which keeps the surface wet and increases danger from damping-off and rot. These soils soon become hard, compact and "dead," and the plants grow slowly, with thick, tough leaves.

Green (Bulletin 61, Ohio Exp. Sta.) gives the following advice upon soils for winter lettuce: "If the market demands head lettuce, then it is of the utmost importance that the soil should have a considerable per cent of sand, and at the same time be sufficiently fertile and have capacity for holding moisture. Non-heading sorts, like the Grand Rapids, are not so particular as to soil, but it is a difficult matter to grow any kind on a soil with much clay in it, by surface-watering, and even if sub-irrigation is practiced such soil should be avoided. It would be futile to attempt to grow lettuce according to methods in vogue in the east on a heavy clay soil. Swamp muck, composted with one-fourth or one-half horse manure, answers very well for either surface or sub-irrigation, particularly for the latter. It has the advantage of being light and easily handled, and never hardens; moreover, it has considerable capacity for water. The addition of fine sand will greatly improve a clay soil, and it is advisa-

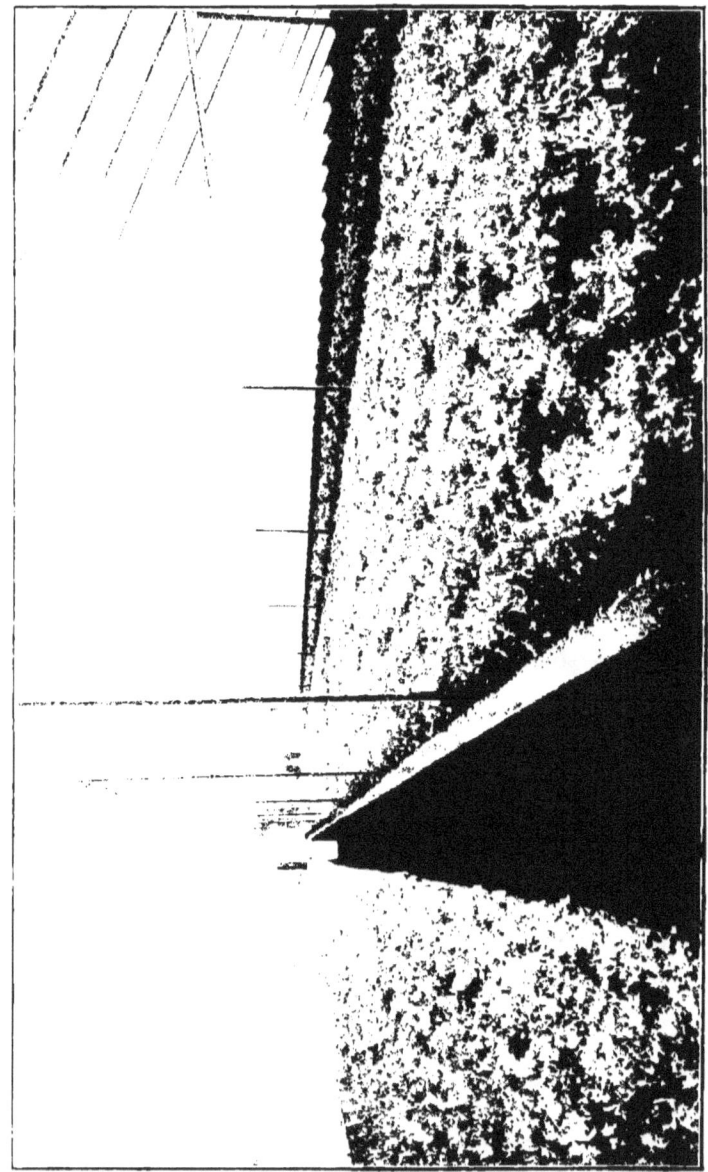

33. *Lettuce of the non-heating type forced in pots.*

ble, if such soil is used, to take it from an old fence row, using the sod only. It may be inferred from the above that lettuce may be successfully grown on almost any soil, and such is the fact, if conditions are thoroughly studied and the details carefully looked after. Nevertheless, it is better to select a soil naturally adapted to the purpose if possible, but in any case such artificial means as composting and sub-irrigation ought not to be neglected."

Growing in pots.—Good lettuce of the leafy or Grand Rapids type can be grown in pots. It is a common practice with gardeners to set pots of lettuce in vacant places in cool houses for the purpose of utilizing the room. Growing in pots is comparatively little used, although now and then a grower follows this method extensively. A most beautiful crop of pot-grown lettuce is shown in Fig. 33 (page 98). The New York State Experiment Station has made some investigations in the pot-growing of lettuce, and has published the results in Bulletin 88 (March, 1895), from which I quote:

"The seed is sown in flats, as usual; that is to say, in boxes about 12 by 10 inches and 3 inches deep. When the plants are about 2 inches high they are transplanted to 2-inch pots. The benches are filled with soil, in which the pots containing the lettuce are plunged so that the tops of the pots are covered with about half an inch of soil.

"Soil for lettuce should not be too heavy, and as the soil which we use for potting is a rather heavy clay loam, sand is mixed with it in preparing it for the lettuce house. The potting soil is composed of three parts by measure of loam, one of manure and one of sand. The soil in the pots is the same as that used on the bench, except that it is sifted, while that on the bench is not. A little drainage material is put in the bottom of each pot. The plants are usually set on the benches about 10 inches apart each way. The roots soon fill the pot and grow

8 FORC.

out into the soil of the bench through the drainage hole in the bottom of the pot. Being thus buried in the soil, the little pots do not dry out as rapidly as they would do were they exposed to the air.

"The soil in the pots is sufficient to support a vigorous growth, and yet when the roots have filled the pots the plants appear to make a more compact growth and head quicker than they do when grown in beds where the extension of the root system is unchecked. Another advantage of this method consists in the fact that the plants are transplanted but once, namely, from the flats to the pots; thus the check to the growth by a second transplanting is avoided.

"The plants may be marketed without disturbing their roots, and for this reason they keep fresh for a longer time than do the plants whose roots are disturbed in preparing them for market. When the plant is ready for market it may be knocked out of the pot and the ball of earth, containing the roots undisturbed, may be wrapped snugly in oiled paper. The earth will thus keep moist for a long time, and furnish moisture to the plant through the roots which are imbedded in it. Local customers may be supplied with lettuce in the pots and the pots returned after the plants are taken from them. Grocers and other retail dealers readily appreciate the advantages of having lettuce grown in this way. It permits them to keep the lettuce on hand for a considerable length of time, and still present it to their customers crisp, fresh and attractive, instead of wilted and unattractive.

"The moment a pot is removed from the bench another may immediately be set in its place without waiting to clear the bench, or any portion of it, of the rest of the lettuce. The method thus proves economical both of time and space.

"This method will undoubtedly commend itself to growers who are forcing lettuce to a limited extent. Whether it can be employed to advantage by those who have extensive houses devoted to lettuce can be decided only by trial. It certainly appears to be worthy of extended trial."

Sowing and transplanting.—If the lettuce crop is to be taken off in early November, from seven to ten weeks should be counted from the sowing of the seeds to the delivery of the product. A midwinter crop may require two to four weeks longer. The heading lettuces generally require a week or two longer than the loose varieties. The time may be shortened ten days to two weeks by the use of the electric arc light hung directly above the house. A single ordinary street lamp of 2,000 normal candle-power will be sufficient for a house 20 feet or more wide and 75 feet long, if it is so hung that the house is uniformly lighted throughout. Our experiments with the electric light, now extended over a period of five years, have uniformly and unequivocally given these beneficial results with lettuce (see page 80).

The first sowing for house lettuce is usually made about the first of September, and the crop should be off in November. The seeds are sown in flats or shallow boxes; it is preferable to prick off the young plants about 4 inches apart into other flats when they are about two weeks old, and transplant them into the beds, about 8 to 10 inches apart each way, when they are about five weeks from the seed. Gardeners often omit the pricking off into other flats, simply thinning out the plants where they stand and transferring them from the original flat directly to the bed; but better and quicker results are usually secured if the extra handling is given. Four or six weeks after the first seed is sown, another sowing is made in flats for the purpose of taking the place of the first crop. The first sowing is sometimes made in the open ground early in September, and this is transplanted directly into the beds.

Following are some actual sample dates of good and bad lettuce growing in our houses, in a climate which is unusually cloudy and "slow" in winter: Landreth Forcing lettuce sown in flats February 24; transplanted to beds, March 17; first heads marketed, under normal conditions, May 10; first heads marketed from a compartment receiving electric light at night (a total of 84 hours), April 30, or 44 days from seed. Simpson Curled was sown October 3; November 7, transplanted to bed. It was desired to hold the crop back, so that the house was kept very cold; and the variety is not well adapted to quick forcing, so that it was January 30 before the entire crop was fit for market, making 119 days from seed. Grand Rapids lettuce sown December 28; transplanted to bed, January 16; began marketing March 21. This makes 72 days from seed, in the dark months; and at least a week could have been gained if we had not been obliged to delay transplanting whilst waiting for a crop of chrysanthemums to come off the bed.

A grower's remarks. — W. W. Rawson, a prominent grower of heading lettuce near Boston, is reported[*] in the following sentences respecting some of the essential points in the management of the crop: "With lettuce planted on the 20th of August, the heads are ready for market on the 20th of October. Every five days I plant 3 ounces of lettuce seed, and this supplies my greenhouses with plants during the winter, one house being set out every week. I transplant twice, first at the fourth week, setting them 4 inches apart; second at the sixth week when they are put 8 inches apart. They head during the seventh and eighth weeks. During December, January, February and March there is a continuous crop. The last crop of lettuces from the greenhouse is in the middle of April. After that I raise them in sashes and in the open air. The house should be ventilated from the ridge; if this is not enough, then from one side also. The temperature should be warmest when the crop is

---

[*]American Gardening, xvii. 197 (March 28, 1896).

heading, and coolest for the three weeks after setting out and just before heading, but not below 35°. As soon as a crop is harvested, the house is fumigated, dug over, and a new crop set out. Not 24 hours is lost in

31. *Boston Market lettuce.*

changing crops. In renewing the beds use light, loamy soil; rotted sod is good, if left in a heap for a year to decompose fully. With regard to mildew of lettuce, if seen soon enough it can be gotten rid of by keeping the house dry and warm for three days, but most people do not discover it soon enough. Fungicides I do not use, but generally, when necessary, smoke the house, or place powdered sulphur on the steam pipes. For smoking, tobacco stems are used. When lettuces grow 'dog-eared' it is the fault of the grower; he has kept the temperature too high."

Varieties. — There are two general types of forced lettuce, the cabbage or heading type, and the loose or leafy type. The former is chiefly desired in the easternmost markets, but is little sought west of New York state. It is more difficult to grow than the loose varieties, being more particular as to soil and treatment, and requiring a somewhat longer season. It is grown to perfection only on loose soils and in solid ground beds. The varieties of the White-Seeded Tennis Ball or Boston Market type are most popular for heading lettuces. The accompanying illustration (Fig. 34, page 103) shows four heads of Boston Market lettuce sent me by W. W. Rawson, Arlington, Mass. The head on top weighed, with roots cut off, 7 ozs., and the one at the left 9½ ozs. The Grand Rapids is a loose-leaved lettuce, shown full grown in Figs. 32 and 33 (pages 95 and 98). It grows rapidly, is of very easy cultivation, and is at the present time the most popular lettuce, except in those particular localities where the heading varieties are preferred.*

Enemies and diseases. — The most inveterate pest of the lettuce grower is the green-fly or aphis. If it once gets thoroughly established, the most strenuous efforts are needed to dislodge it. The pest is most frequent in houses that are kept too warm. The plants may be sprinkled with tobacco dust, or tobacco stems may be strewn upon the ground between the plants and in the walks, and either treatment may be expected to keep

---

*A test of the varieties of lettuce for forcing purposes is recorded in Bull. 43 (1892) of the Ohio Exp. Sta.

down the aphis. It can easily be kept out of the houses by fumigating twice a week with tobacco, and probably with the rose leaf extract of tobacco. Do not wait until the insect appears. Begin fumigating as soon as the plants are first pricked off, and continue until within two or three weeks of harvest, or longer if necessary.

The rot often ruins crops of lettuce. The outer leaves decay, often quickly, and fall flat upon the ground, leaving the central core of the plant standing. Fig. 35 is a fair sample of a plant collapsed by rot. I once lost an

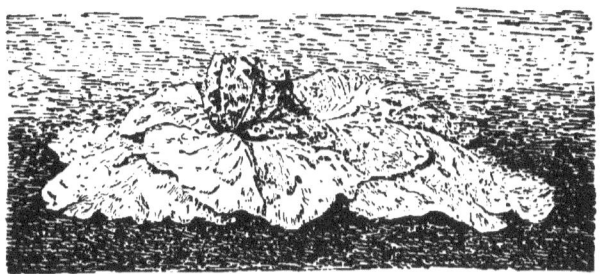

35. Lettuce plant collapsed by the rot.

entire crop by this disorder. The plants were about two-thirds grown and in good condition. The house was rather over-piped for lettuce, and we kept it cool by careful attention to ventilation. It became necessary to be absent three days in midwinter. Careful instructions were given a workman concerning the management of the house, but he kept it too close and too wet, and at the end of the three days the crop was past recovery.

This lettuce rot is due to a fungus (*Botrytis vulgaris*) which lives upon decaying matter on the soil, but when the house is kept too warm and damp, and the lettuce becomes flabby, it invades the plant and causes irreparable ruin. There is no remedy, but if the soil is sandy and "sweet" and the house properly managed as to moisture and temperature, and top dressings of manure are avoided, the disease need not be feared. Particular care should be taken to avoid having any water on the leaves at night, particularly in dull, cold weather. When an attack becomes apparent, the best thing to do is to raise the temperature, give plenty of air (but avoid draughts), and dry the house off. Galloway speaks of the rot as follows, in the article already quoted: "Wet rot of the lower leaves, and rotting of the stems and consequent wilting of the plant, are seldom troublesome in this [Boston or sandy] soil if properly handled, because the surface is at all times comparatively dry. Wet rot is produced by a fungus which may be found at any time on pieces of sticks and straws scattered through the soil. The fungus does not have the power of breaking down the uninjured tissues of the plant, excepting possibly in very rare cases. When the tissues become water-soaked, however, as they do when in contact with wet soil, the fungus, which is also most active in the presence of moisture, readily gains entrance and soon develops sufficient energy to become an active parasite."

The mildew (*Peronospora gangliformis*) is the staple lettuce disease of the books, but it is much less frequent than the rot. It is induced by sudden changes of temperature, soft, flabby plants, and too much water at night. Fumes of sulphur may be expected to keep it in check when the sanitary conditions of the house are set at rights. No doubt much of the trouble ascribed to mildew is really the rot.

Leaf-burn is a dying of the tips of the leaves when the plant is nearly or quite mature. It is particularly troublesome on the heading varieties, in which the slightest blemish upon the leaves detracts greatly from the selling qualities of the lettuce. This difficulty, according to Galloway, is attributable largely to the soil: "Top-burn, one of the worst troubles of the lettuce grower, does comparatively little injury on this Boston soil, providing the proper attention is given to ventilation and the management of the water and heat. Burn is the direct result of the collapse and death of the cells composing the edges of the leaves. It is most likely to occur just as the plant begins to head, and may be induced by a number of causes. The trouble is most likely to result on a bright day following several days of cloudy, wet weather. During cloudy weather in winter the air in a greenhouse is practically saturated, and in consequence there is comparatively little transpiration on the part of the leaves. The cells, therefore, become excessively turgid, and are probably weakened by the presence of organic acids. When the sun suddenly appears, as it often does after a cloudy spell in winter, there is an immediate, rapid rise in temperature and a diminution of the amount of moisture in the air in the greenhouse. Under these conditions the plant rapidly gives off water, and if the loss is greater than the roots can supply the tissues first wilt, then collapse and die. The ability of the roots to supply the moisture is affected by the temperature of the soil, the movement of water in the latter, and the presence or absence of salts in solution. In this soil the temperature rises rapidly as soon as the air in the greenhouse becomes warm, and the roots in consequence immediately begin the work of supplying the leaves with water. The movement of the water in the soil is also rapid, so that the plant is able to utilize it rapidly."

CHAPTER V.

CAULIFLOWER.

There is probably no vegetable which is capable of profitable forcing in America concerning which so little has been written in reference to its treatment under glass as cauliflower. It is true that the literature of vegetable forcing is very meagre in this country, and it is, therefore, little wonder that the cauliflower, which is scarcely known as a winter crop outside the establishments of wealthy persons who employ gardeners, should have received so little attention from writers. It should be said that in speaking of the forcing of cauliflowers, reference is made to the practice of growing them under glass to maturity in the cold months, and not to the much commoner practice of growing them to a large size under frames or sash-covered houses and stripping the sash off upon the approach of warm weather and allowing them to mature without cover. The management of cauliflowers under glass is a simple matter, particularly in houses which are adapted to lettuce, so that it is unnecessary to make any extended account of the operation. A sketch of some of the experiments made at Cornell will sufficiently indicate the methods to be employed.

Unsuccessful experiments. — In our first crop, the seeds were sown in "flats" or shallow boxes, and the young plants were transplanted into pots. When the plants were 8 or 10 inches high they had been shifted to 8-inch pots, and knowing that cauliflowers delight in a low temperature, the pots were set upon the **ground**

in a cool lean-to house, where the temperature often went below 40°. The floor of this house was cold and wet, and it was soon evident that the plants were suffering. They were removed, therefore, into an intermediate temperature. Growth soon began again, and small heads began to form before the plants had reached the proper size. These heads, however, soon split or "buttoned," and none of them were merchantable. The lesson was evident. The plants had been checked, and under the sudden stimulus of a new growth the premature heads were ruptured. The experiment was repeated the following winter in a small way, the attempt being made to keep the plants in a uniform condition of vigor and growth throughout their life time. This attempt was successful, and it led to two larger experiments. In this second trial, the plants were grown in 6-inch pots, but this was thereafter abandoned as too expensive and troublesome.

The successful crops. — The house in which the two first successful crops were grown is a low two-thirds span, facing the south, 60 ft. long by 20 ft. wide. It is built upon a side hill, and it has three benches, the two lower ones being used for the cauliflowers. The lowest bench, against the south wall, has a board bottom underneath 7 or 8 inches of soil, and is supplied with mild bottom heat from two 1¼-inch steam pipes. The main or central bench, 7 feet wide, is solid: that is, it is a ground bed, and has no bottom heat. The soil in this bed is about 8 inches deep, and it rests upon a natural subsoil of very hard clay. The soil in both beds was placed upon them in the preceding fall, and it was made of good garden loam with which a very liberal supply of old manure was mixed. One load of manure mixed with three or four of the earth makes a good soil; and if it is somewhat heavy or pasty, sand must be supplied to it to afford perfect drainage and prevent it from getting "sour" or hard. The lower bed, which had bottom heat, did so poorly

56. *Winter cauliflowers ten weeks after planting in the bed.*

under both crops that I shall dismiss it at once from this account. The plants were later than those in the solid bed, and never equaled them in size and percentage of good heads; and they were conspicuously lacking in uniformity. So few good heads formed that the bed did not return the labor expended upon it.

Seeds for the first crop were sown in boxes on August 24. The plants, having been once transplanted, were set in the beds October 4 and 5, about 16 inches apart each way. Three varieties were used, — Extra Early Dwarf Erfurt, Gilt-Edge Snowball and Early Snowball.

The plants were watered two or three times a week, as occasion demanded, and the ground was frequently stirred with a hand weeder. An abundance of air was given during the day, a row of small ventilators along the peak of the house being thrown open even in sharp weather if the sun was bright and there was little air stirring. From 60° to 70° during the day and about 50° at night were considered to be the ideal temperatures, although in very bright days the mercury might register 80° for a time and the night temperature several times sank below 40°. There was a tendency for the plants to damp off soon after they were set, but care in not watering too much (particularly close about the plant) and in giving an abundance of fresh air seemed to keep the trouble in check; and new plants were set into the vacancies. We were obliged to contend with two other enemies, the green-fly or aphis, and the common green cabbage worm. The aphis is readily kept in check by tobacco smudge. The first cabbage worms were noticed November 21, and for a couple of weeks they had to be carefully picked. The boxes of young plants had stood out of doors during September, and it is probable that eggs were laid upon the plants at that time.

The first week in December, heads were beginning to form. The first heads were sold January 13, four and a-half months from the sowing of the seed. The Erfurt gave the earliest and evidently the best results. The plants had been somewhat checked late in their history by very dark weather and possibly by some inattention in management, and many of the heads began to "button," or to break into irregular portions, with a tendency to go to seed. The house was needed for other experiments, and on January 20 the plants were all removed. At this time nearly three-fourths of the crop had matured sufficiently to give marketable heads, although many of the heads were small. Winter cauliflowers, in common with all forced crops, should be harvested when small, for products of medium or even small size sell for nearly or quite as much as large ones in winter, and the cost of raising them is much less. A head 4 inches across is large enough for January sales, and many of the heads which we sold were considerably smaller than this. These heads sold readily at our door for 20 cents apiece.

January 25, a second crop of cauliflowers was set in the beds, comprising Early Snowball and Dwarf Erfurt. Seeds for this crop were sown in flats October 21. On November 5 the plants were transplanted to other flats, and on December 16 shifted to 3-inch pots, where they remained until set in the bed. On April 8, the plants had reached the size shown in the photograph in Fig. 36 (page 110). At this time they completely covered the ground, and choked out lettuce which had been placed between them. About the 20th of March, heads were found to be forming in the Early Snowball. In the former experiment, Erfurt gave the first heads. A week later than this, Snowball had heads 3 to 4 inches in diameter, while Erfurt showed none. The first heads were sold on the 29th of March, about five and one-third months from the time of sowing. It will be observed that the time between sowing and harvest is greater in the second crop than in the first. This is because the plants were wholly grown in the dark and short days of midwinter. It should be added, also, that the climate of Ithaca is excessively cloudy, and that the forcing of plants presents special difficulties here.

An attempt was now made to keep the plants in a uniform but not exuberant state of vigor to prevent the heads from buttoning. The crop held up well, and on the 1st of May, when the experiment closed, there were many merchantable heads unsold. Ninety per cent of the plants made good heads, which is a very large propor-

37. A head of winter cauliflower.

tion, even for the best field culture. In this crop, the heads were allowed to attain a larger size than in the midwinter crop, the average diameter being about 6 inches. A good head of Snowball is shown in Fig. 37.

It is rarely necessary to bleach the heads, as is done in field culture. Late in the season, in April, it may be necessary to break a leaf down over a head now and then to protect it from too hot sun, but ordinarily the heads will be perfectly white under glass, when full grown. The heads are as sweet and tender as the best field product, and we have rarely grown a crop under glass, either of vegetables or flowers, which was so satisfactory and which attracted so much attention as these crops of cauliflowers. As to varieties, there is evidently little choice between the Erfurt and Snowball strains. In the last and most successful crop, the Early Snowball was the earlier, but otherwise it had little if any superiority over the other.

Subsequent experience has confirmed the methods detailed above, and has convinced us that cauliflower is one of the most satisfactory plants for forcing, so far as the growing of them is concerned. It is a question whether they would bring sufficient price in the market to warrant the raising of them in winter. The grower would certainly need to have a special market, for it is not a staple commodity. Field-grown cauliflowers are now kept in cold storage, which would still further reduce the demand for forced heads. It should be said, in closing, that cauliflower seed is very expensive, and that only the very best seed can be relied upon for good results.

CHAPTER VI.

RADISH.

CORNELL EXPERIENCE.*

THE radish is generally considered to be a vegetable which may be forced without any special difficulty. The prevalence of this opinion is probably due to the fact that the plants are grown out of doors without any trouble, and also to the still common practice of growing them in hotbeds. Under these various conditions, nearly all varieties of radishes thrive; but, nevertheless, it is a fact that the radish is one of the most sensitive of all the vegetables forced for market. It is impatient in a high temperature, slow and unsatisfactory in a cold one; it imperatively demands light, and the least shade causes the stem to elongate so that the foliage may be as near as possible to the sunshine; it becomes tough and unpalatable in poor soil, while in rich earth, with plenty of moisture, it yields readily to the attacks of the various damping-off fungi; and it must be grown quickly ("forced") in order to make the flesh crisp and of a delicate flavor. Conditions which will meet these requirements are not found in all forcing establishments. Radishes often thrive between cucumbers, when these plants are grown as a late winter crop, following lettuce.

Sowing.— Radishes are always propagated from seeds.

---

*By E. G. Lodeman. More detailed results may be expected, in bulletin form, when the experiments which are now in progress mature.

These are fairly large, and as a rule they possess strong powers of germination. The starting of the plants is, therefore, an easy matter; the seeds may be sown in drills from one-fourth to one-half an inch deep, the greater depth being preferred for light, sandy soils. They are generally sown thickly, and the seedlings are afterwards thinned to the desired distance; but if the seeds are fresh they may be planted at intervals of about one-fourth inch in the drills. This should insure a good stand. A convenient method of making the drills in hotbeds and benches is to fasten to one side of a lath a strip that is about a quarter of an inch thick and as wide as the drill is to be deep. This is nailed edgewise along the center of the lath (Fig. 38), and the drills are made by pressing the projecting piece into the soil until the lath will allow it to go no further. It is then carefully withdrawn, and if the soil is properly prepared and not too dry, a perfect groove will be formed. A very uniform depth can be attained in this manner.

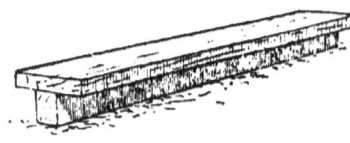

38. *Planting stick.*

Soil.—The soil for radishes should be what is known as warm and quick. Sand should predominate, but plenty of humus and well rotted-stable manure must be mixed with it. By composting thinly-cut sod growing upon sandy loam with one-third its volume of stable manure, a good radish soil will be formed. It will be ready for use in about a year, and if at the end of that time the vegetable fiber is not thoroughly decayed, it will not matter. Such a compost is suitable for nearly all vegetables grown in greenhouses, but it is especially valuable for rapid-growing crops. When placed upon a layer of ashes, coarse gravel, inverted sods, or some similar open material, the drainage is perfect, and the plants have an excellent opportunity for rapid growth.

SOWING THE SEED. 117

The amount of soil required by radishes varies with the varieties grown. The small, spherical-shaped sorts do well in a depth of only 3 or 4 inches, while the long-rooted varieties require almost twice as much. After the soil has been placed in the benches it should be made moderately firm by packing it with some heavy object; a brick

39   *A bunch of winter radishes.*

answers the purpose well. If it is inclined to be dry, it should be moistened, for when in proper condition for seed sowing it may be worked to the best advantage.

General management.—The drills may be made 3 or 4 inches apart for the smaller and more rapidly maturing varieties; for the others, 5 or 6 inches between the rows will be sufficient.

After the seed has been sown and the earth above has been well firmed, no watering will be necessary until the seedlings appear, unless the soil was too dry to begin with. In that case, water as freely as necessary; there is little danger of applying too much. The seedlings should appear in four or five days, and a week or ten days later they may be thinned. The small kinds will do well if two or three are left to the inch; the large ones require more room, and one plant to about an inch of space will be found none too thin. When this work has been done, nearly all the further attention necessary will be to maintain a proper temperature and to apply water when it is needed. Weeding, and an occasional cultivation with a hand weeder, should not be neglected.

As has already been said, the successful forcing of radishes is not such an easy matter as it would at first appear. The more important of the difficulties will now be considered in detail.

The conditions found in a hotbed which is almost spent are very nearly ideal for forcing radishes. In the first place, the temperatures of the soil and the air under the glass are as nearly right as they can well be made. As a rule, the radish is believed to do best in a cool house, one having a temperature of 40°-60°.* The soil in such a house should not be much warmer. But in a hotbed it is warmer, and frequently very much warmer. This explains the rapid and luxuriant growth which may be produced apparently without effort on the part of the

---

*"It adapts itself to hotbeds and forcing-houses quite well, but it objects to an overheated forcing-house as much as to an excessively exposed coldframe. It grows too many leaves and becomes pithy in one situation, and in the other case its growth is stunted or wholly checked, and under severe freezing it dies. Its proper temperature is from 40° to 65°, with plenty of fresh air. In rich soil, with sufficient water, it is a quick cropper, sometimes being ready for market in 21 days from the seed." * * * "The wholesale market price of radishes at Philadelphia in winter may be quoted at $2 to $4 per 100 bunches."—*Dreer's Vegetables Under Glass,*" 57, 59.

grower. Repeated trials in growing radishes in large houses having different temperatures have shown plainly that during the first two or three weeks, at least, radishes will bear well a soil temperature of fully 65° F., and 70° has not proved too much in several instances. If sufficient moisture is present the plants must grow, and they must mature quickly.

But although a high soil temperature is desirable, it does not follow that the atmosphere should be equally warm. On the contrary, if the temperature of the house can be kept about 10 degrees below that of the soil, the tendency to leaf formation will probably be checked. The hotbed may again serve as a guide. Here the heat is in the soil, bottom heat, as it is called, and the large amount of glass, as compared with the amount of air-space, must have a strong tendency to lower the temperature about the foliage; that surrounding the roots is much less affected.

Another important point,— one which has not been duly emphasized in connection with this crop,— is the amount of light received by the plants. Few plants show the want of light more quickly than radishes. If the shadow of a steam pipe or of a board falls upon the bench, the plants soon become drawn; the shadow cast by tall-growing varieties causes the shorter ones to grow more upright; a roof having small panes of glass and a comparatively large amount of wood-work has a strong tendency to prevent the plants from forming bottoms, unless the glass is close to the foliage; and if no direct sunlight is allowed to reach the plants, no swelling of the stem may take place, but the plants will grow very slender, and finally die, as if attacked by some unknown malady. If radish seed is sown very thickly, a similar result may occur even in places which are fairly well lighted. The strong growth of foliage excludes practically all the light from the soil, and the plants will form no bottoms.

The above remarks seem to show the necessity of thinning plants properly if the finest and most tender radishes are wanted. Thinning allows light and air to enter freely to all portions of the plants above ground, and the conditions are consequently favorable to rapid growth.

A moderately moist atmosphere appears to be favorable to the strong and quick development of radishes. When this crop is forced in hotbeds, the sash are necessarily lowered at times, and a confined air surrounds the plants, frequently for considerable periods. They appear to thrive under such treatment, and it is desirable to produce the same condition when growing the plants in greenhouses.

It is rare that the soil in a hotbed is more than 12 or 15 inches from the glass. This allows an abundance of light to reach the plants. The benches in a forcing-house cannot be so favorably placed in all their parts, and the best way of correcting the fault is to use large glass and a light framework in the roof. Under such conditions the plants will frequently do fairly well 8 or 10 feet from the glass. But with a light roof, the panes being at least 12 x 14 inches, the conditions approach more nearly those existing out of doors, and this explains the fact that the plants do not become drawn or "leggy."

Varieties.—There are a great many varieties of radishes; they differ mostly in form, color, and time of maturity. Those which mature rapidly are the ones most commonly forced, and a greater number of crops may be removed in a given time. Several mature, under favorable conditions, about three weeks from the time of seed sowing. These are nearly all red in color, and mostly of a spherical or olive form. The following may be recommended: Ne Plus Ultra, New Rapid Forcing, Extra Early Carmine Olive-shaped, Earliest Carmine Turnip, Early Scarlet Globe, Twenty-day Forcing, Earliest White, New White Forcing.

Among the best of those which mature about a week

later than the above, may be named New Crystal Forcing (white), New White Lady-Finger, Succession, French Breakfast, Long Scarlet Short-top, Long Cardinal. As already stated, the long radishes are not so satisfactory for forcing as the smaller varieties are. It must also be borne in mind that varieties of radishes, as of most other vegetables, are constantly changing, so that the varieties which are recommended to-day may not be recommended a year from now.

WASHINGTON EXPERIENCE.*

In the vicinity of many of our large cities the growing of radishes in greenhouses may, if properly done, prove a profitable industry. The following notes on the subject are based upon work carried on during the past four or five years, supplemented by observations extending over a longer period:

Houses adapted to growing radishes.— Radishes may be grown in almost any kind of a greenhouse, and for this reason the crop is a valuable one to work in with others, such as lettuce, tomatoes, cucumbers, etc. We do not advocate, however, the practice of growing radishes in a house with other crops, unless it is in certain special cases, where there is ground to spare and requirements for each crop are approximately the same. As is the case with all plants under glass, better results will follow if an entire house is devoted to one crop, thus making it possible to furnish, without fear of injury to other crops, the necessary requirements for growth.

Three-quarter span houses, 18 feet wide, with two walks and three beds, will be found as convenient as any for the crop. Three-quarter span houses with one path will also be found useful. Such a house, with young radishes just coming through the ground, is shown at Fig. 40.

---

*By B. T. Galloway, in American Gardening, xvii. 609, 610 (Sept. 26, 1896).

The walks should be from 14 to 18 inches wide, depending on the depth, and should have their sides made of 2-inch hemlock or cypress boards, fastened to sawed cedar or other durable posts. Good crops may be grown in even-span houses, and even a lean-to may be used, if proper facilities for heating and ventilating are present.

The soil.— In order to obtain solid, crisp radishes, the soil must not contain too much manure, nor should sand predominate. Ordinary garden loam, containing about 7 per cent clay, makes the best soil. To this should be added well-rotted manure in the proportion of one part manure to three or four parts soil.

We prefer solid beds to benches, as the conditions are more uniform in the former and the expense of maintaining them is less. The beds should be from 6 to 8 inches deep, but good crops may be grown on 4 inches of prepared soil. In the latter case it is necessary to add a little manure after each crop, while if deeper beds are used the same soil will answer for the entire season's work. If the radishes are followed by cucumbers, the manure necessary for the latter will serve for next season's radishes, but it will be necessary in such cases to remove about 2 inches of this extra manured soil and replace it with loam from the outside. The new loam should then be thoroughly mixed with the soil already in the house, and when this is accomplished the seed may be planted.

Planting the seed.— Radishes which come into the market before Thanksgiving are seldom profitable, and for this reason it is best to postpone the first seed-sowing until about the middle of October. Previous to this time the house may be used for growing stock plants of lettuce. By this we mean that lettuce sowed in the house, September 1, and transplanted 4 by 4 inches September 15, will be large enough by the first week in October to transplant to other houses, where it is to head.

Previous to sowing the radish seed, the ground should

be made smooth and as free from lumps as possible. By means of a light pine board 4 inches wide, rows 4 inches apart are marked off. The edge of a common lath is then placed in the marks and gently pressed into the soil until a narrow furrow one inch deep is made. The seed is then dropped in the furrow about half an inch apart, covered, and pressed down with the hand. Working in

40. *A three-quarter span radish house.*

this way, two men can plant almost 150 square feet an hour, and will use about 3 ounces of seed. As soon as the radishes are up and the seed leaves are well formed, the plants should be thinned out to 1½ to 2 inches apart.

It is of the highest importance to have all the radishes attain marketable size at the same time, and to accomplish this it will be necessary to use only the large seed. Where the seed as ordinarily obtained in the market is used, about 35 per cent of the crop will reach marketable size in from 35 to 40 days, 28 per cent will require 15 days longer, while the rest will in all probability never be worth anything. By using only the large seed, 90 per cent of the crop will come in at one time, thus making it possible to pull practically all the crop at once and immediately replant. As obtained in the market, about one-third of the seeds are too small to use, and consequently are thrown away.

Two pounds of seed was screened so as to separate the large from the small seed. In this case there was obtained from the 2 pounds of seed 19½ ounces of large seed and 10⅔ of small. The remainder was made up of pieces of gravel and crushed seed, bits of sticks, etc. The seed cost wholesale 60 cents per pound, and if one-third by weight is thrown away it brings the cost up to 80 cents per pound. This is a very small matter, however, in view of the many advantages resulting from the use of the large seed.

For screening the seed we use a sieve made as follows: A circular piece of thin sheet brass 6 inches in diameter has holes 2·25 of an inch (2 mm.) in diameter punched or rather cut in it, the holes being about 1-16 of an inch apart. The perforated sheet is then provided with a rim of brass or tin 2 inches high. We have then nothing more than a shallow cup or basin, with numerous holes in the bottom. A handful or more of seed is placed in this cup, and a few minutes' shaking will cause all the small seed to drop through the holes, while the large ones which cannot get through remain behind.

Varieties to plant.—In our experience, most of the markets prefer a bright scarlet turnip-shaped root. The pure scarlets always sell better than those tinged with purple, or having white tips. Ne Plus Ultra, Roman Carmine and Prussian Globe have proved the three best kinds for forcing. We have tried 20 or 25 other varieties, but soon gave them up on account of various undesirable qualities.

Preparing the crop for market.—When the crop is ready to market, which will generally be about 40 days from the time of planting, the roots are pulled and tied 6 to 8 in a bunch, or 12 to 16, as the market may require. Everything is pulled clean, and when a sufficient number of bunches is obtained they are thrown into a tank, tub or barrel and washed in clean water. Ordinarily there is very little soil adhering to the roots, so that the washing is a comparatively easy matter. Care must be exercised, however, in keeping the water clean, otherwise the radishes will go to market lacking the gloss that helps to sell them.

As soon as the plants are pulled the ground should immediately be forked over, smoothed, and planted, as already described. Following the foregoing plan, the first crop will be ready for market about Thanksgiving, the second crop January 5 to 10, the third crop the last week in February, and the fourth crop the first week in April. After this the house will pay better planted to cucumbers, which should by this time be in 6 or 8 inch pots.

Approximate yields per square foot.—A square foot of ground should yield on an average 16 bunches of radishes, 6 to 8 in a bunch, in the period extending from October 15 to April 10. The price will average 2 cents per bunch, making the returns 32 cents per square foot.

Temperature, moisture, insects and diseases.—The radish cannot be pushed by heat. A night temperature of 45° to 50°, with 20° to 25° more during the day, is about right. If too much bottom heat is given the plant will run to top. Watering should be carefully done, and in no case should the soil be allowed to become dry enough for the plants to wilt. In such cases a heavy watering is likely to cause the radishes to crack, thus rendering them unfit for market.

Insects and diseases cause very little trouble. Greenfly sometimes proves difficult to manage, but a light fumigation every two weeks with tobacco stems will keep the pest in check. The only disease worthy of mention is the cracking, to which reference has been made. Too much manure in the soil and the improper use of water are largely responsible for this trouble. The remedy is obvious.

Summary.—(1) Radishes may be successfully grown in almost any kind of a house.

(2) The soil should be moderately heavy, and hold water, but not bake or crack.

(3) Solid beds are preferable to benches, because the conditions of moisture and heat may be kept more uniform and the expense is less.

(4) Two men should plant 150 square feet per hour, using 3 ounces of seed in the work.

(5) The seed should be screened and all less than 2-25 of an inch in diameter should be thrown away. By following this plan 90 per cent of the crop will attain marketable size at the same time.

(6) Ne Plus Ultra, Roman Carmine and Prussian Globe have proved the best varieties for forcing.

(7) Four crops may be grown from October 15 to April 10, and the returns should average 30 to 32 cents per square foot.

CHAPTER VII.

ASPARAGUS AND RHUBARB.

Asparagus and rhubarb are generally forced from transplanted roots. That is, strong plants, four or more years old, are dug from the field and taken to the house for forcing. The crop is produced chiefly from the nourishment which is stored in the roots, and the roots are exhausted by the crop, and are then thrown away.

Inasmuch as the plants do not grow by becoming rooted and established in the soil after their removal to the house, it follows that they do not demand direct sunlight. In fact, the product may be tenderer and more saleable for being grown in a dull or even a nearly dark place. The roots are usually set underneath the benches in the glass house, but they may be set in the potting-room (if warm enough), or even in the cellar near the heater. The most rapid growth will be secured when the temperature is high (even as high as 70° at night), but a stockier and better product may often be grown when the temperature is somewhat lower.

There are various means of forcing asparagus and rhubarb where they stand, in the field. One of the commonest is to place the half of a barrel over a clump in very early spring, and then to pile fermenting horse manure about the barrel. The heat from the manure will start the plant into a precocious growth. In Europe, asparagus is sometimes forced where it grows by piling manure into trenches which are dug (and sometimes bricked up, with openings in the walls) between the rows. These

128 ASPARAGUS AND RHUBARB.

trenches are sometimes heated by hot-water pipes. In some instances, sashes are placed over the plants temporarily.

These various practices have suggested the idea that asparagus, rhubarb, sea-kale, and the like, might be permanently grown in a house with a removable roof, so that heat could be applied to them late in winter, and the roof then be removed and the plants find themselves growing out of doors in normal conditions. If the ground were well enriched, it would seem that such plantations

41. *Frame-work and heating pipes of Cornell asparagus house.*

ought to be able to be forced for several or many years in succession. Acting upon this suggestion, an asparagus house has been erected at Cornell. The experience with this house has not been sufficiently extended to warrant any conclusions from the experiment, but it promises well, and a description of it may be suggestive to the reader who is interested in the forcing of asparagus or rhubarb.

This Cornell asparagus house — if it may be called a house — is about 2c x 50 ft., and the frame is made of steam pipes (Fig. 41, page 128). The sides or walls are only 18 in. high, and the frame consists simply of a ridge and three pairs of rafters. The steam-heating pipe, or

42. *The asparagus house covered with canvas.*

riser, is seen at A, just beneath the ridge, and this feeds two returns upon either side of the house, next the walls. When it is desired to force the asparagus, canvas or muslin is stretched over the frame (as in Fig. 42). No difficulty has been found in starting the asparagus into growth in January and February. The cover is left on and the heat kept up until all danger of frost is past, when the canvas is removed and the plants grow naturally out of doors. It is probable that some such plan as this will be found to be perfectly practicable in the forcing of asparagus and rhubarb, and thus obviate the wasteful methods now in use of forcing and destroying transplanted roots. The secret of this method will no doubt be found to lie in allowing the plantation to become very thoroughly established (at least three or four years old) before forcing is attempted, in the very best tillage and fertilizing during the summer whilst the plants are growing, in taking off the cover just as soon as settled weather comes, and in not cutting the plants after that time.

ASPARAGUS.

The most essential point in the forcing of asparagus from transplanted roots, is to have very strong roots. They should not be less than four years old from the planting of the bed, and five and six-year roots are commonly better. It is often almost impossible to secure good roots, for the best roots are the ones which the asparagus grower most desires to keep in his plantation. The two circumstances which yield the best roots, as a rule, are the growing of the plantation for this particular purpose, and the taking out of alternate rows in plantations which have become too crowded. The grower is often obliged to take the roots from old and partially spent beds, but the best results are not always secured from such stock.

The roots are dug as late in the fall as possible, care being taken not to break the clumps, and to retain as much soil as possible, and they are then piled in a shed or cold cellar where they can be had as wanted. In this storage, they should be covered with earth or litter to prevent them from drying out, and freezing is supposed to add to their value for forcing.

The roots are commonly forced under the benches of a forcing-house. They may be handled in a hotbed, but as hotbeds are outside the purpose of this book, this method of forcing will not be discussed in detail. It may be said, however, that forcing in hotbeds differs in no important respect from forcing in the house. A space is made under the bench at least 3 inches deeper than the clumps which it is desired to force. This space may be either a pit dug into the ground, or it may be formed by boards upon top of the earth. The pit will generally need to be at least a foot deep. In the bottom is placed a couple of inches of good soil, and upon this soil the clumps are solidly placed, standing them as close together as possible. Earth is now filled in between the clumps, and the crowns are covered with earth at least an inch deep. If it is desired to bleach the asparagus, 6 or 8 inches of soil should be covered over the clumps.

The temperature should be kept rather low for a few days, until the roots become thoroughly settled in place. After that, the temperature may be raised to that required for roses, or even higher. Very high temperatures give spindling shoots. It is essential that the roots be profusely watered. New roots are brought in every three or four weeks, to give a succession.

The following are actual dates of asparagus forcing, under benches, at Cornell: Plants taken from an old patch November 20, 1893, and set under benches three days later. December 4, plants just pushing through. December 8, first shoots cut, averaging 9 inches long. December 14, first good cutting, shoots running from 6 to 15 inches long. December 18, second good cutting. December 26, a good cutting, some of the shoots having remained too long and become woody; some of these shoots were 2 ft. long. January 10, a heavy cutting. January 19, cut about half as many shoots as on the 10th. January 30, cut about as much as on the 19th, but shoots growing smaller. February 10, small cutting of weak shoots. Beyond this time there were no shoots worth cutting. These plants were forced most too rapidly at first, with the result of getting too many spindling shoots.

John Gardner's method.*—"I prefer roots three or four years old for forcing; but the age is immaterial, provided a vigorous growth has been made the previous season. The roots are originally planted out in rows 5 feet apart and a foot apart in the row, covered with 3 inches of soil, and cultivated as for an ordinary crop. When wanted for forcing the roots are plowed out, with as little damage to them as possible. In neighborhoods where asparagus is grown for market, farmers will often plant as above, and then, in the third or fourth year, will plow out every other row to be used for forcing, leaving permanent rows 10 feet apart. At this distance the ground can be thoroughly tilled, and abundant light, warmth and air will make strong crowns, so that an early crop of the first quality can be expected. Roots to be forced are placed in a pit under the benches and heated with hot water. They are placed on 2 inches of soil, and covered with 4 to 5 inches to blanch the shoots. Cutting will be in order about 15 days after the roots are put in, and the same roots will produce profitable shoots for six weeks. Asparagus can be forced on greenhouse benches, in frames or in hotbeds, where the manure is not too fresh, so as to generate too much heat and steam. I have seen the best of 'grass' grown in a common frame, with 18 inches of leaves and manure to ferment and give heat, and a covering thrown over the frame at night. It should be remembered that asparagus starts with very little heat, 45 degrees being sufficient to start it in the soil."

Forcing in hotbeds.†—"A most suitable place for forcing asparagus is a frame about 4 feet deep, with one 4-inch hot-water pipe running around it. About 2½ feet of fresh

---

*Garden and Forest, ii. 598 (Dec. 11, 1889).

†William Scott in Garden and Forest, vii. 478 (Nov. 28, 1894).

stable litter should be put into the frame and firmly packed, with an inch or two of sand spread over it. This bed should be allowed to stand until the heat of the ma-

43. *Rhubarb under a forcing-house bench.*

nure has declined to about 70 degrees, and not below 65 degrees, before the crowns are placed on it. For this work advantage should be taken of a day when the weather is mild, as the crowns are easily damaged by frost. Large crowns five or six years old are preferable to smaller ones for forcing. They may be placed rather closely together in the frame, but the distance apart must be regulated by their size. The roots should be spread evenly over the surface and covered with 6 inches of sand. Little water will be required, as the steam from the manure affords considerable moisture, but if the bed should become dry it may be moistened with water of the same temperature as the soil in the frame. A little air may be admitted when the day is bright and warm, to keep the temperature from rising above 80 degrees. When the points of the shoots begin to appear above the sand the crop is ready to cut. Where ground is plentiful a supply of forcing crowns can be kept up by sowing a little seed every year, having five or six successions, the oldest plants being forced for cutting."

RHUBARB.

The forcing of pie-plant does not differ essentially from the forcing of asparagus. Thoroughly established clumps are dug in the fall, and these are packed in beds underneath the benches, sifting the soil in tightly between the clumps, and then covering them with 2 to 6 inches of soil. The temperature should range as for lettuce or roses, or for very quick results it may be considerably higher. The length of time required for securing the saleable product is about the same as that required for asparagus, or perhaps a little longer. About four or five weeks after the planting under the benches is the usual time required for the first profitable cutting. Paragon and Linnæus varieties may be used for the earliest results, but the best crops are to be obtained from some of the larger kinds, like Victoria and Mammoth.

CHAPTER VIII.

MISCELLANEOUS COOL PLANTS.

PEA.

PEAS are very little known as a winter crop, although there is no particular difficulty in growing them. The yield is so small and the price so little that they are not often profitable, yet a few persons have found them to pay. They may be grown in narrow boxes (about 6 inches wide and as many inches deep), and these boxes are then placed in odd or vacant places about the house. If the boxes are 3 feet or more in length, the soil can be kept in a uniform condition of moisture without great trouble. The boxes should be kept very cool for a time — not much above freezing, — but when the plants appear they may be given the temperature of lettuce or carnations. The greater yields are obtained from the pole varieties, but the earlier results from the dwarf varieties like American Wonder.

Experiments at Cornell.[*] — During the past few years, peas have at various times been grown in the forcing-houses at Cornell with the intention of determining their value as a commercial crop, and also to study their behavior under glass. The forcing of peas has been carried on in northern Europe for many years, although on a somewhat different plan from that undertaken at this Station. Foreign gardeners generally grow the winter

---

[*] E. G. Lodeman, Bulletin 96, Cornell Exp. Sta.

crop in frames or hotbeds. In the neighborhood of Paris such protection is unnecessary, and successive sowings are made in the open ground from November to March, one of the most popular varieties for this purpose being St. Catherine (*Pois de Sainte-Catherine*). This variety is particularly well adapted to late fall and early winter sowings. In more northern latitudes, either coldframes or hotbeds supply the necessary protection for maturing the crop. Ringleader, Early Dwarf Frame, and Caractacus have been very popular in England. The second named variety is especially adapted for growing in hotbeds. It is exceedingly dwarf and matures very quickly, so that considerable quantities of peas may be harvested from a small area. Taller varieties are generally bent over to admit of their proper growth.

Peas thrive in a cool temperature, and the protection afforded by comparatively little glass or wood is sufficient to carry them through moderately cold weather. In the northern states, artificial heat must be given if the crop is to be grown during the winter months. As this cannot be done conveniently in frames, larger structures must be employed, and these may easily be supplied with a proper amount of heat for growing this vegetable. A night temperature of 40° to 50°, and a day temperature 10 to 20 degrees higher, will be sufficient to cause rapid growth and fairly prolific plants. Peas succeed best, as a rule, if grown in solid beds of rich, sandy soil that is well supplied with water. If peas grown under glass are subjected to the above conditions, their cultivation presents no serious difficulties, and it will scarcely be necessary to mention the details of more than one crop which we have grown.

Seeds of two varieties of peas were sown January 6, 1894; they were Extra Early Market and Rural New-Yorker. They were planted at the same depth as in outdoor culture, but the seed was sown more thickly, and the rows were as close to each other as the after culture

PEAS IN WINTER.

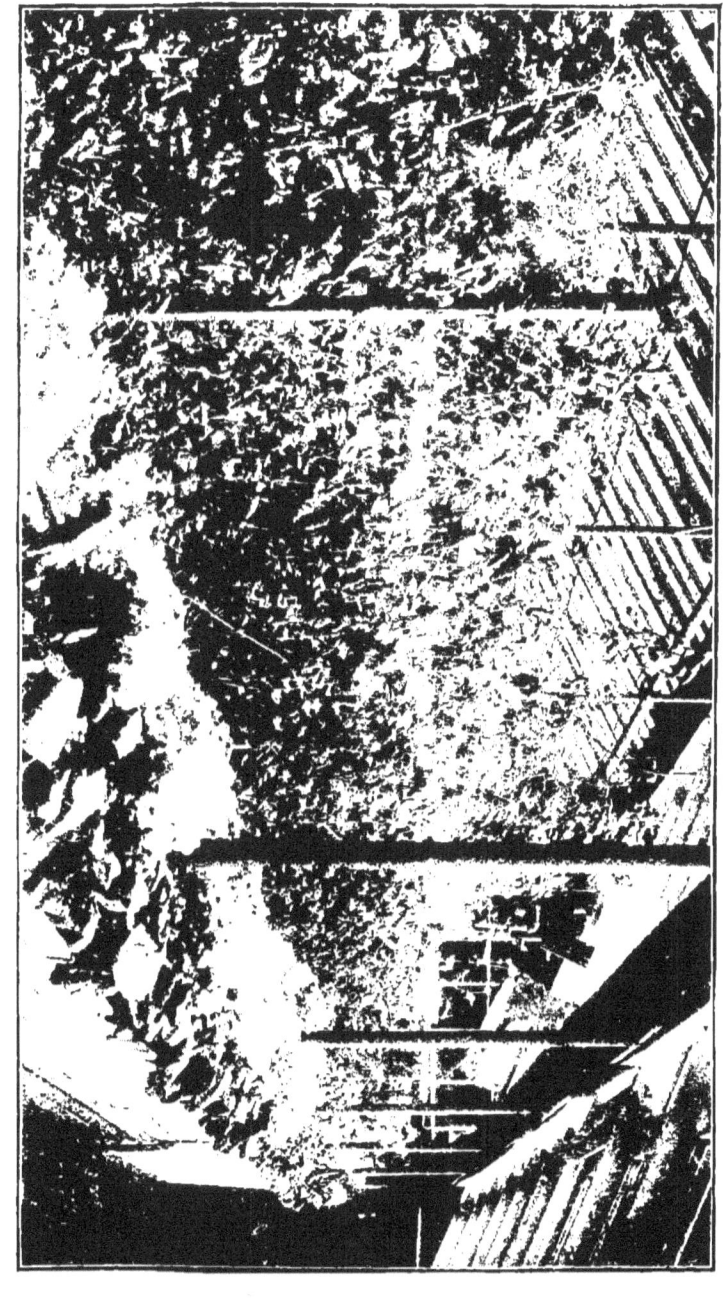

41. A bed of winter peas. Cinerarias in front.

of the crop would allow. Very dwarf varieties, such as Tom Thumb and American Wonder, may be planted in rows 3 to 5 inches apart, depending on the richness of the soil and the general care given the plants. Tall-growing varieties, as Champion of England, may be sown in rows running in pairs, the distance between the rows of each pair being from 6 to 10 inches, while the pairs are separated by spaces 15 to 18 inches wide. This will allow working-room among the plants and still admit of heavy planting.

One of the essential points in the successful growing of peas, whether in a greenhouse or out of doors, is the use of fresh seed. Garden peas retain their vitality from three to eight years, but the shorter period may be considered as more nearly correct when applied to varieties which are to be forced, since the loss of a week or two under glass is expensive, and two sowings cannot well be afforded. The seedlings began to appear eight days after seed sowing and they grew vigorously from the start. February 23, Rural New-Yorker showed the first opened blossoms, Extra Early Market at the same time having buds which were about to open.

On the 20th of March, or about 73 days from sowing the seed, both varieties had matured sufficiently to supply pods that were fit for market, but no picking was made until 11 days later, when the plants yielded pods at the rate of 6½ quarts for each 30 feet of double row. There was practically no difference between the two varieties as regards earliness or the amount of yield obtained. Two weeks later, a second and last picking was made, the plants yielding only one-half as much as before. This brings the total yield to a little over a peck. This is scarcely a profitable crop, especially since the varieties grown are quite tall, and required a trellis.

Formerly, the trellises used consisted of branches forced into the ground so that they would afford support to the vines; but with the crop here considered, a more satisfactory trellis was made by using a wire netting having large meshes. This was fastened between the rows by means of stakes, and thus each strip of netting served as a support for a double row. This forms the neatest and most substantial trellis here used for supporting the vines.

The yields from extremely dwarf varieties, such as Tom Thumb, have proved unsatisfactory. The plants require no support, but they yield only one picking, and this is so light that their culture under glass cannot in all cases be advised.

Peas grown under glass are sensitive to heat, and the warm spring days, when accompanied by sunshine, check their growth to a marked degree. The most healthy growth is made during the cold months of the year, and after April 1 not much should be expected from the vines unless steps are taken to keep the house as cool as possible. This may be accomplished by shading, and by a free use of water upon the walks of the house.

From a financial standpoint, the growing of peas can scarcely be advised, but amateurs may derive much satisfaction from their cultivation, as the plants are easily grown, they require little care, and the quality of the peas is especially appreciated when no fresh ones are on the market.

CELERY.

Celery practically goes out of the market in April. The stored crop is then exhausted, and until the earliest field product is received, in July, celery is not to be had. There should be some means of supplying the demand in May and June. Some three or four years ago, we turned our attention to this problem, and we now feel that it is a comparatively easy matter to grow celery for late spring and early summer use.

We sow the seed in late fall or early winter, in flats

or seed-pans. The young plants grow very slowly, and we make no effort to hasten them. About a month after the seeds are sown, the plants are pricked out into other flats, where they are allowed to stand 3 or 4 inches apart each way. A month or so later, they are transplanted into beds, following lettuce, cauliflower, chrysanthemums, or other crops. It will thus be seen that for two months or more the plants take up little or no room, for the flats are placed in vacant places here and there throughout the house, and they need little other care than watering. They should be kept cool — in a house used for lettuce, violets, carnations and the like — for if one attempts to force them they will likely run to seed. When the plants are finally transplanted, we prefer to put them in solid beds without bottom heat.

In six weeks to two months after the plants are turned into their permanent quarters they will be ready to bleach, and this operation has caused us more trouble than all other difficulties combined. Our first thought was to set the plants very close together, so that they would bleach themselves, after the manner of the "New Celery Culture," but it would not work. The plants ran too much to foliage, and they tended to damp-off or rot where they were too close. We next tried darkening the house,

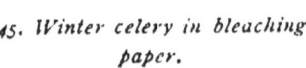

45. *Winter celery in bleaching paper.*

but without success. We then attempted to bleach the plants by partially burying them in sand in a cellar, but this also failed. Finally, we tried various methods of tying up or enclosing each midwinter plant as it stood in the bed. Tiles placed about the plants — which are so successful in the field,— rotted the plants in the moist air of the forcing-house. Heavy bibulous paper did the same. But thick, hard wrapping paper, with an almost "sized" surface, proved to be an admirable success. The stalks were brought together and tied, and a width of paper reaching to within 2 or 3 inches of the tips of the leaves was rolled tightly about the plant. As the plant grew, another width of paper was rolled about the first, and again reaching nearly the top of the plant. Two applications of the paper are sufficient. A month to six weeks is required to bleach the celery by this process in a cool house in April and May. Fig. 45 (page 140) shows the method of bleaching with the paper.

The seeds for one of our crops of house celery were sown December 10, 1894; pricked off, January 8; planted in beds, February 6; first tied up in paper, April 12; second tying, May 9; celery fit to use, May 21 to June 20. The Kalamazoo celery is well adapted to house cultivation. The quality of this house-grown product is equal to that grown in the field.

SALADS, POT-HERBS, AND MINTS.

Water-cress. — Persons who are fond of water-cress should know that no plant is easier to grow under benches in greenhouses. If there is an earth floor under the benches of a cool or intermediate house, the plant will take care of itself when once introduced, provided, of course, there is sufficient moisture. Fig. 46 (page 142) shows a mat of water-cress growing under a bench in a general conservatory house, near the overflow of a tank. It is not necessary to supply water in which the plant may grow, but it thrives well, with its characteristic flavor, in soil which is simply uniformly moist and cool. The plants may be gathered from brooks or other places where it is established, and planted at intervals under either north or south benches, and when once colonized it needs no renewing.

Garden-cress.—The ordinary French or garden cress (varieties of *Lepidium sativum*) also thrives well under glass. We have grown both the plain and curled-leaved forms upon benches or beds along with lettuce and spinach. The seed is sown directly where the plants are to stand. The plant grows quickly, and the early, tender leaves should be used before it runs to seed.

16. *Water-cress under a bench.*

Parsley.—No vegetable is more readily grown in winter than parsley. The seed is sown in the open in spring, and the plants receive the ordinary care during the summer. In the fall, the strong roots are lifted and planted in a bed or bench in a lettuce house. The plants are headed down when transplanted, and the sunlight is kept off them for a few days until they are thoroughly established. After that, they need no extra or unusual care. Parsley will thrive well in the dark end of the house, or in almost any odd corner, as behind a door or in the shade next the wall. The plants should be renewed each year. The most satisfactory variety is the Curled or Fern-leaved.

Spinach was formerly grown in frames and hotbeds, and sometimes in glass houses, but the length of time required to bring it to maturity, and the competition of the southern-grown product, make it unprofitable. Only now and then is a man found who is able to make frame-grown spinach pay. We have grown it in the forcing-house, and find that it forces readily with the same temperature and treatment which are given to lettuce.

Mustard. — Any of the pot-herb mustards are easily grown in a lettuce or carnation house. One of the best types is the Chinese mustard. This makes an attractive edging to chrysanthemum or lily beds. The seeds are sown where the plants are to stand, although they may be sown in pots or flats and the plants transplanted to their permanent quarters.

Dandelion. — This plant is grown somewhat extensively in the open in parts of the eastern states, particularly about Boston, for greens. It is also occasionally forced. Spring-sown plants are lifted in the fall and transplanted to a cool house. The leaves should be ready for cutting by the holidays. As soon as the cutting is completed, the crowns are thrown out and the bed or bench is used for other crops. The French improved varieties are the kinds of dandelions to be grown. The crop of these may be followed by lettuce, White Spine cucumbers or radishes.

Mints of various kinds are readily grown in cool houses, such as are adapted to lettuce and violets. The species most commonly grown are sage and spearmint (*Mentha viridis*), for which there is generally a good demand, in eastern cities, at Thanksgiving and Christmas. Sods of the sage or mint may be dug and placed directly in the house, care being taken to cut the sods very deep, and not to break them in the transfer. Better results are obtained, however, by planting the mint permanently in a solid bed, and covering it over with sash at forcing time. Heating pipes should be laid alongside the bed. From six to eight weeks are required to bring the mint to cutting size.

ONION.

We have had good success in growing multiplier or potato onions under glass, planting them in a lettuce bed, where they will give bunch onions in six or seven weeks. In a warmer temperature, they become very strong in flavor. We have not been able to accomplish any useful results with onions from seeds, however, because they grow too slow and are not inclined to bottom. Neither have we succeeded with onions from sets, although we have given them a fair trial in different houses. The following statements upon forcing onions from sets are by W. Van Fleet, of New Jersey, in answer to inquiries respecting the forcing of bunch onions for winter market :*

"Three or four inches is about as thick as they can be grown ; 3 x 6 is safer. If grown 3 x 4 inches, alternate rows may be taken out as soon as large enough for market. Use one-fourth to one-third rotted manure, the rest good, sandy garden loam or rotted sods ; 1-50 bone dust, or 1-150 (in bulk) good fertilizer may be added after growth has begun. They can endure more cold than lettuce or radishes, but are easily checked by low temperature when in full growth. Give them an average of 70° F. As the leaves do not cover the soil and prevent evaporation, there is little danger from over watering ; nevertheless, onions do not like sodden ground. Have the benches well drained ; water thoroughly, and let the top soil dry perceptibly before repeating. The quick-growing American varieties give best results ; Philadelphia, Silverskin and Yellow Globe Danvers are excellent. The sets should be carefully selected, of uniform shape, and less than one-half inch in diameter. Onions are rarely forced under glass now, and are of doubtful profit, owing to competition from the Egyptian and other hardy perennial onions, which grow throughout the winter in the south and are shipped to the northern markets as early as February. There is a possible

---

* Rural New-Yorker, liii. 777 (December 8, 1894).

profit in growing the Egyptian onion under glass in cold localities, but I am not aware that it has been tried commercially. The bulblets, which form in place of seed, could be planted in flats of rich earth, 6 inches deep, well watered and attended to until freezing weather, when they could be covered thickly with straw until needed, or brought under glass at once. The after treatment would be similar, except that a temperature below 65° would prove most satisfactory."

BEETS, CARROTS, AND TURNIPS.

The root crops grow readily in lettuce beds, but their commercial value is so small and the length of time required for their growth so great that they are rarely profitable. Beets are occasionally grown between the late winter crops of tomatoes or cucumbers. If the house has grown lettuce or other cool crops, the beets may be transplanted into the beds in rows about 3 feet apart, setting the cucumber plants between the rows. The beets should be off by the time the other plants demand all the room. The turnip beets (like the Egyptian), half-long carrots and early varieties of turnips are the varieties

47. *A bunch of winter carrots.*

best adapted to forcing. Carrots are slowest to mature, and also find the smallest demand in the market. From three to four months are required to secure good bottoms on carrots. For home use these root crops may be grown in a few square feet of soil on benches which grow lettuce and carnations or even roses.

POTATO.

Potatoes can be grown on spent rose or lettuce beds, or under benches which open out to the light. We have grown a bushel of tubers in a thick row under the edge of a carnation bench some 40 feet long. They need no special care. Potatoes are sometimes planted in ground beds in forcing-houses in late winter or early spring after the legitimate winter crops are harvested.

PEPINO.

The pepino or melon shrub is practically unknown as a forcing-house product. The first critical study of the plant in this country was made at the Cornell Station in 1891, but Professor Munson, in Maine, seems to have been the first person to make a success of it as a fruit-bearing plant under glass.* The plant is an undershrub, making a neat and spreading bush 2 or 3 feet high when a year old. The fruits are oblong and somewhat egg-shaped, with a solid and seedless flesh and a cantaloupe-like flavor. It more closely resembles the eggplant in botanical features than it does any other fruit plant of our gardens. It is propagated by cuttings of the young shoots in the same way as the geranium or tomato. Cuttings made in March or April may be expected to make fruit-bearing plants by the following January or February. The plants should be carried through the summer in 4-inch or 5-inch pots and transferred to 6-inch pots on the approach of winter. They should be grown in

---

*W. M. Munson, in Garden and Forest, v. 173 (Apr. 13, 1892), with illustration.

a cool house, with no bottom heat. A lettuce house suits them well. In such temperature strong plants may be expected to yield two or three fruits to each cluster.

History and description of the pepino.—This interesting plant is so little known that I append a somewhat full account of it :*

Within the last few years a novelty has appeared in the seedsmen's catalogues under the name of Pepino, Melon Pear, Melon Shrub, and *Solanum Guatemalense*. Its botanical affinities, as well as its horticultural merits, have been a perplexity. The plant is a strong-growing herb or half-shrub in this climate, becoming 2 or 3 feet high and as many broad. It has a clean and attractive foliage, comprised of long-lanceolate nearly smooth very dark green entire leaves. It is a profuse bloomer, the bright blue flowers reminding one of potato flowers. But one fruit commonly sets in each cluster, and as this grows the stem elongates until it reaches a length of from 4 to 6 inches. The fruit itself is very handsome. As it ripens it assumes a warm yellow color, which is overlaid with streaks and veins of violet-purple. These fruits are somewhat egg-shaped, conspicuously pointed, and vary from $2\frac{1}{2}$ to $3\frac{1}{2}$ inches in length. The illustration, Fig. 48 (page 148), shows an average specimen about two-thirds natural size. If the fruits are still green upon the approach of frost, they may be placed in a cool dry room, where, in the course of two or three weeks, they will take on their handsome color. If carefully handled or wrapped in paper, the fruits will keep until midwinter or later. The fruit is pleasantly scented, and the flavor of it may be compared to that of a juicy, tender and somewhat acid eggplant. It is eaten either raw or cooked.

Upon the approach of winter we dig up some of the plants and remove them to the conservatory or forcing-house. As ornamental plants they will prove to be

---

*From Bulletin 37 (Dec. 1891). Cornell Exp. Sta. (now out of print).

11 FORC.

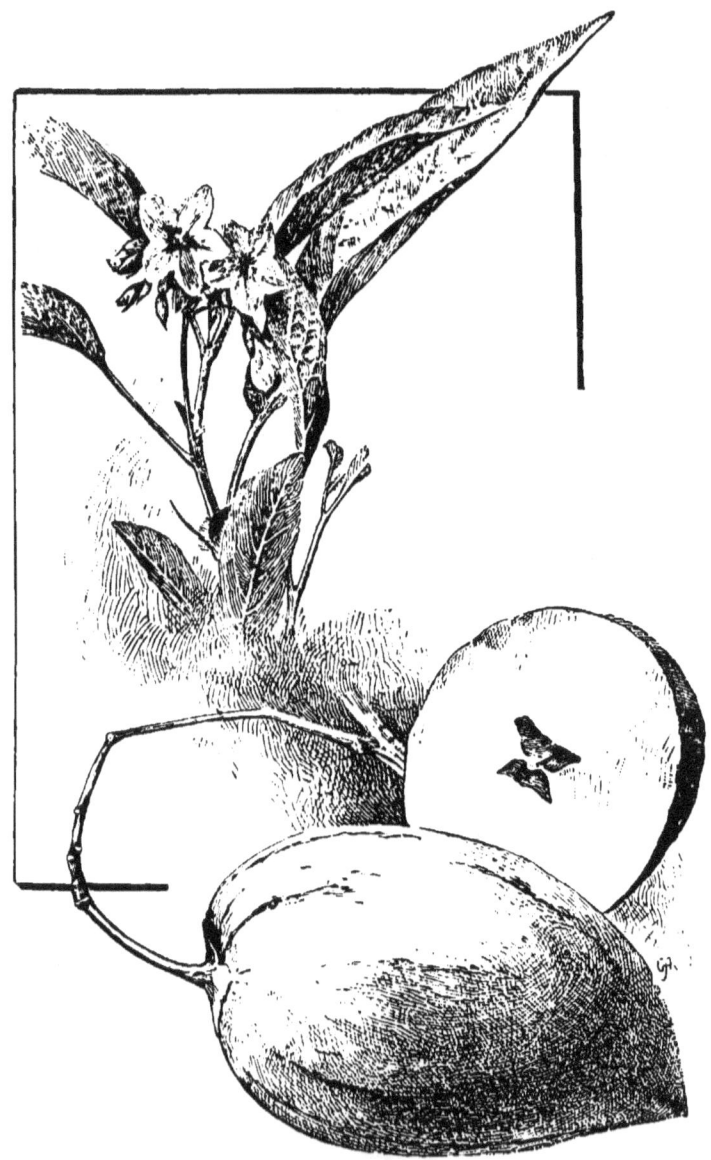

48. *Spray and fruit of the pepino.*

very useful in this latitude. The habit is attractive, the flowers bright and pleasant, and the fruit is highly ornamental and curious. The plant will stand a little frost.

The plant does not fruit freely with us, however, although it blooms profusely. We have endeavored to insure fruiting by hand pollination, but without success. The anthers give very little pollen. Perhaps half the plants succeed in setting two or three fruits apiece. All the fruits which we have raised have been entirely seedless, and this appears to be the common experience. The seed-cavities remain, however, as shown in the cross-section in Fig. 48. The plant must be propagated by cuttings or layers, therefore. We obtained our stock from a botanical specimen which I obtained from Florida, and which was not thoroughly dried.

This plant was introduced into the United States from Guatemala in 1882 by Gustav Eisen, of California.* There has been much speculation as to its nativity and its true botanical position. At first it was thought by some to be a variety of the eggplant,† but it is very distinct from that species. But the plant is by no means a novelty to science nor even to cultivation, for it was accurately described and figured so early as 1714 by Feuillée in his account of travels in Peru.‡ He called it *Melongena laurifolia*. At that time the plant bore "several little lenticular seeds, one line broad." It was carefully cultivated in gardens, and the Indians ate it with delight. The taste is described as somewhat like a melon. Eating too heartily of it was supposed to bring on fevers. In Lima it is called Pepo. In 1799 it was again described and figured by botanists visiting Peru, Ruiz and Pavon.‖ They described the fruit as "ovate, pointed, smooth and shining, white variegated with purple, hanging, of the

---

* Orch. and Gard. x. 61 (1888).
† Gard. Monthly, xxix. 24, 48, 84, 120, 355 (1887).
‡ Journ. Obs. Phys. Math. et Bot. 735, t. 26.
‖ **Flora. Peruviana**, ii. 32 t. 162 a.

shape of a lemon." They say that it was much cultivated in Peru, and added that it was propagated by means of cuttings. It was called "Pepino de la tierra." In 1785, Thouin, a noted French gardener, introduced it into Europe, and four years later Aiton, of the Royal Garden at Kew, England, named it *Solanum muricatum*.* The specific name, *muricate* or *prickly*, was given in reference to the rough or warty character of the sprouts which spring from the root, and which are often used for propagation. And now, over a hundred years later, it has found its way to us.

Mr. Eisen's account of the pepino will be interesting in this connection. "The Central American name of this plant," he writes, "is pepino. Under this name it is known everywhere in the Central American highlands, and under this name only. But as pepino in Spanish also means cucumber, it was thought best to give the plant an English name. I suggested the name melon shrub, but through the error or the wisdom of a printer the name was changed to melon pear, which I confess is not very appropriate, but still no less so than pear guava, alligator pear, rose apple, strawberry guava, mango apple, custard apple, etc. * * * As to the value of the fruit and the success of it in the states, only time will tell. The fact that I found the plant growing only on the high land, where the temperature in the shade seldom reaches 75° Fahr., suggested to me the probability that it would fruit in a more northern latitude. In California it has proved a success in the cooler parts, such as in Los Angeles city, and in several places in the coast range, and will undoubtedly fruit in many other localities where it is not too hot. * * * My friend, the late Mr. J. Grelck, of Los Angeles, had a plantation of 10,000 pepinos, which grew and bore well, and he sold considerable fruit. * * * In pulp and skin the pepino

---

*Hort. Kew. i. 250.

resembles somewhat the Bartlett pear, but in taste more a muskmelon; but it has besides a most delicious acid, entirely wanting in melons and quite peculiarly its own. In warm localities this acid does not develop, and this fact is the greatest drawback to the success of the fruit. The fruit has no seed, as a rule. And in all, I have found only a dozen seeds, and those in fruit which came from Salama in Guatemala, a place rather too warm to produce the finest quality of fruit. The botanical name of the pepino is not known to me with certainty. The same was described by the Franco-Guatemalan botanist, Mr. Rousignon, as *Solanum Melongena Guatemalense*, but it is to me quite evident that this solanum is not, nor is it closely related to the *S. Melongena* or eggplant, which latter is a native of Central Asia. The pepino is probably a native of the Central American highlands, and appears to have been cultivated by the Indians before the conquest by the Spaniards."* Last year Mr. Eisen writes that "it has only succeeded in Florida, but has there proved of considerable value."†

The greatest fault of the pepino appears to be its failure to set fruit. Mr. Eisen states that in Guatemala it "yields abundantly, in fact enormously, 100 to 150 fruits to a vine 4 feet in diameter being nothing uncommon. I have seen it yield similarly in California, but whenever exposed to too much heat and dryness, it is very slow to set fruit."‡ He recommends that it be shaded if it refuses to set fruit. Martin Benson, Dade Co., Florida, writing to the *American Garden*,‖ says that he has had great success with it. "I counted the fruit on a medium-sized plant and found it bore 60 of all sizes, from those just set to some nearly matured and weighing upwards of

---

* Gard. Monthly, xxix. 84 (1887).
† Gard. and Forest, iii. 471 (1890).
‡ Orch. and Gard. x. 61 (1888).
‖ ix. 265 (1888).

a pound. The fruit varies considerably, but averages about the size of a goose egg. The fruit is the most perfectly seedless of any I have ever seen, without a trace of a seed. It requires cool weather in order to set fruit, and never does so excepting a norther or other cool spell, when the fruit sets in great quantities." Mr. Benson's letter is accompanied by an admirable illustration of the fruit. In the northern states it has always proved a shy bearer, if I may judge from such records as exist. "D," writing to the *Gardener's Monthly*, says that he had "only about two pears to each plant, among literally hundreds of blossoms." *Orchard and Garden* comments upon this feature as follows: "The general experience with it here [New Jersey], thus far, seems to justify us in calling it exceedingly shy in setting fruit, and if this tendency to abortive blooming cannot be overcome, the melon pear must be considered without practical value." These remarks are certainly counter to the statements and pictures made by some seedsmen in regard to its productiveness. Professor Munson, as we have seen, has found it to be fairly productive under glass when grown in a low temperature.

CHAPTER IX.

TOMATO.

NEXT to lettuce, the tomato is probably the most important vegetable grown in American forcing-houses. Its only close competitor for this honor is the cucumber. Winter tomatoes always find a ready sale at prices ranging from 25 to 75 cents per pound. Even after the Florida tomatoes come upon the market in late winter, a good quality of house-grown fruits continues to sell well in every good market. The crop is one which demands a high temperature, an abundance of sunlight, and great care in the growing, but the profits, under good management, are correspondingly high.

The house. — A light and tight house is essential, and it must be high enough to allow of training the plants (that is, at least 5 feet above the soil in all parts). Our preference is a sash-bar frame house, something like those shown in Figs. 12 and 13. A north-and-south house would be preferable, probably, because of the more even distribution of light. Tomatoes may also be grown for a late spring crop in a carnation or lettuce house (see page 98).

The importance of direct and strong sunlight was well illustrated in one of our experiments. At one end of the house is a low building which shaded a part of the plants after two or three o'clock. The plants within 3 or 4 feet of this building, which were thus deprived of direct sunlight for half the afternoon, bore no fruits whatever, although they were strong and vigorous. At 6 and 7 feet away some fruits were borne, but it was not until about 15 or 20 feet from the building that a full crop was obtained. The ill effects of shade are also visible upon the north benches of houses running east and west, where the plants are shaded somewhat by those in the center of the house. During the middle of winter the north bench in the house will ordinarily produce no more than half as much fruit, even in an unequal-spanned house, as those in direct sunlight. The plants in partial shade grow as well and as large as those in full sun, and they often blossom well, but the fruit does not set.

The proper temperature for tomatoes is from 60° to 65° at night, and 10° higher for dull days. On bright days it may be allowed to run higher, although we always wish to ventilate at 75°, but a temperature of 90° or even 100° can do no harm. Until fruit begins to set, the atmosphere should be kept moist, especially on bright days, but the setting of the fruit is hindered by a humid atmosphere.

Soil and fertilizers.—Nearly all writers upon house cultivation of tomatoes assert that the soil should be only moderately rich, because heavily manured plants are over-vigorous in growth, are generally unproductive, and are particularly liable to disease; and the additional cost of training is said to be considerable. Our experience emphatically contradicts this supposition. Heavily manured plants undoubtedly require more care in the pruning, and it is possible that when not properly handled they may be more liable to mildew, because of the dense and crowded growth; but, on the other hand, we always get the best yield from the strongest plants, and we find the extra cost of training to be of little account. We grow the plants in rich garden loam, to which is added a fourth or fifth of its bulk of well-rotted manure, and when the plants begin to bear, liquid manure is applied nearly every week, or a top-dressing of manure is given. To those unaccustomed to forcing-house work this may seem extravagant fertilizing; but it must be remembered that in house cultivation the roots are confined in a small space, and they have little chance to search for food. And as a matter of practice, we find this heavy manuring to be essential to best results. It is strange that the notion that tomatoes require a comparatively poor soil should ever have become so widespread. It has been held also in regard to outdoor tomatoes, but our own experiments, and those of others, have shown that that it is generally erroneous (consult pages 53 to 61).

Raising the plants, and bearing age. — Tomato plants are usually grown from seeds, but sometimes from cuttings.

49. *Box cultivation of winter tomatoes.*

Seeds are sown in flats or pots, and the plants are handled at least twice before they go into permanent quarters. Cuttings are taken from strong, well-developed branches, and are made of the upper 4 or 5 inches of the shoot. Cutting-plants struck at the same time as seeds are sown will bear sooner than seedlings. Cutting-plants (if made from well-matured shoots) generally bear nearer the ground than seedlings. Fig. 50 shows cutting-plants in bearing.

In this latitude it requires from four to five months to bring a forced tomato plant into bearing. A few statistics will show the time required from seed to fruit. Seeds which were sown August 9 gave plants fit for transplanting early in September. These were planted in permanent quarters in the tomato house October 15, and the first fruits were obtained December 28. They con-

50. *Cutting-grown tomato plants in a shallow bench.*

tinued in bearing until near the end of February, when they were trained for a second crop. Plants started November 10 were transplanted into 4-inch pots December 8, and from these pots into permanent quarters February 25. The first fruits were picked May 6, and May 12 the first market picking was obtained. On the first of June they were in full bearing. It will be noticed that the second lot grew much more slowly than the first one. This is because the plants were growing in the short and dull days of midwinter. Market growers like to sow seeds or take cuttings in August for the holiday crop. The second crop is ready to go on the benches early in January. A commercial grower in Ontario informs me that when he sows seeds the middle of January he expects to put the plants on the benches on the first of April and to make the first picking the 20th of May.

Beds, benches and boxes. — There are various methods of growing house tomatoes. Much depends upon the height of house and arrangement of benches and heating apparatus. They may be planted in the ground or floor of the house, but this is not advisable, as it does not allow of the application of bottom heat, and the plants grow slowly ; and it is frequently an advantage to shift the plants somewhat during subsequent treatment. They require brisk bottom heat, and it is necessary, therefore, to place them upon benches.

The plants may be grown in shallow beds upon the benches, or in boxes or pots. Many persons prefer to grow tomatoes in 18-inch-square boxes. Fig. 49 (page 155) shows the arrangement of such a tomato house. The return pipes lie close upon the ground, and are covered with a low platform or bench, made of 3-inch slats with inch spaces between them. The boxes are placed 10 inches or a foot apart, and four plants are set in each of those which are 18 inches square and a foot deep. A plant, therefore, occupies about $1\frac{1}{2}$ square feet of floor space. We have grown them in 10-inch-square boxes, and also in 10-inch pots, but these dry out so quickly that we do not like them. One or two narrow cracks are left in the bottom. A good layer of potsherds or clinkers is placed in the bottom for drainage, and the box is then filled two-thirds full of soil. When the fruit begins to set, the box is nearly filled with rich soil and manure. The object of not filling the box at first is to confine the roots

in a smaller space, and therefore to hasten fruitfulness —
perhaps an imaginary advantage — but more particularly
to allow of an additional stimulus to be given the plant
at fruiting time by the addition of fresh soil.

On the whole, however, we prefer to grow tomatoes
on benches, with about 7 or 8 inches of soil. Fig. 14
shows tomatoes growing upon a floor which lies directly
over the heater, a place which gives most excellent results. In this bed we set the plants in rows 24 inches
apart, and 18 inches apart in the row. This house is

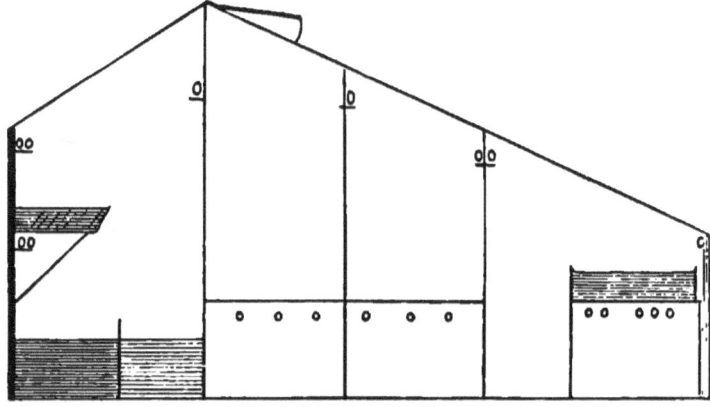

51. *Forcing-house for tomatoes, heated with water.*

very light. In darker houses the plants cannot be set so
close. Fig. 50 (page 156) shows a bed 3 feet wide (and
only 4 inches deep) in which but a single row of plants is
grown. We have grown an excellent crop of tomatoes
on a bean bench, from which three crops of beans had
been taken during the winter. After each crop of beans,
the soil was loosened up and manure or manure water
added if needed. The soil was again manured before
the tomatoes were set. The bed is 6 inches deep. Upon
this bed the plants were set 2 feet apart each way, and
each plant was trained to two shoots. We sometimes
carry a late crop of tomatoes upon benches which grow
peas and lettuce during the winter. Such houses are not

warm and light enough for winter tomatoes, but a crop may be had by late May or June.

In comparing benches and boxes, Munson* obtained the better results from the latter. The experiments were made in a broken-span house (Fig. 51, page 158) "20 x 50 feet, and about 11 feet high at the ridge. The central bed is supplied with six 2-inch hot water pipes, the flow being carried overhead to the further end of the house. Each year a dozen or more plants of each of several varieties have been grown in boxes, while duplicate lots have been grown in open beds. These beds were 2½ to 3 feet wide and 8 inches deep. They were built across the central bench, and thus received the same bottom heat as the boxes." "In almost every instance the better results were obtained from the boxes. With one or two exceptions, the first fruits were matured from one to thirteen days earlier; the weight of the crop was greater, and the individual fruits averaged larger. The average results for the whole time may be summarized as follows:"

Varieties and treatment.	Number of fruits per plant.	Weight of fruit per plant—lbs.	Average weight of individual fruits—ozs.
Golden Queen—			
Box	9.8	1.84	3.0
Bed	9.0	1.31	2.2
Ithaca—			
Box	11.3	1.73	2.5
Bed	10.3	1.51	2.1
Long Keeper—			
Box	10.9	2.01	3.0
Bed	8.9	1.19	2.3
Lorillard—			
Box	11.5	1.54	2.3
Bed	8.7	1.08	2.0

* Rept. of Maine Exp. Sta. for 1894.

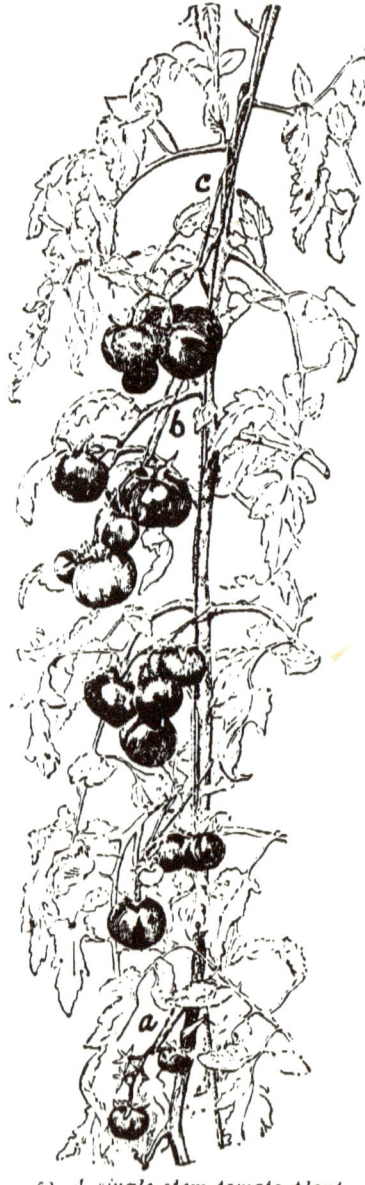

52. *A single-stem tomato plant.*

Training. — The plants must be trained. For midwinter, when it is necessary to economize sunlight, I much prefer to train plants to a single stem. Strong flax cord, the size of wool twine, is used for support. A single strand runs perpendicularly from each plant to a horizontal wire or rafter extending lengthwise the house under the roof. The plant is secured loosely to this support at intervals of a foot or so by means of some broad and soft cord, as bass or raffia. Fig. 49 (page 155) shows the young plants being trained, and Fig. 52 shows a mature vine supported by the cord. All side shoots are pinched off as soon as they appear, and the leader is "stopped" or pinched off as soon as it reaches the glass, or sometimes when fruits begin to form. In houses of sufficient height, I like to train the plants fully 6 feet high. In midwinter it may be necessary to cut away some of the older leaves or to cut them in two near the middle in order to let in light. As the fruit sets the leaves near the base of the plant begin to die, and they should be picked off. Healthy plants in full bearing are often bare of leaves for the first 2 feet. The fruit is borne on one side of the stem, and it is a common notion that the plants must be so placed that this side of the stem shall be toward the sun. This precaution is entirely unnecessary.

When the plants are set in benches, at distances of 2 or 3 feet, two or three shoots may be trained out upon diverging strings, in fan-shaped fashion. If the fan stands north and south it will probably interfere least with the light. Tomatoes are sometimes trained along under the roof as rafter plants, but this system is not adapted to commercial purposes, as it darkens the house so much that few plants can be grown, and the rafter plants are likely to suffer from cold.

As soon as the fruit becomes heavy the largest clusters will need to be held up. A sling of raffia is caught over a joint of the plant and is passed under the middle of the cluster, as seen in Fig. 52 (at a, b, c, page 160), which shows the bearing portion of a good average plant.

Upon very strong vines the clusters sometimes "break," or push out a shoot from the end. This shoot should be cut off. Tomatoes upon clusters where this abnormal shoot was allowed to grow were generally smaller and more irregular than upon clipped shoots.

Watering.—During all the early growth of the plant the atmosphere may be kept moist, particularly in sunny days, when it is customary to wet down the walks. Care must be taken in watering. It is best to soak the soil pretty thoroughly at each watering, yet it should not be drenched. Careless watering usually leaves the surface wet, while the under soil remains dry. This must be avoided. In midwinter we water our plants thoroughly about twice a week, giving no water directly to them between times. If the red spider should attack the plants, the atmosphere must be kept moist, and in bad attacks the foliage should be syringed. Every care should be taken to keep the plants free from the spider, for the pest cannot well be overcome after the fruit begins to set, at which time the house should be kept dry. If fungi begin to attack the plants, however, the atmosphere will need to be kept drier.

Pollination. — When the flowers begin to appear, the atmosphere must be kept dry during the brighter part of the day in order to facilitate pollination. The pollen is discharged most profusely in dry, sunny days. In the short, dull days of midwinter, some artificial aid must be given the flowers to enable them to set. The common practice is to tap the plants sharply several times during the middle of the day with a padded stick. This practice is perhaps better than nothing, although tests which we once made upon the value of this operation as compared with no attention were entirely indifferent in results. During the past winter (1895-6) we tested the value of this jarring with the transfer of pollen by hand, and obtained more fruits from the jarring method, but their total weight was much less. I am strongly of the opinion that it will pay the commercial grower to transfer the pollen by hand during midwinter. At this season the flowers are most likely to fail and the product is the most valuable; and the tests which I am about to report concerning the influences of different quantities of pollen strengthen this advice. There are various methods of pollinating the flowers. The most expeditious and satisfactory method which I know is to knock the pollen from the flowers, catching it in a spoon, watch-glass, or

53. *Ladle for pollinating house tomatoes.*

other receptacle, and then dipping the stigmas of the same or other flowers into it. A good implement is shown in Fig. 53 (page 162). This is made by glueing a small watch-glass to the end of a wooden ladle. There is a time in the life of the flower when the pollen falls out readily if the atmosphere is dry enough to hold dust. This is when the flower is fully expanded and somewhat past its prime. The flower is tapped lightly with a lead pencil and the light yellow powder falls out freely. The house must be dry and warm at the time. C. J. Pennock, Kennett Square, Penn., a grower of winter tomatoes for market, writes me as follows concerning the pollination of the flowers: "During the short days of winter I pollinate carefully every day, and I consider the operation necessary. I use a tool of my own make. It is a light piece of wood about 16 in. long and one-half in. square, one end of which has a slight saucer-like depression. This stick is held in the left hand with the depression under the blossom to be pollinated. Another light stick or reed is used to tap the blossom and shake out the pollen, the end of the pistil being pressed into the accumulated pollen in the depression at the same time. On a sunny day, when the house is dry, the operation can be performed rapidly. I have tried jarring the plants and have seen a brush used, but do not consider either as good as the above method." In the brighter days of March and later I have found no other attention necessary than keeping the house dry at midday.

But there appears to be further reason why hand pollination is profitable. In my earliest experiences in tomato forcing I was impressed with the fact that indoor tomatoes are smaller than those grown out of doors, and the midwinter fruits are usually smaller than those produced under the same circumstances in late spring. There is also a marked tendency in house tomatoes to be one-sided, as indicated in Fig. 54. It was a long time before any

54. One-sided tomato.

reason for these facts suggested itself. I finally came to feel that this irregularity and perhaps the smallness were often due to irregular or insufficient pollination, although it is probably true that lack of sunlight has something to do with the inferior size. The first definite aid towards the solution of the problem was the result of an experiment performed by my former assistant, W. M. Munson.* Mr. Munson pollinated two fruits upon the same cluster with pollen from one source, but in one flower very little pollen was used, and it was applied upon one side of the

55. *The effects of much and little pollen.*

stigma only, while the other flower received an abundance of pollen over the whole surface of the stigma. The result is shown in Figs. 55 to 57 (pages 164 and 165). In Fig. 55, the large fruit received the more pollen, and it is fully four times as large as the other, which received a very small amount. Moreover, the large fruit was practically symmetrical, while the small one was one-sided. Figs. 56 and 57 (page 165) show cross sections of these

---

* A report of fuller studies in this direction by Professor Munson may be found in the Annual Report of the Maine Experiment Station for 1892, Part ii.

fruits. The larger fruit (Fig. 56) has all the cells developed and seed-bearing, while the smaller one (Fig. 57) has seeds upon one side only, and the other or unfertilized side is seedless and nearly solid. The original central division of this fruit is shown at A B. This experiment has been repeated several times with substantially the same results. The flowers, of course, were emasculated in the bud, and were securely covered with bags to prevent any interference.

56. *Effects of liberal supply of pollen.*

Four important lessons are to be drawn from these experiments: 1. One-sidedness appears to be due to a greater development of seeds upon the large side.* 2. This development of seeds is apparently due to the application of the greater part of the pollen to that side.

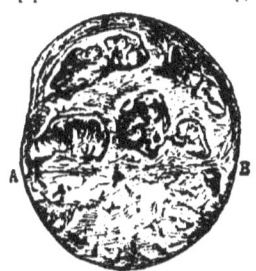

57. *Effects of scanty supply of pollen.*

3. An abundance of pollen applied over the entire stigmatic surface, by increasing the number of seeds increases the size of the fruit. 4. The pollen, either directly or indirectly, probably stimulates the growth of the fruit beyond the mere influence of the number of seeds; the growth of the solid part in Fig. 57 appears to indicate this. This secondary influence of the pollen in increasing the size of fruits, both by means of increasing the number of seeds — which necessarily demand a larger envelope or receptacle — and

---

*For similar results in the pollination of apples, see Bull. 31, Mich. Agr. Coll. 91 (1887).

by some stimulating influence which it may have upon the pericarp itself, is well known as a scientific fact. If I have interpreted these experiments correctly, they mean that a part, at least, of the smallness and perhaps all of the one-sidedness of house tomatoes are due to insufficient pollination, and that it will pay the grower in midwinter to pollinate by hand and to exercise pains to apply an abundance of pollen over the whole surface of the stigma. This conclusion is further emphasized by the experiment which I have already reported (page 162), in which the fruits upon jarred plants (and which undoubtedly received comparatively little pollen) were smaller than those which were hand-pollinated. It is possible that the same principle can be applied to some other fruits, and our experiments with other plants in this direction have already been considerable.

The development of the hard and seedless part of the small tomato (Fig. 57) is perhaps the most interesting feature of the experiment from a scientific point of view. This part must have developed because of some entirely secondary stimulus of the pollen upon the pericarp, or else because of the stimulus afforded by the growth of the seeds in the other half; if neither of these propositions is true, it must follow that seedless tomato fruits may develop without any aid of pollination whatever. In any case, the query is raised if it will ever be possible to grow perfectly seedless tomatoes. We have already grown them, but can make no definite report upon the subject.

Second crop.—The crop from the one or two or three trained shoots of house tomatoes does not exhaust the vitality of the plant; consequently when the crop is well along, one or two new shoots may be trained out from near the base of the plant to produce a second crop. If the plant is carrying a load of fruit when these second shoots are being trained, liquid manure should be given once or twice a week, or a fresh mulch of old manure may be added. In the dark days of midwinter there may not be enough light to make these new shoots strong in such close planting as we practice, and it is better, therefore, to delay starting them until the fruit from the first crop is nearly all full grown. But in late February and March the new shoots may be allowed to become 3 or 4 feet long before the old shoots are cut down. Of course, much will depend upon the distance at which the plants are set, the lightness of the house, and the fertility of the soil. Shoots which were about a foot long when the old tops were cut down the first of March gave ripe fruits the first and second weeks in May. We have noticed that strong and stocky shoots from 6 inches to a foot long give fruits about as early as weak and slender shoots 3 and 4 feet long, and they make better plants. With judicious treatment, the second crop can be made to follow the first with an interval of four to six weeks only, although this is difficult with the close planting which we have employed. One shoot may be trained out from each plant to take the place of the old top, or two shoots may be allowed to grow and some of the old plants cut out entirely. The advantages of either practice are about equal in the box system of growing. Mr. Pennock trains his plants to a single stem for winter bearing. For later fruiting, he trains out two or three shoots from each plant. But Mr. Pennock grows his plants in beds or benches and sets them $2 \times 2\frac{1}{2}$ feet.. In any case, each of the second shoots should bear as much as the first one did, and usually more, because of the greater amount of sunlight later in the season. The old top is cut off an inch or so above the junction of the new shoot.

Another method of obtaining the second crop is to bury the old plants. As soon as the fruit is off, the soil is removed between the plants, and the stems, deprived of lower leaves, are coiled down into the hole until only a foot or so of the tip projects. The earth is then filled in over the plants, and the tip grows the same as a young plant. We have not found this method quite so satisfactory as the training out of new shoots. The yield has not been quite so heavy as from single second shoots, although fruits were obtained fully as early as from shoots which were a foot long when the test was started. But it is a somewhat laborious operation, and some of the stiffer plants are apt to be cracked in the handling; and in box culture it is necessary to pull out one or two of the four plants in order to make room for the operation.

A third way of obtaining the second crop is by means of new seedling plants. This is the common method. Plants are started from seeds two or three months beforehand, and are transplanted two or three times into pots. At the final shifting they are taken from 4- or 5-inch pots and placed in permanent quarters. At this time they should be from 18 inches to 2 feet high, or ready for the first tying up. We find that seedlings will bear about the same time and to the same extent as sprouts which are of equal length to begin with. The preference would seem to be, therefore, for sprouts, as they avoid the previous labor of sowing and handling; and the seedlings take up valuable room while growing. But accidents are likely to occur to the old plants; and an advantage which seedling plants have over sprouts lies in the complete change of soil which is possible when seedlings are grown.

An experiment made (in boxes) at Cornell (in midwinter) upon the comparative merits of seedling, buried and sprout-made plants (one sprout being allowed to grow from the stump of the old plant) gave the following data:

```
Average yield from seedlings . . . . . . .  9    fruits per plant.
   "      "    "   buried plants . . . . .  7      "    "    "
   "      "    "   sprouts . . . . . . . .  9.2    "    "    "
Highest production in seedlings . . . . . . 13.5   "    "    "
   "        "      " buried plants . . . . 11.5   "    "    "
   "        "      " sprouts . . . . . . . 13.5   "    "    "
```

This test showed that the seedlings and sprout-made

plants were of equal value, but the buried plants were distinctly inferior. It should be said, however, that such tests are of comparatively little value, because the merits of the buried and sprout-made plants depend very much upon the vigor and healthfulness of the parent plants. As a result of several years' experience, we now habitually grow our tomato plants from seeds.

Yields and prices. — It will be seen from the foregoing discussion that any statement of the yield per plant of house tomatoes must be utterly valueless unless the method of training is given. The yield from two-stemmed plants may be twice as great as that from single-stem training, and the yield from double cropping of one plant will be from two to four times as much as from a single crop; and much will depend upon the time of year. Some of the reports which have been made of enormous yields must be untrue. The true way to estimate yield is by the amount of floor space covered.

In our experience we obtain from 1½ lbs. to 2 lbs. per stem (or plant) in midwinter, and about twice to three times as much in spring, or an average of 3 lbs. or more for the season. This amount is produced on 1½ to 2 sq. ft. of soil. Mr. Pennock obtains from 8 lbs. to 10 lbs. to the plant for the season, but his plants cover 5 sq. ft. The practical results of the two systems are therefore about the same — about 2 pounds to the square foot;[*] but the uniform single-stem system has some advantages in ease of manipulation, and the plants are so numerous that the loss of one by any accident is not so serious as in the other case. It should be said that the reported yields of house tomatoes are usually made from the spring crop, not from the winter crop. A winter crop, to be profitable, should average at least 2 lbs. to the plant, in close planting and single-stem training, and a spring crop

---

[*] This is over three times the yield per square foot in field culture in this latitude.

should average 4 lbs. to the plant. In a good crop of tomatoes, the fruits should average about three to a cluster in winter, and about four or five in spring. Fig. 58 (page 171) shows a good cluster of forced tomatoes.

We have made experiments to determine if the second crop from the plant is influenced by the amount of the first crop. The tests were made with both buried and sprout plants. For one series we used the plants which bore the heaviest midwinter crop, and for the other those which stood in partial shade and had borne nothing. The results show that the first crop did not influence the bearing capacity of the second stage so long as the parent plants remained healthy. And they also show that amount of crop is not a fixed trait of the individual plant; *i. e.*, a plant which bears little at first may bear heavily the second time, and *vice versa*.

The actual figures of yields and prices of commercial growers of forced tomatoes will be helpful. In a certain crop of Lorillard tomatoes, 673 plants, the total pickings were as follows:

For March	15 lbs.
" April	783 "
" May	802 "
" June	905 "
" July	338 "
	2,993 "

This is is an average of 4.3 lbs. per plant. This is a large average yield. In midwinter, the crop could not be expected to be much more than half this amount. These plants were trained to a single stem.

Following are extracts from the letters of four growers:

"We set our plants about 2 x 2½ ft. One house, 112 ft. long by 23 ft. wide, had 8 rows of plants and about 54 per row, and yielded over 4,000 lbs. of fruit from December 20 to July 1. My recollection is that you grew much closer together and had about the same yield per

sq. ft., and thought it a safer plan, as a dead plant meant less loss. My judgment would be that your plan would require much more labor in setting and caring for the plants, and in practice we rarely lost a plant. When I commenced forcing tomatoes I found that the price was extremely low until the last of December, but now the price is good in November. Prices have varied in the past two years from 7 cts. to 50 cts. per lb. An average price during December, January, February and March has been about 30 cts. to 35 cts., I think."

"We plant our benches with tomatoes from 3-in. pots along in January and February as carnation stock is ready, growing them along at carnation temperature until we have taken off the last crop of carnation cuttings; then we give a little more heat, and have a crop of tomatoes about the last of May, through June, and have them all off early in July. We have generally had an average of 6 to 6½ lbs. per plant. There is much variation in average price, according to time we get the main crop on, from, I suppose, 10 cts. to 15 cts. per lb."

"Our experience with tomatoes extends only with one house and for one season. They were in for six months and one week. We sold 2,669 lbs.; gross receipts, $598.72, or an average of 22½ cts. per lb.; variety, Lorillard; house, 100 x 20 ft."

"We grow tomatoes only as a second crop in spring, bringing them in about the first of May and continuing through June. From two houses (20 x 115 ft. and 20 x 100 ft.) we picked 3,500 lbs. of fruit, which brought an average price of 12 cents per pound."

Varieties. — We have forced Dwarf Champion, Lorillard, Ignotum, Ithaca, Golden Queen, Golden Sunrise, Volunteer, Beauty, Potato Leaf, and others. Of these, the Dwarf Champion is least satisfactory. It does not grow high or free enough to allow of convenient training, and the fruit is small and ripens slowly. Among the others there is little choice. Perhaps the Ithaca is the least desirable of the remaining ones, because of its irregularity. But I cannot look upon the irregularity of house tomatoes as wholly a varietal character. All tomatoes, apparently, tend to be more irregular indoors than out, a tendency for which I can not yet give any sufficient reason. The form seems to vary somewhat in the same variety at different times, and it is probably closely associated with the moisture of the soil and the incidental treatment of the plants. The Ignotum seemed to be somewhat more irregular in the house the first winter than the second. Lorillard and Ignotum seem to hold the first place among the varieties which we have tried, although Volunteer is scarcely inferior. The Golden Queen is perhaps the best yellow. Yellow tomatoes are in little demand, but a few plants may prove profitable from which to sell fruits to those who desire to make table decorations. If we could have but one variety, we would choose the Lorillard.

Munson makes the following comments upon varieties:* "Some varieties seem specially adapted for culture under glass, while others fail to give satisfactory results. Why this is so we do not know; but for the purpose of determining the most promising, we have grown several of the best known varieties for several seasons. Naturally, as the days grow longer in April and May the fruit will be of larger size and the product per plant will be greater than is the case with the first crop — in January and February. The figures given below represent the average results obtained, including both crops, for several seasons. Several other varieties — including Ignotum, Perfection, Peach, Prelude, Dwarf Champion, etc. — have been grown, but those named in the table have proved most satisfactory:

---

*Rept. Maine Exp. Sta. for 1894.

Variety.	Average number fruits per plant.	Average weight of product— lbs.	Average weight of individual fruits— ozs.
Chemin Market	12	2.29	3.0
Golden Queen	12	2.22	3.8
Ithaca	11	1.69	2.5
Long Keeper	10	1.86	3.0
Lorillard	13	2.05	2.7
Optimus	13	1.96	2.5

"The ideal tomato for forcing should be of medium size — about 2½ ounces preferred — and should be uniform, smooth, regular, and of firm texture. All things considered, Lorillard answers these requirements more completely than any other sort we have grown; though Optimus has usually done well. Chemin Market is very attractive in appearance, and is of good size, but it lacks solidity.

"No collection is complete without a few plants of Golden Queen. This is especially valuable for the pleasing contrast when served with the red or purple fruits.

"There is a marked difference in the adaptability of varieties for house culture, among the best of those tried being Lorillard, Optimus, Chemin, Golden Queen, Ithaca and Long Keeper.

"All things considered, the Lorillard has proved the most satisfactory tomato for forcing."

Marketing. — The tomatoes are usually marketed in small splint baskets holding from 4 to 10 pounds of fruit. Each fruit is wrapped in tissue paper, and if to be shipped by rail, the baskets should be lined with rolled cotton. In midwinter an average price of 40 cents a pound should be remunerative; in spring and fall 25 cents a pound should pay. In midwinter our fruits average from 2 ozs. to 2½ ozs. each, but in late March and

April the average will rise to 3 ounces and more. In May, well pollinated fruits often weigh 7 or 8 ounces. The weight of the best fruits is often increased by cutting off the smallest and most irregular ones. The largest forced tomato which I have ever seen was grown by John Kerman, Grimsby, Ontario. It weighed 24½ ounces. It was an Ignotum, and was picked in June. Mr. Kerman reports* another fruit of the same crop which weighed 27½ ounces.

A grower of house tomatoes gives me a description of his method of marketing: "In shipping I use small packages. The flat-bottomed splint basket, holding about 8 qts., with handle, is excellent, and can be bought for $6 or less per gross. They hold 10 lbs. each. In packing, line the basket with at least two thicknesses of medium-weight wrapping paper, turning down the corners even with the top of the basket, or have it cut to exactly fit. Newspapers can be used, but are not so neat. Two inches of excelsior shavings is placed in the basket after being lined with the paper. The tomatoes are wrapped singly in tissue paper, cut by manufacturers in convenient sizes, two sizes being sufficient. Two layers of tomatoes are packed in each basket, with a layer of excelsior between each layer and on top of the upper layer. I have found these baskets to hold just 10 lbs. of tomatoes without undue crowding or rubbing the side of the basket. The grower's name and net weight of tomatoes should be placed, by means of a neat label, inside of the basket, and the basket wrapped in paper, all tied securely and neatly, with label on outside for shipping direction, to include consignor's name, and grade and weight of package. The tomatoes should be sorted into at least three grades — firsts or choice, seconds, and culls."

Animal parasites. — A white scale (*Aleyrodes vapor-*

---

*Canadian Horticulturist, xix. 260 (August, 1896.)

ariorum) is a common pest here on tomatoes. The imperfect insect is a small white scale-like body, preying upon the under surface of the leaves, and the mature form is a minute fly-like insect which flies about the house. It can be kept in check by fumigating with tobacco smoke.

A much more serious pest is a small spotted mite, scarcely larger than the red spider (*Tetranychus bimaculatus*, of Harvey). The mites feed upon the under sides of the leaves, causing the upper surfaces to appear speckled with white, as shown in Fig. 59. They attack many plants, but tomatoes and cucumbers are favorites. We have tried numbers of remedies with great thoroughness, but the first way we discovered of keeping them in check was to syringe with water so forcibly

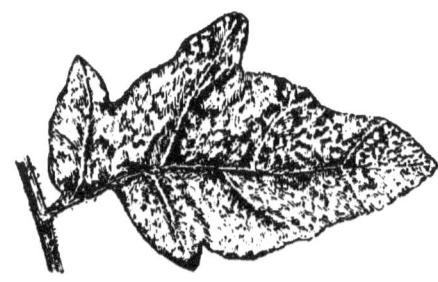

59. *Work of the mite.*

once or twice a day as to knock them off. By the time they were fairly resettled on the plants we would knock them off again. By this alternating warfare, aided by picking and burning the worst leaves, we kept our plants in tolerable order. Later, however, we have found that Hughes' fir-tree oil is fatal to them, as also to all kinds of lice and scales. For the mites, we use a half pint of oil to two gallons of water, and the material may be applied with a syringe or knapsack pump. In more recent experience, we have not had so good success with this oil. We now keep them in check by exercising every care to have the house free of the pests before setting in the plants, and by spraying the leaves (particularly beneath) with a fine nozzle every bright morning. If the mites once get a thorough foothold upon a plant it is almost impossible to thoroughly eradicate them.

The root-gall, caused by a nematode worm (*Heterodera radicicola*), often does great damage in tomato houses (Fig. 29, page 87). The treatment is to use only soil which has been thoroughly frozen, as explained on page 85. After cleaning the benches of infected soil, it is well to wash them in strong lye.*

Diseases. — We have had serious difficulty with diseases. The rot of the fruit has been one of the worst, and this has appeared chiefly upon the first fruits. This disease appears to originate as a physiological trouble (not from the attacks of fungi, as commonly supposed), and the proper treatment is to keep the house dry and sweet.

The tomato blight or rust (*Cladosporium fulvum*) is frequent in tomato houses, particularly towards spring. Fig. 60 shows the patches of

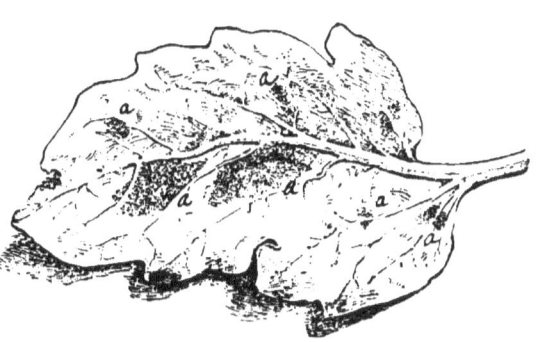

60. *Tomato blight* (*Cladosporium fulvum*).

the fungus at the points marked *a*. It causes rusty patches upon the leaf, and the foliage soon shrivels and dies. It is very likely that the disease may be brought into the house in soil upon which diseased plants have been grown. If it appears, the plants should be thoroughly sprayed at once with Bordeaux mixture.

The dropsy or œdema of the tomato is a physiological disease produced in house tomatoes by a too succu-

---

*For a fuller account of the root-gall on house tomatoes, see Bulletin 43, Cornell Exp. Sta. (Sept. 1892).

lent growth consequent upon a dark house, over-watering, and unskillful attention to ventilation. Outgrowths or swellings closely resembling fungous infections appear upon the leaves and stems, and the leaves finally curl up (Fig. 61). This trouble has been made the subject of a special study by Atkinson,* whose "summary for practical purposes" is as follows:

"The œdema of the tomato is a swelling of certain

61. Œdema of the tomato.

parts of the plant brought about by an excess of water which stretches the cell walls, making them very thin and the cells very large. The excess of water may be so great that the cell walls break down, and that part of the plant dying, exerts an injurious influence in adjacent parts.

"The excess of water in the tissues is favored by the following conditions:

"1. Insufficient light. The long nights of the early winter months, numerous cloudy days, and in part, the walls and framing of the forcing-house, deprive the plants

---

*Bulletin 53, Cornell Exp. Sta. (May, 1893).

of needed light. By a process known as transpiration, plants are relieved of much water when well lighted, but in poor light, since the roots are absorbing water, it is apt to accumulate to excess. Well lighted parts of the house, then, should be selected for the tomatoes.

"2. Too much water in the soil. Water in excess can be withheld from the soil and prevent the trouble, and yet provide enough for the plants to grow.

"3. The temperature of the soil may be too near that of the air. A high temperature of the soil makes the roots active, and if the temperature of the air is not considerably higher an excess of water is apt to accumulate in the plant. The aim would be, then, to have the temperature of the air considerably higher than that of the roots.

"Lack of proper light also brings about the following harmful conditions:

"1. Acids in the plant accumulate in the dark, and in strong light they decrease. When there is an abundance of water in the plant these acids draw large quantities into the cells, causing the cells to swell, resulting many times in œdema, or in the killing of the protoplasm, so that these parts of the plant die and become brown or black.

"2. Lack of light causes weak cell walls. It is only when well lighted that plants are capable of making substances to build up cell walls with. Therefore, lack of light not only favors the accumulation of water, if other things are favorable, but it prevents the plants from building up strong tissues. In such cases plants can *grow themselves to death*. Possibly artificial light might be used to advantage.

"A quiet and close atmosphere also favors the accumulation of water in the plant. Good ventilation should then be secured. Some means for the artificial agitation or exchange of the air at night might probably be profitably devised.

"Varieties of tomatoes more subject to the œdema: those with a tendency to a very rapid and succulent growth are more liable to the trouble; tomatoes which develop a firm, woody young stem are less liable to it."

The most serious disease of forced tomatoes which I have yet encountered is what, for lack of a better name, I called the winter blight,* and which is the concern of the remainder of this chapter. This disease was first described in Garden and Forest in 1892.† The disease first appeared in our house in the winter of 1890-91, when about a dozen plants were somewhat affected. At this time the trouble was not regarded as specific; the plants were old, and had borne one crop, and it was thought

62. *Winter blight of tomato.*

that they were simply worn out. In some of our experiments it became necessary to carry about a dozen plants over the summer, and these were introduced into the house when the forcing season opened the next October. From this stock the trouble again spread, and in six or eight weeks it had become serious, and there was no longer any doubt that we were contending with a specific disease.

This winter blight attacks the leaves. The first indi-

---

* In Bulletin 43, Cornell Exp. Sta.
† A New Disease of the Tomato, by E. G. Lodeman. Garden and Forest, v. 175 (Apr. 13, 1892).

cation of the trouble is dwarfing and slight fading of the leaves, and the appearance of more or less ill-defined yellowish spots or splashes. These spots soon become dark or almost black, and the leaf curls and becomes stiff, the edges drawing downward and giving the plant a wilted appearance. This condition of the leaf is well shown in Fig. 62 (page 180). The spots grow larger, until they often become an eighth of an inch across, or even more, and they are finally more or less translucent. This injury to the foliage causes the plant to dwindle, and the stems become small and hard. Fruit production is lessened, or if the disease appears before flowers are formed, no fruit

63. *A plant attacked by winter blight (at the back), compared with a healthy one.*

whatever may set. In two or three instances, in which young plants were attacked, the disease killed the plant outright, but a diseased plant ordinarily lives throughout the winter, a constant disappointment to its owner, but always inspiring the vain hope that greater age or better care may overcome the difficulty. Fig. 63 (page 181) is a graphic illustration of the appearance of the disease. The box contains two plants, the lower one of which is healthy.

It is probable that this disease is the work of germs. Examination of the diseased tissue has discovered the presence of micrococcus, but the true relation of the organism to the disease has not been made out.

Various treatments have been tried upon this disease. Our first attempt was thorough spraying with ammoniacal carbonate of copper, and this is the one which first suggests itself to growers. Our efforts, although carefully made at intervals, were wholly unsuccessful. It was then thought that treatment of the soil in which new plants were set might prove effective, and as our crop was grown in boxes, the experiment was easily tried.

Boxes in which diseased plants had grown were emptied and the insides were thoroughly washed with various substances, as follows: Three with dilute solution of ammoniacal carbonate of copper; two with lime whitewash; one with Bordeaux mixture, and two with lye. Fresh soil was placed in these boxes and healthy young plants were set in them. The boxes were then placed in the tomato house, near both healthy and diseased plants. For three or four weeks the plants appeared to be healthy, but after that time the disease attacked them all without respect to treatment. The same result followed thorough watering of the soil with ammoniacal carbonate of copper, nitrate of soda, and lye. Late in the winter the remaining plants were removed from the box, the soil was again treated with ammoniacal carbonate of copper, and fresh seedlings were set in it; but these plants also contracted the disease. Just before this last treatment was given, a 10-inch pot was filled from the soil in the box, and a seedling from the same lot as those placed in the box was planted in it. The pot was set in the tomato house. This plant showed the disease in less than three weeks. The question at once arises if the disease was not communicated through the air from infected plants, rather than through the soil. This I cannot answer, but it is certain that the disease travels from plant to plant which stand in separate boxes, and whose tops do not touch. Through what distance this transfer can take place I do not know. We observed it to have occurred through a distance of 2 or 3 feet, but a plant which stood 15 feet from diseased plants, but separated from them by a glass partition in which two doors stood open, did not take the blight.

All our experiments, therefore, simply lead us to the conclusion that the best treatment for this winter blight is to remove all diseased plants at once, and if it becomes serious to remove all the plants and soil in the house and start anew. They emphasize the importance of starting with new plants and fresh soil every fall. And all our experience has shown that the disease is fatal to success in tomato forcing, for we lost our crop in an endeavor to treat it. Since clearing our houses thoroughly of this infection, we have never had it again.

CHAPTER X.

CUCUMBER.

The cucumber contests with the tomato the merit of being the most popular of the "warm" plants for forcing. In America the extensive forcing of cucumbers for market is of recent origin. In England, on the other hand, the species has long been forced, and as a consequence there has developed in that country a peculiar type of fruit, which is even yet not popularly known in the United States. The Americans desire the short cucumbers with which they are familiar in the open garden. So it happens that there are two branches or types of the species to which we need to address our attention.

THE ENGLISH FORCING TYPE OF CUCUMBER.

The English forcing varieties represent the most improved type of the cucumber, and many of them are so distinct in appearance from our common kinds that visitors to our houses often fail to recognize them as cucumbers. They deserve to become better known in this country. It is undoubtedly true that the market demand is more or less confined to particular cities, but it is increasing for these, as for all the better winter products of forcing-houses. The smaller and cheaper varieties are better adapted to the general market, but the careful grower, who has access to the larger markets, by rail or otherwise, should be able to control a select and very profitable trade in the English sorts, particularly

when grown in connection with tomatoes, beans, and other winter crops. Good fruits sell at from 25 to 75 cents apiece, and on special occasions even higher.

General requirements. — The general requirements of houses, temperature and moisture are essentially the same as for the forcing of tomatoes and beans. The temperature demanded by English cucumbers is 60° or 65° at night and 70° to 75° in the shade during the day. They must have bottom heat, and are, therefore, grown on benches. Cucumbers are vigorous feeders, and water must be abundantly supplied to prevent flagging. In bright weather the air should be kept moist by wetting the walks, both to assist growth and to check the ravages of red spider. The greatest care is necessary, however, to dry the house off thoroughly every day or two (particularly in dull weather) to prevent attacks of mildew. These cucumbers have been developed in the mild and humid atmosphere of England, and they seem to be particularly liable to injury by hot suns. We have the best success in growing them under shaded roofs.

In preparing the beds, which should be 6 to 8 inches deep, we generally place about an inch of clinkers or potsherds on the boards; then follows 3 or 4 inches of partially decayed rich sods, preferably from an old pasture, and the bed is then filled with good, rich garden soil, to which has been added one-fourth part of well-rotted manure. If the soil is somewhat sticky when a damp portion of it is pressed in the hand, enough sand is added to make it loose and porous. During the winter liquid manure is applied as occasion seems to demand. It is imperative that the soil be very rich. Productiveness in the cucumber is almost entirely a question of food. Most gardeners suppose that three or four of these large cucumbers are all that a plant can bear at one time; but the crop will depend very greatly upon the food, and the room which they have on the bench. We have had as many as 14 large cucumbers on a vine at one time. If the fruits are picked as soon as they arrive at edible size, the crop will be the larger.

The plants are started in flats, upon small squares of inverted sods, or in pots. I prefer the pots. We use 3-inch rose-pots, filling them only a third full of earth. When the plant has formed a pair of true leaves and stands well above the brim, the pot is filled with earth. This affords additional root space and renders transplanting unnecessary. When the pots are well filled with roots, the plants are transferred directly to the beds. Now comes one of the most critical times in cucumber forcing. The young plants are very liable to the attacks of aphis and fungi, and any failure in the bottom heat will seriously affect them. There are very few vegetables which require such careful attention until they become established. The aphis — which is mentioned later on — must be kept off, or the plant will be ruined, even in a few days. A stunted cucumber plant will make a short, bunchy growth at the top, and the leaves will be small and yellowish; it may remain almost stationary for some weeks. Even if it finally resumes vigorous growth, it rarely becomes a profitable plant. Some plants become stunted without apparent cause. A prolific source of poor plants is the growing of the seedlings in fall before the fires are started, for if the young plants become cold at night they will almost surely be ruined. To insure a good stand, I advise starting three or four times as many plants as are needed. The most vigorous ones are set out a foot or foot and a half apart upon the benches. As soon as the plants are established, the weaker ones are destroyed, leaving the remaining individuals from $2\frac{1}{2}$ to 3 feet apart. A good plant will grow vigorously from the start, and sometimes the lower leaves will fall off, giving it a scraggly and diseased appearance; but so long as the growing portions are vigorous and the leaves are not attacked by mildew, the plant is in good condition.

Training. — The plants must now be trained. We make a simple trellis of No. 18 annealed wire. When there is sufficient room above the benches the plants are trained upon a perpendicular trellis, but on low benches they are trained along the roof. The wires are stretched lengthwise the house in parallel strands from a foot to a foot and a half apart, and cross-wires are run down from the rafters every 4 or 5 feet to pre-

65. *A large crop of English cucumbers.*

vent the strands from sagging. The vines are tied upon the wires with raffia or other soft cord. Two or three strong main branches are trained out, and only enough side shoots are allowed to grow to cover the trellis, the remaining ones being pinched out as soon as they appear. It is essential that the plants do not become "choked" or overcrowded with young growth, and some of the large leaves may be taken off in the dark days of midwinter if the foliage becomes very dense.

The branches are all headed-in as soon as they reach the top of the trellis or begin to encroach upon the space allowed for neighboring plants. If the plants grow very rapidly and the trellis is large, some preliminary heading back may be useful, but we have not practiced the very close pinching-in system recommended by English growers.

Bearing age. — Growers who find no difficulty in forcing the common cucumbers in winter often fail with the English sorts. I am convinced that this failure comes mostly from two errors: insufficient bottom heat, and impatience for quick results. The grower must understand that earliness is not a characteristic of the English cucumbers. From the sowing of seed to marketable fruits, in midwinter, is an average of 80 to 100 days, in our experience. From a month to six weeks is required for the fruit to attain saleable size after the flower is set. A writer in *Revue Horticole* in 1874, records the growing of Telegraph in 65 days from seed, which was the quickest time on record in his vicinity. This experiment was made from February to April, however, when the days are lengthening. The plants continue in bearing for three or four months under good treatment, and a plant ought to yield at least eight goods fruits. If the plants are pinched-in after the English custom, and allowed to bear but two or three fruits at a time, the fruiting season can be extended, and probably a larger number of fruits can be obtained; but it is probably more profitable, especially in small houses, to secure the returns more quickly, in order to obtain a larger supply at any given time. Care must be taken not to allow the heavy fruits to pull the vines off the support, and those which do not hang free should be held up in slings, for if allowed to lie on the soil, they do not color evenly. Fig. 65 (see opposite page) shows (two fruits at the right) the method of swinging the fruits in slings. This swinging also appears to exert some influence upon the shape of the fruit, as will be discussed farther on. The figure (made from life) shows a successful cucumber house in full bearing.

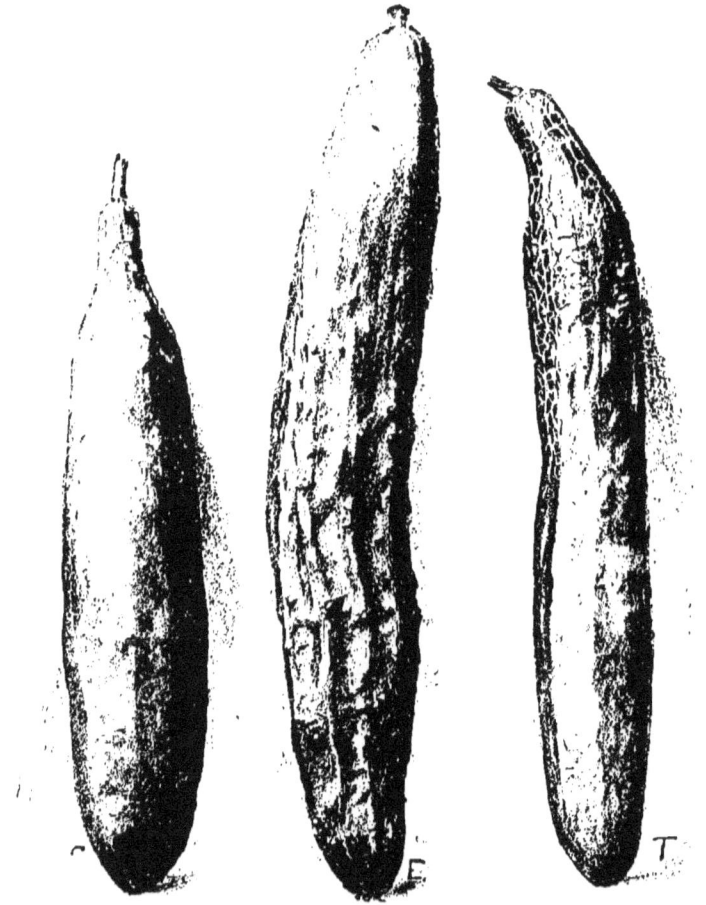

66. *Three prominent varieties: S, Sion House; E, Duke of Edinburgh; T, Telegraph.*

Varieties.—There are many good varieties of English cucumbers. We have grown Sion House (S, Fig. 66) most largely, and for general purposes we prefer it. It is of medium length, averaging a foot or 14 inches when fully mature, smooth and regular. It would probably sell better than the larger sorts in markets which are unaccustomed to the large English varieties. Telegraph (T, Fig. 66) is also a favorite and productive variety, and is probably the most popular one with commercial growers. It is a smooth, slender, and very handsome fruit, ordinarily attaining a length of 18 or 20 inches. English authorities say that this variety is very liable to mixture, but we have never had such experience. Kenyon (*Lord Kenyon's Favorite*) is also an excellent smooth, slender sort of medium length. Edinburgh (*Duke of Edinburgh*) is a spiny and somewhat furrowed variety, attaining a length of 20 to 24 inches (E, Fig. 66). It is not an attractive variety, and we prefer others. Lorne (*Marquis of Lorne*) is one of the best of the very large sorts. We have grown a fruit of this 33½ inches long, and it was a perfect specimen. Blue Gown is also an old favorite.

Very large fruits are less popular than those of medium length. They are too large for convenient table use, and they are apt to be inferior in quality to those a foot in length. The flavor of English cucumbers is somewhat different from that of the common field sorts, the texture being, as a rule, somewhat less breaking. But this is not an evidence of poor quality; it is simply a different quality, and evidently belongs to these fruits as a class. The English sorts retain their green color longer than the field varieties. They are ordinarily picked before they attain their complete growth, although they remain edible for some time after they have reached maturity.

The reader will now be able to understand what the English mean by "prize cucumbers." Specimen fruits are exhibited at the shows, and there are certain customary scales of points for determining the merits of individual fruits, such as the age of the specimen, the ratio of thickness to length, the shape of the shoulder or stem end, the color of the tip, and the like.

Origin of this type of cucumber.—To the student of plant variation, the forcing cucumbers possess unusual interest. As a class, these cucumbers are very distinct from all others, and yet they are known to have come in recent times from the shorter and spiny field sorts, at least those particular varieties which we now grow. It is not improbable that very long cucumbers were known some centuries ago. The *Cucumis longus* of Bauhin, 1651, is figured, as pointed out by Sturtevant*, "as if equaling our longest and best English forms." But these older types do not appear to have been the ancestors of our modern forcing kinds. Our types all appear to have originated within the present century. The English have always been obliged, because of their climatic limitations, to grow cucumbers largely by the aid of artificial heat, and since the improvements inaugurated by M'Phail† over a century ago, and extended by others shortly afterwards, special pits or houses have been designed for them. "Under these conditions," as Vilmorin remarks,‡ "the race could not fail to greatly improve in appearance and size, earliness and hardiness being regarded as qualities of secondary importance. This has actually occurred, and there are now in cultivation in England about ten or a dozen varieties of the long green cucumber, all bearing long and nearly cylindrical fruits, nearly spineless, with solid flesh, and seeding very sparingly." M'Phail and other early writers do not speak of special or named kinds for forcing, showing that there had been little departure at that time from common sorts. The earliest mention which I find of

---

* Amer. Nat. 1887, 909.
† A Treatise on the Culture of the Cucumber, by James M'Phail, Second ed. 1795.
‡ Les Plantes Potagères, Second ed. 187.

a named long forcing cucumber was written in 1822.* It recites that in 1820 Patrick Flanagan, gardener to Sir Thomas Hare, sent two specimens of cucumbers, one green and the other ripe, to the London Horticultural Society. The green one measured 17 inches in length, was nearly 7 inches in circumference, and weighed 26 ounces. The ripe one was 25½ inches long, 11½ inches in circumference, and weighed 6 lbs. The record continues: "Mr. Flanagan states that he has frequently grown these cucumbers in high perfection for the table, near 2 feet long; in 1811 he produced one in a stove which measured 31 inches in length, was 12 inches in circumference, and weighed 11 pounds. This is a remarkable variety of the cucumber, combining with such extraordinary vigor of growth so much excellence of flavor as to make it particularly deserving of notice. Some seeds were communicated to the society, and have been distributed under the name of Flanagan's cucumber. The sort was obtained by Mr. Flanagan in 1804, from a friend in Buckinghamshire. It keeps true to itself, without variation; but it is difficult to make it yield seed. It requires to be grown in high temperature." The surprise which these fruits occasioned among a body of gardeners indicates that they were novelties. I cannot understand the great weight of the large cucumber. Our specimens of larger size weigh only about a third as much. The oldest of the varieties which we now cultivate appears to be the Sion House, a product of the gardens of the Duke of Northumberland, at Brentford, in Middlesex, to which the gardening world is indebted for many achievements. I presume that the first record which was made of this variety is that written by the conductor of the *Gardeners' Magazine* early in 1831, as follows:† "An excellent variety of cucumber is grow-

---

* Trans. London Hort. Soc. iv. 560.
† Gard. Mag. vii. 101.

ing in the forcing houses at Syon.* The fruit is long, perfectly smooth, and the leaves extremely large (18 inches across); they are grown in boxes placed over the back flue of the pine-pits, and the shoots trained under the glass over the pits. Mr. Forrest [gardener] has gathered fruit daily since October last, and will continue to do so, if he chooses, all the year round." In his first edition of *Plantes Potagères*, Vilmorin says that the Sion House was raised from the White cucumber, but he omits the statement in the second edition; and I am unable to find any confirmation of it.

From this comparatively recent beginning the English cucumbers have diverged widely from their parents. In all the following characters they differ, as a rule, from common cucumbers. The fruits (and ovaries) are very long and slender, cylindrical (not ridged or furrowed), spineless or nearly so at maturity, remain bright green until full maturity, and seeds are produced sparingly; the flowers are very large; the vines are very vigorous and long, with long and thick tendrils; and the leaves are very broad in proportion to their length, and the full grown ones appear to have a tendency to make shallower sinuses or angles than do the field kinds. But the most remarkable peculiarity is the habit of producing seedless fruits, which is discussed farther on.

In 1859, Naudin† grouped all cultivated cucumbers under four divisions: Small Russian, Common Long, White, and Sikkim (later described by Sir J. D. Hooker as *Cucumis sativus* var. *Sikkimensis*). Recently Sturtevant,‡ omitting the Sikkim cucumber, has grouped them under six heads: Common cucumbers; "a second form, very near to the above, but longer, less rounding, and more prickly;" "smooth and medium-long cucumbers;" English or forcing kinds; white; Russian. I am not

---

* *Sion* appears to be the later and preferable spelling.
† Ann. Sci. Nat. Bot. 4th Ser. xi. 28.
‡ Amer. Nat. 1887, 908.

sure that this latter classification is a practicable one, but it is certainly well to place the English forcing varieties in a group alone.

Pollination — Ill-shaped fruits. — Cucumbers are monœcious plants : that is, the sexes are borne in separate flowers on the same plant. Fig. 67 represents the two kinds of flowers on the common field cucumber. P is the pistillate or fruit-bearing flower. The young cucumber, or ovary, can be seen below the petals or leaves of the flower. S shows the staminate flower, which persists only long enough to supply pollen to fertilize the pistillate flowers. The staminate flowers are more numerous than the pistillate, and they begin to appear

67. *The pollen-bearing and fruit-bearing flowers.*

earlier; a sufficient supply of pollen is therefore insured against all exigencies of weather or other untoward circumstances. Out of doors the pollen is carried from the staminate to the pistillate flower by insects, but pollen-carrying insects are absent from the greenhouse. If the flowers are fertilized in the house, therefore, the pollen must be carried by hand. It is certain that some plants of English cucumbers will set fruit to perfection without seeds and entirely without the aid of pollen, but other plants (and in our experience they have been greatly in the majority) utterly refuse to do so. I do not know if this is true of the common cucumbers, but we have made several unsuccessful efforts to grow Medium Green (*Nichol's Medium Green*) in the house without pollination. In the early days of cucumber forcing, hand pollination was practiced, but it has been abandoned by many growers.* It is possible that the forcing cucumber sets more freely now without pollen than it did before its characters were well fixed, or perhaps the early gardeners performed an unnecessary labor. We have sometimes thought that the fruits set more freely without pollination as the plants become mature. As a result of several years' experience, however, we find that hand pollination is essential to the certainty of securing a crop.

Many gardeners suppose that pollen causes the fruit to grow large at the end, as in Fig. 68, and they, there-

---

*"Fertilization was formerly considered necessary for the setting of cucumbers, but it has long been proved to be needless. Indeed, fruits intended for eating are better without, as the seeds in them are not so numerous. For seeding purposes fertilization is decidedly required, if good, heavy seed be needed."—*Kitchen and Market Gard.* 150 (London, 1887).

"Except for seeding purposes, it is not necessary that the latter [pistillate flowers] should be fertilized, the fruit reaching the same size, and being all the better for the absence of seeds. In winter time, or in the case of weak plants, the whole of the male flowers might with advantage be kept removed."—*Nicholson's Dict. Gard.* I, 405.

General Russell Hastings, of Bermuda Islands (whose house is shown in Fig. 64, page 185), writes me as follows upon this question of pollinating the forcing cucumbers: "I am growing the English frame cucumber, many fruits growing 2 feet long and weighing as high as 3 pounds. When I first began, some six years ago, having read of the necessity of pollinating by hand, I used to perform this work; but I became neglectful, and it seemed entirely unnecessary to pollinate, as my growth was fully as good as before my careful attention. I went so far in my experiment as to select a pistillate bud which, if left alone, would have opened the following day, and with care cut off the bud and destroyed the pistil. From this I raised a very large cucumber, but, of course, without a seed from one end to the other. When I first began with my glass house, I had no bees, and never saw one in the house, but for the past two years I have had bees not far from the house, and as the sash stands open nearly every day, it is, of course, constantly visited by bees. The result in the number and growth of cucumbers is no better than when I did not pollinate, nor when there were no bees around."

fore, aim to produce seedless cucumbers for the double purpose of saving labor and of procuring straighter and more shapely fruits. For several years we have made experiments upon these questions, but we are not yet able to make many definite statements concerning them; we think, however, that the large thickened ends of fruits like Fig. 68 are caused by the production of seeds in that portion. The early flowers nearly always fail to set if pollen is withheld, but late flowers upon the same plant may set freely with no pollen. Fruits which have set without pollination are uniformly seedless throughout, as shown in Fig. 69 (page 198), the walls of the ovules remaining loose and empty. Pollination does not occur when the fruits are left to themselves in the forcing-house, especially in midwinter, when pollen-carrying insects are not present. Upon old plants we often prevent pollination, for experimental purposes, by tying together the flower tube, or occasionally by cutting off the flower bud altogether from the top of the ovary or young cucumber, but this latter method is uncertain.

In pollinating, we follow the same method advised by Abercrombie and other writers of the last century,— pick off a staminate flower, strip back the corolla, and insert the column of anthers into a pistillate flower.

68. *A misshapen fruit.*

The production of misshapen fruits is one of the difficulties of cucumber forcing. The commonest deformity is the large end shown in Fig. 68. English gardeners often grow the fruits in glass tubes to make them straight. The cause of the deformities, particularly of the swollen end, is obscure. The forcing cucumber pro-

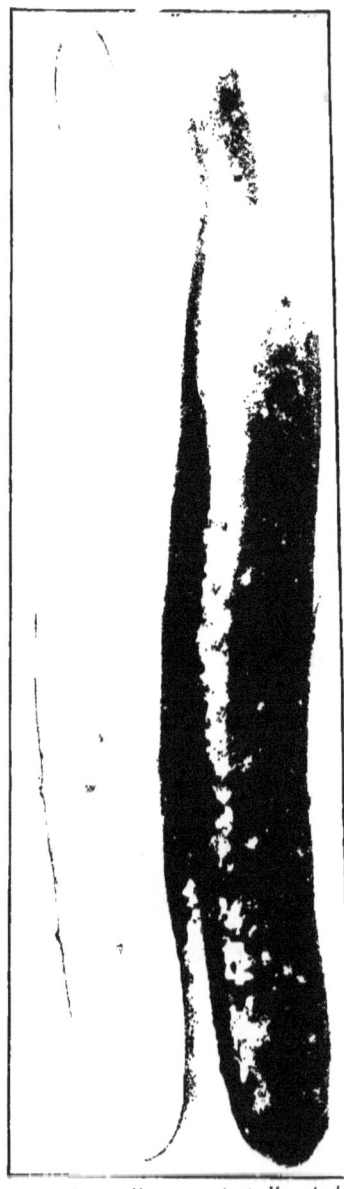

69. *A seedless (not pollinated) fruit. The Berkshire Champion cucumber.*

duces seeds only near the blossom end, the ovules in the remaining half or two-thirds never filling out, no matter how much pollen is applied to the stigma. It would seem, therefore, that if all these ovules in the blossom end were to develop into good seeds, the fruit must be larger at this point. And it would also seem as if accidental application of pollen to one side of the stigma must make the fruit one-sided by developing one cell at the expense of another, for this actually occurs in tomatoes and apples. But we have found that seed-bearing is not necessarily associated with a swollen end to the fruit, and pollination of one side does not appear to destroy the symmetry of the fruit. We have performed many experiments upon the influences of different amounts of pollen, but find that there is very little difference in external results, whether little or much pollen is used. This is directly contrary to our experience with winter tomatoes. Little pollen (30 to 50 pollen grains) may produce fewer seeds than much pollen (200 or more pollen grains), but the shape of the fruit is not necessarily influenced. And yet there are instances in which pollination appears to make the fruit unshapely, but why it should exert this influence at some times and not at others I am unable at present to state. It appears to be often a peculiarity or variation of individual plants. There were two plants in our house one winter which invariably produced deformed fruits when pollen was used, although fruits on other plants alongside were not influenced by pollen. Upon these susceptible individuals we found that the pollinated fruits would grow to uniform thickness if they were swung or tied up, as recommended on page 189. It is probable that much of the irregularity in shape is but an expression of plant variation, rather than a result of particular treatment. It is an interesting fact in the variation of plants under domestication that the long English cucumber cannot produce seed in its lower half, although ovules are usually present. It is probable that the fruit has been developed to such a length that the pollen-tubes cannot reach the remote ovules.

Crosses. — The English forcing cucumbers cannot be successfully grown in the field, but they possess some points of merit for a field cucumber, as smoothness and cylindricity, length, and great vigor of vine. We therefore attempted some crosses in the winter of 1889-90 between the Sion House and Medium Green, hoping to produce a superior sort for outdoor use. Our results have been exceedingly interesting from a scientific point of view, although we have not yet procured the cucumber which we sought. Fruits of unusual promise have been obtained, but they have not produced good seeds. Some of the mongrel fruits developed a peculiar weakness in the tendency of the placentæ or cell walls to decay. The seeds did not mature, and the soft, pulpy tissue about them solidified. Near the apex of the fruit the placentæ tended to break away from the body, and in the cavities decay set in and extended finally to the base of the fruit. All the fruits upon one of the mongrel plants behaved in this manner. In no case had the fruit been injured, nor was the decay visible upon the exterior until it had extended well down the fruit. I am unable to account for it.

In most instances, the mongrel vines resembled the Medium Green (the staminate parent) more than the Sion House. The fruits were generally intermediate, although almost every gradation was observed. Sometimes the fruits would vary widely upon the same plant. A number of vines bore beautiful fruits twice longer than the Medium Green, nearly cylindrical, with very few spines; and we are looking for good results from this or some similar cross.

Enemies. — The most serious enemy with which we have had to contend in cucumber forcing is the spotted mite, which feeds upon the under surface of the leaves, destroying the green tissue. This pest is treated in the preceding chapter (page 176).

A large coal-black aphis or plant-louse (probably *Aphis rumicis*, Linn.), has been a serious pest. It is the worst aphis with which I have ever had experience, and every effort should be made to prevent its becoming established upon the plants. It can be destroyed by persistent fumigation, but it must be remembered that the cucumber cannot endure a very heavy smudge.

The root-gall (already described on pages 84 and 85) is often serious in cucumber houses.

The powdery mildew (*Erysiphe Cichoracearum*, or *Oidium erysiphoides* var. *Cucurbitarum*) is a serious enemy to cucumber culture if it once gains a good foothold. It will soon ruin the plants. The disease is superinduced by too close and moist atmosphere and a too soft condition of the foliage. It usually begins as light green or yellowish ragged spots — a quarter-inch or half-inch across — on the leaves, and generally soon develops into frosty patches. When it appears, dry off the house, raise the temperature, and give plenty of air (without any draughts). It is also a good plan to dust the foliage thoroughly with powdered sulphur. If the disease threatens to become serious, sulphur should be evaporated in the house. Flowers of sulphur is placed in a small basin and set upon a small oil stove (Fig. 31, page 92). The house is tightly closed, and enough sulphur is evaporated to completely fill the house with strong fumes for a half hour. Care must be exercised that the sulphur does not take fire, for burning sulphur is very injurious to plants.

THE WHITE SPINE TYPES OF CUCUMBER.

The forcing of the White Spine types of cucumber is not greatly different from that of the true forcing types. The chief points of dissimilarity to be borne in mind are these: The White Spine types are shorter-lived than the others, and tend to ripen up their crop at once; they are less succulent in growth, and demand full sunlight for their best development; they can be readily grown under glass in summer, after the house is cleared of its winter crops, thereby giving a crop much in advance of the outdoor plants; they seem always to require pollination, either by hand or by bees; they are less rampant growers, and bear smaller leaves than the others, and may, therefore, be planted somewhat closer.

With these contrasts in mind, the reader who has followed the discussion of the English cucumber in the preceding pages will have no difficulty in apprehending the essential points in the management of these American cucumbers. The plants will mature the crop in about three months from the time they are put on the benches. A certain house of 68 plants yielded, in three months, 6,180 fruits, or an average of 90 to the plant. This was possible because every fruit was picked the

202 CUCUMBER.

70. House of White Spine cucumbers.

moment it was fit for sale, and the crop was grown from April to June. A common method of growing them is to let them follow lettuce. Two or three crops of lettuce can be taken from a house by early spring (say by March), and cucumber plants may then be ready to be set in the beds. These four crops should bring in a gross return of 30 to 50 cents a square foot of ground, the income depending mostly upon the man. Even in winter, these plants can be grown in houses which were designed for lettuce, if the temperature is kept pretty high, for these types of cucumbers do not demand bottom heat so imperatively as the English kinds do. A cucumber forcer tells me that he generally receives $3 per dozen for extra quality of White Spine (or Boston Market) cucumbers, and $4 per dozen for the forcing kinds.

CHAPTER XI.

MUSKMELON.

"There is not, I believe, any species of fruit at present cultivated in the gardens of this country," wrote Thomas Andrew Knight, in 1811, "which so rarely acquires the greatest degree of perfection, which it is capable of acquiring in our climate, as the melon." The melon is particularly prized in England, for, because of the coolness of the climate, it is generally grown to perfection only under glass, and is thereby appreciated; and it is in England, too, that one finds the most expert methods of growing it. The melon is treated there, however, as a spring or early summer, or late fall, crop.

The forcing of melons for delivery in midwinter is practically unknown. The fruit is often grown as an early winter crop, ripening in October and early November, and the seeds are often sown in January and the melons matured in May and June. Gardeners now and then ripen a few melons in midwinter, but the fruits are almost invariably very poor, or even disagreeable, in quality. The writer has long been convinced that it is possible to secure good melons in December, January and February, and to grow them nearly as cheaply as the English or frame cucumbers. The attempt was first made in the winter of 1889-90, and it has been repeated more or less persistently until the present time, and the results during the past two years have been satisfactory. The melon is certainly the refinement of the vegetable garden. To get it in midwinter, with the sweetness and fragrance of August, is no mean ambition. Then, if at no other time, one may exclaim with Thoreau—

"And what saith Adshed of the melon——?
"'Color, taste, and smell,—smaragdus, honey, and musk;
Amber for the tongue, for the eye a picture rare;
If you cut the fruit in slices, every slice a crescent fair;
If you have it whole, the full harvest moon is there.'"

In order to satisfy the reader's curiosity at the outset, I will say that the essentials for growing midwinter melons, as I understand them, are these: *High temperature from the start* (80° to 85° at midday, and 65° to 70° at night); *the plants must never be checked, even from the moment the seeds germinate, either by insects, fungi, low temperature, or delay in "handling"; dryness at time of ripening; a soil containing plenty of mineral elements, particularly, of course, potash and phosphoric acid; polliniferous varieties; the selection of varieties adapted to the purpose.* All these requirements seem to be easy enough of attainment as one reads them, but it has taken us six years to learn them. Others would no doubt have been more expeditious; but it should be said that no one of these conditions will insure success, but *all of them must be put together.*

Watermelons are not forced, as they demand a too long season, make too rampant growth, and probably would not develop their best quality in midwinter. I have seen them ripened in a glass house in early summer, following winter crops, with fair success. It is probable that forcing varieties could be developed, but it is doubtful if the fruits would be large enough to meet with ready sale.

The house.—A house which is adapted to the growing of English cucumbers or tomatoes should grow melons. The first requisite is heat. The capacity of the heating system must be sufficient to maintain a high temperature in the coldest weather. The house should

MUSKMELON.

71. *A bench of melons six weeks after transplanting. Eggplants on the right.*

be free of draughts and large leaks. Our melon house opens into sheds at both ends, so that no outside air ever blows into it; yet even here we lock up the house from the time the melons begin to form, to prevent persons from passing through it. We like to keep the room close. It should be capable of being kept dry. There should be ample room over the benches for training the vines 5 to 6 feet. We use benches, for melons must have strong bottom heat. Fig. 71 (page 206) is a view in our melon house, taken on the 3rd of October (at this time many of the melons were as large as one's fist), the plants having been set in the bench on the 20th of August, and the seeds sown the 20th of July. For myself, particularly where such high temperatures are wanted, I prefer steam heat. A melon house should receive direct sunlight through an unshaded roof. In this respect melons differ from the English or frame cucumbers, which generally thrive best under a shaded roof. The burning of the foliage by the sun is avoided by the use of glass which does not possess waves or varying thicknesses in the panes. The bubbles, flaws and "tear drops" in glass are not the cause of burning. Fig. 3 (page 18) shows a cross-section of the house in which we have grown melons, and which is also shown in Fig. 71. We have used benches A, B and C. The lower bench, D, has too little head room, and, being the lowest, it is too cold for melons.

The soil should be very fertile. We have had good success with clay sod, which had not been manured, pulverized and mixed thoroughly with about one-quarter the bulk of well-rotted stable manure (but fresh or rank manure should not be used). Such a mixture contains enough quickly available nitrogen to start the plants off strongly, whilst the mechanical condition of it is so friable that all the mineral elements are easily obtained by the plants. It should be well firmed, after it is placed in the bench, by pressing it down with the hands or by pounding with a brick. An occasional light application of potash and phosphoric acid worked into the soil will be found to be useful. Very much of the ultimate behavior of the plants will depend upon the proper selection and mixing of the soil, and one who has had no experience in forcing-house work will rarely obtain the best results for the first year or two in preparing the earth. The mechanical condition of this soil is really more important than its fertility, for plant food may be added from time to time, but the soil itself cannot be renewed whilst the crop is growing; and, moreover, the plant food is of little avail unless the soil is well drained and aërated, not too loose nor too hard. It is impossible to describe this ideal soil in such manner that the beginner can know it. Like many other subjects of handicraft, it can be known only by experience. It may help the novice, if I say that soil which will grow good melons in the field may not be equally good in the house. Under glass, with the fierce heats in full sunshine and the strong bottom heat, heavy watering, as compared with normal rainfall, is essential, whilst the rapid drainage and the evaporation from both the top and the bottom of the bed, impose conditions which are much unlike those of the field. But the ideal condition of the soil to be maintained in the house may be likened to the warm, mellow, rich and moist seed-bed in which every farmer likes to sow his garden seeds in spring. There is no sub-soil indoors to catch the drainage, and a mellow field soil is often so loose and porous that the water runs through the benches and carries away the plant food. The house soil must, therefore, be retentive, but then there is danger that it will become puddled or sodden, or arrive in that condition which a gardener knows as a "sour" soil. This condition may be avoided by the use of the stable manure to add fiber to the soil, by the very frequent stirring of the immediate surface with a hand weeder, and particularly by great care in watering. As the fruits begin to mature, water the house very sparingly. "The less water given, the higher will be the flavor of the fruit."* Inasmuch as old or fruiting plants require a dry house, and young plants thrive best in a moister atmosphere, it is not advisable to attempt to grow successive plantings of melons simultaneously in the same house.

Recent English instructions, by James Barkham,† give the following advice about melon soil: "The top spit from an old pasture is what I prefer, if such is obtainable, soil such as a good, strong, yellow loam being most suitable. This should be broken up with the spade to about the size of a duck's egg. Do not use any manure, but to every cartload of loam add two barrowloads of old mortar or plaster, broken up and run through an inch mesh sieve, and one barrowload of half-decayed leaf soil, turning the whole two or three times, so as to thoroughly mix it. Mistakes are often made in preparing soil for melons by making it too rich by adding manure, which encourages a too luxuriant growth. When this is so, it is an impossibility to obtain satisfactory results, as the growth becomes so succulent that instead of the fruit setting it turns yellow and decays."

The bench should not be above 7 inches deep, and perhaps 5 inches is better. If the soil is too deep, the plants grow too much, and are late in coming into bearing. If the bench is 4 feet wide, two rows of plants, 2½ feet apart in the rows, may be grown; but if the bench is an outside one, it may be handier in training if there is but a single row, with the plants about 18 inches apart. It should always be borne in mind, however, that at least twice the number of plants should be set in the beds which are ultimately to grow in them,

---

*George Mills, A Treatise on the Cucumber and Melon, 73.

†James Barkham, F. R. H. S., in Journal of the Royal Horticultural Society, xx. p. 1 (1896).

for there will almost certainly be accidents and black aphis, and mildew, and damping-off. When the plants have stood in the benches two or three weeks, the weak ones may be pulled out. It is a good practice, when but a single row is planted, to set the plants nearer one side than the other, and then leave the wider side of the bench empty, and add the soil to it as the plants need it. In this way fresh forage is obtained for the roots in soil which has not been leached of its plant food nor impaired in its mechanical condition; and the plants will make a steady growth from start to finish, rather than an over-vigorous one at first. If there is too much soil, the roots spread through it quickly and the plants run at once to vine.

Sowing and transplanting. — The seeds should be sown in pots. We like to place a single seed in a 2-inch pot, and in about three weeks — if in summer or fall — to transplant the seedling into a 4-inch pot. In two or three weeks more the plant may be set permanently in the bench at the distances indicated in the above paragraph. It is a most excellent plan (as explained for cucumbers) to fill the pots only half full of earth or compost at first, and then fill the pot up as soon as the plant overtops the rim. The record of one of our crops is as follows: Seeds sown August 4; repotted August 30; transplanted to bench

72. *Melon plant (in 4-inch pot) in fit condition for transplanting into bench.*

September 10; first fruit picked December 6; crop all harvested for Christmas.* If a crop is desired on the first of November, the seeds should be sown from the middle to the 25th of July. Fig. 72 (page 210) shows the size of a good melon plant as it leaves a 4-inch pot for the bench. It is very important that the plants should not become pot-bound, nor stunted in any other way. It is only strong, pushing plants which give satisfactory results.

Training.—The plants are "stopped"—the tip of the leader taken off—as soon as they become established in the bench. This pinching-in is practiced for the purpose of setting the plant at once into fruit-bearing, and to make it branch into three or four main shoots. All the weak or "fine" shoots are removed as fast as they appear, so that the plant does not expend its energy in the making of useless growth. The three or four main vines or arms are trained divergently upon a wire trellis, and as soon as a shoot reaches the top of the trellis—4 or 5 feet—it is stopped. Some growers prefer to have a leader 4 or 5 feet long, and only two laterals and of about the same length as the leader. The trellis is made simply of light wire, strung both horizontally and vertically, with the strands about a foot apart in each direction. To these wires the vines and fruits are tied with raffia, or other soft, broad cord. It must be remembered that the fruit is borne along the main branches, and that all small or "blind" growths from the main stem and branches should be nipped out as soon as they start. The fruits should hang free from the vine, never touching the ground. It will generally be necessary to hang them to a wire, as shown in Fig. 73 (page 212), by making a sling of raffia, or resting them

---

* It should be said that the forcing season at Ithaca is unusually cloudy, and that, consequently, these dates of maturity are somewhat later than they may be in sunnier regions.

upon a little swing with a block or wood for the bottom (as in Fig. 77, page 217). They will then not hang too heavily on the vine, nor break off,—as they sometimes do if unsupported.

Barkham, whom I have already quoted, writes as follows of the training of melons: "Train the plants to a neat stake until the trellis is reached; rub off all growths as they show from the stem below the trellis; train the growths right and left, and allow the leading

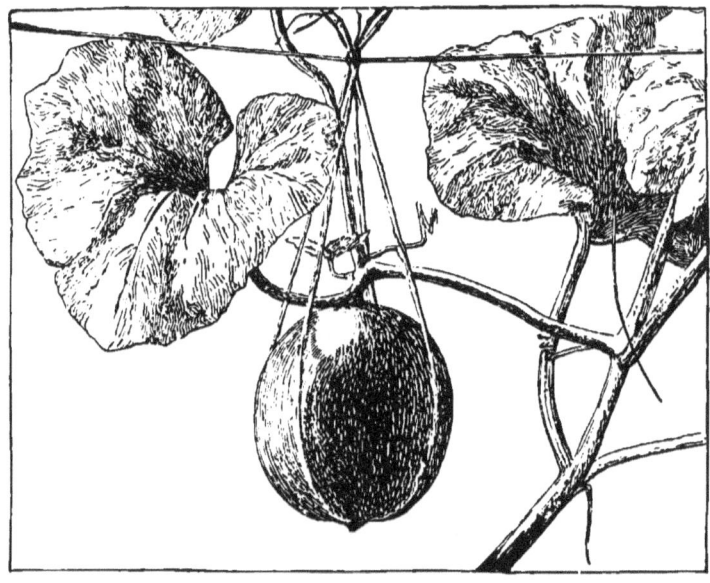

73. *Melon in a sling of raffia.*

stem to grow up, without stopping, to within a foot of the top. If the side shoots are likely to be crowded, pinch out some at first sight, as the melon will not endure thinning so severely as the cucumber; therefore the growths should be stopped and thinned early enough for those remaining to just cover the trellis with well-developed foliage, and no more. The first laterals which are formed at the bottom of the trellis should be stopped at the second or third leaf, and by the time the sub-laterals show fruit other fruits will be showing on the first laterals higher up. The plants, whether growing in houses or pits, should be gone over twice or three times a week for the purpose of stopping and removing any superfluous growth, so as to allow of the principal leaves being fully exposed to the light. Stop at the first joint beyond the fruit, and remove all weak growths and laterals not showing fruit.

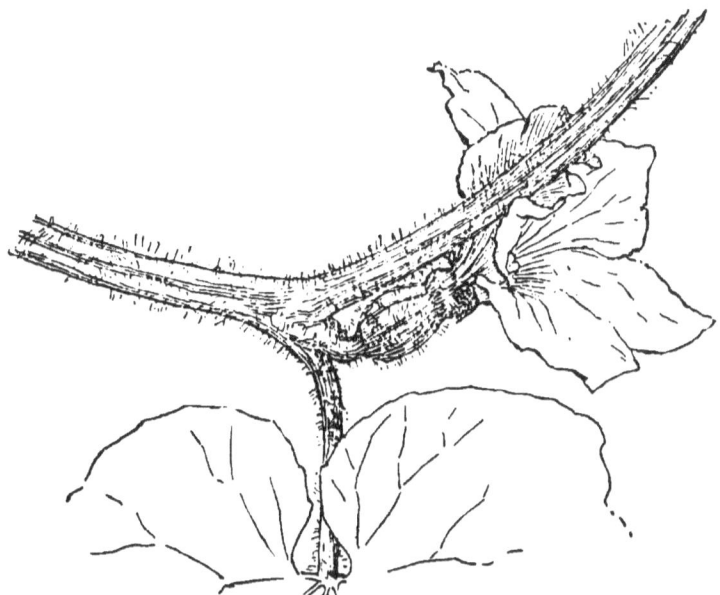

74. *Pistillate flower of melon. Full size.*

"Overcrowding is the greatest evil in melon culture, because the excessive foliage must be thinned, and its removal results in exudation from the wounds, gangrene sets in, and the affected parts perish through 'wet-rot' (bacteria and bacillus growths). To arrest these, antiseptics must be used; the safest is quicklime, rubbing it well into the affected parts, and repeating as necessary. But the worst effect of removing a large quantity of growth is giving a check to the fruit, not unfrequently causing it to cease swelling, and it becomes hard in the flesh; fungoid germs fasten upon the exudation, and the fruit decays when it should ripen. These disasters are generally preventable by attending to the thinning and stopping of the growths in time."

Pollinating. — The flowers must be pollinated by hand. Melons are monœcious, — that is, the sexes are borne in separate flowers on the same plant. The first flowers to open are always males or staminates, and it may be two weeks after these first blossoms appear that the females or pistillates begin to form. There is nearly always a much larger number of males than females, even when the plant is in full bearing. Fig. 74 (page 213) is a female or pistillate flower, natural size. It is at once distinguished by the little melon, or ovary, which is borne below the colored portion of the flower. The male or staminate flower is seen in Fig. 75. It has no enlargement or melon below, and the flower perishes within a day or so after it opens. Pollination is performed in the middle of the day, preferably when the house is dry and the sun bright, so that the pollen is easily detached from the male flower. A male flower is picked off, the petals or leaves stripped back, and the central

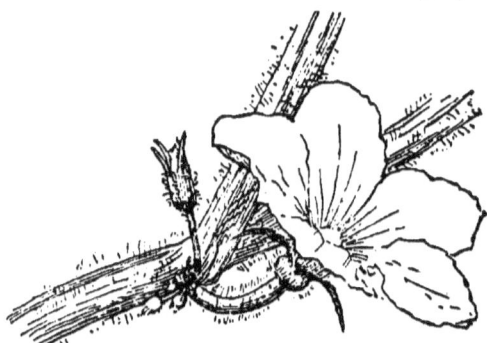

75. *Staminate flower of melon. Full size.*

or pollen-bearing column is then inserted into a pistillate flower, and there allowed to remain. That is, one male flower is used to pollinate one female flower, unless there should happen to be a dearth of male flowers, in which case two or three female flowers may be dusted with one male. If the house is too cool and too moist, the pollen will not form readily, and there are some varieties which are poor in pollen when grown under glass.

Every pistillate or female flower, except the first two or three which appear, should be pollinated, although not more than four or five on each plant should be allowed to perfect fruit. It is very rare that even half of the female flowers show a disposition to set fruit. It is best to ignore the very first flowers which appear, for if one strong fruit is set much in advance of the appearing of other pistillate flowers, it will usurp the energies of the plant, and the later fruits will be likely to fail. Upon this point Barkham remarks: "Never commence fertilizing the blooms until there is a sufficient number ready at one time, or within an interval of three days, to furnish the crop. If one or two fruits are allowed to swell off first, the later-set fruit will not swell, but die away. Indeed, if only one fruit is set in advance of the rest, it will monopolize all the strength of the plant, and prevent any more fruit from setting. When a sufficient number of fruits is set, select the largest and best shaped, taking off all small and misshapen ones. If large fruits are wanted, leave from four to six fruits to each plant, or if smaller fruits are desired, allow eight or ten to remain." Mr. Barkham here speaks of the spring crop (seeds sown in January or later), and his plants are about 3 feet apart each way.

Varieties. — The general varieties of field melons do not succeed well in the house. We have tried various common melons for forcing, but the only one which was adapted to the purpose is Emerald Gem. We have had the best success with the English frame varieties, particularly with Blenheim Orange. All these melons are small (winter specimens weighing from $1\frac{1}{4}$ to 2 lbs.), with thin netted rinds, and a red or white flesh of high quality.

Blenheim Orange (Fig. 76, page 216) is a red-fleshed

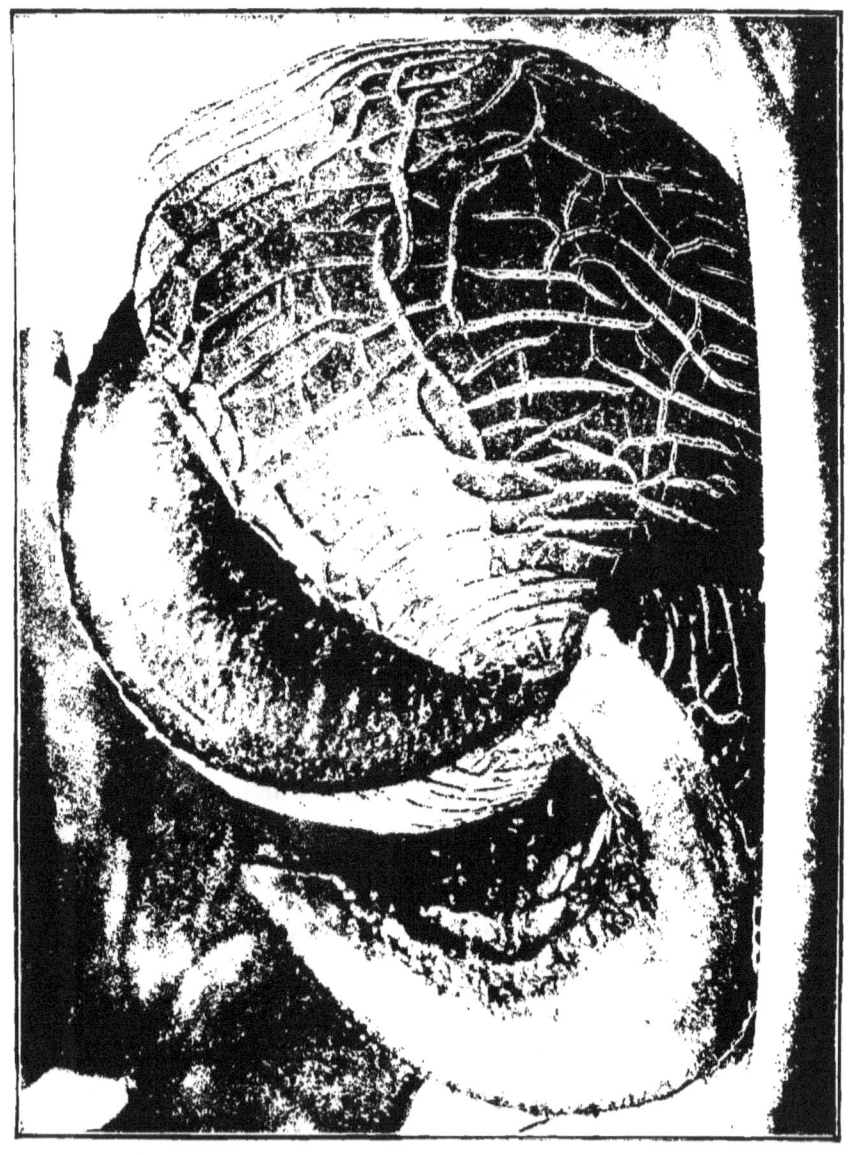

melon of medium to medium-large size, with a very irregularly and variously barred rind, scarcely ribbed, short-oval in shape, highly perfumed, and of the very highest quality. This has been our favorite winter melon. In midwinter we have had it with all the characteristic flavor and aroma of autumn fully developed. It is also an early melon, in season coming in just after Emerald Gem.

77. *Hero of Lockinge melon.*

Hero of Lockinge (Fig. 77). This ripens just after Blenheim Orange. It is a firm melon of medium size, with white flesh, dark in color, with a few very prominent irregular bars, not ribbed, globular, the flesh tender and excellent, but less aromatic than Blenheim. This is one of the best of the frame melons, and is very striking in appearance.

Lord Beaconsfield follows Lockinge, but it has not been valuable with us. It is a dull green, globular-conical, misshapen melon, without ribs or netted markings, and a soft, green flesh, which is rather poor.

Little Heath is a melon of medium size, slightly oblong, dark lemon yellow, with no bars or markings;

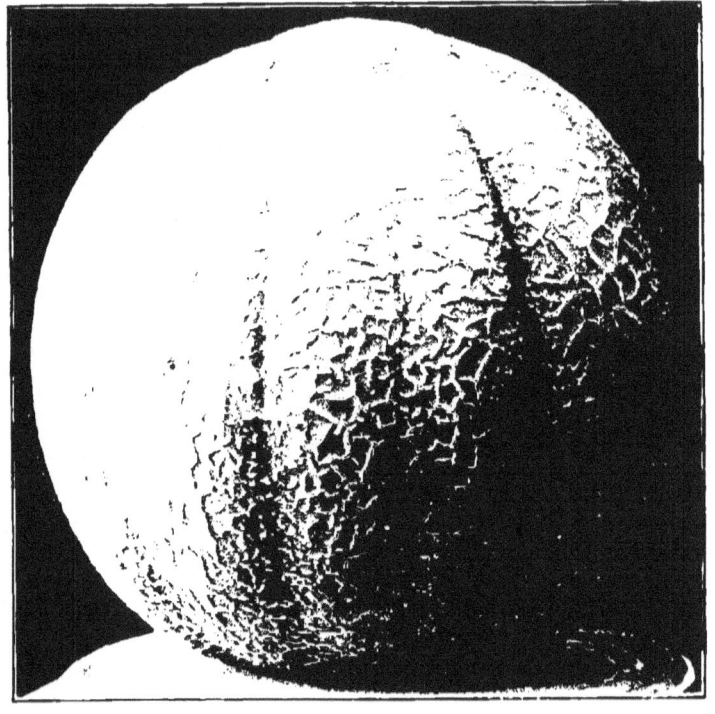

the very best, ripening ten days or two weeks after Blenheim Orange.

Empress. A globular melon of rather small size, ribless, but marked with very coarse angular bars; flesh pale orange, of good quality, but occasionally inclined to be somewhat acid. A pretty little melon, with curious markings, ripening with Masterpiece. Less desirable than Blenheim or Masterpiece.

Monarch. A good-sized melon, with sparse markings, except about the blossom end; dull yellow in color, not ribbed; flesh described as thick and solid, red, of excellent flavor. Ripens with Masterpiece. Our stock of this melon appears to have been mixed, and we have also grown a cross with Lockinge. Because of its variable character and somewhat unattractive appearance, we prize it less than some other varieties; but it is probable that a pure stock would have given more satisfactory results. From one stock we got green-fleshed fruits of best quality. We do not know which is the true Monarch.

Other varieties we have tested as follows: Sutton A 1, good size (a fruit picked January 26 weighed 2 lbs. 3 ozs.), very prominently and beautifully barred, the flesh orange, quality of the very best; Perfection, slightly furrowed and scarcely netted, green outside, the flesh green, but good and rich, though not so musky and aromatic as Masterpiece; Sutton Scarlet, flesh red, of excellent quality; Imperial, a rather soft, green-fleshed melon, but the best variety (in a lot of a dozen or more) tested in the season of 1895-6 (best fruit weighed 1 lb. 14 ozs.); Windsor Castle, large (specimen picked January 20 weighed 2 lbs. 6 ozs), with no ridges or bars (occasionally a vestige of bars), flesh green, quality fair to good. Amongst our own crosses, Masterpiece × Lockinge is perhaps the best. It has a pale-red or sometimes lemon-colored flesh, and is somewhat variable in quality, but generally very excellent. A sample of this fruit was sent to a connoisseur on the 15th of January, who wrote as follows: "The melon was by far the most toothsome article that has passed my lips this winter. Its flavor carried me back to early fall, and made me doubt my senses when I looked out of the window and saw snow on the ground, and saw by the calendar that we had begun the new year. I am greatly obliged to you for being able to satisfy a summer taste in midwinter."

The varieties, then, which we chiefly recommend for forcing, are Blenheim Orange, Hero of Lockinge, Masterpiece, Sutton A 1, Imperial, with, perhaps, Emerald Gem for early.

Yields and markets. — A good crop of melons in the winter months is an average of two to three fruits to the plant. This means that some plants must bear four or five melons, for there will almost certainly be some plants upon which no fruit can be made to set. The larger the fruits, the fewer each plant can mature. Four or five pounds of fruit to the vine is all that can reasonably be expected after November. In fall (that is, early November or earlier) and late spring crops, the grower should expect four to five melons to the plant (with the plants 2 feet apart each way); this is about all that one can obtain, even from small varieties like Emerald Gem. Of the larger sorts, like Blenheim Orange, three or four fruits is a good crop. In midwinter, we have not yet been able to average above two good melons to the plant, at 2 feet apart each way. The fruits will continue to ripen for a week after they are picked. Ordinarily, if seeds of Emerald Gem, Blenheim Orange, Hero of Lockinge, or other early varieties, are sown August first, fruits may be expected early in November. If the fruits are desired in January, there should be two or three weeks' delay in sowing. All plants grow slowly in the short, dark days of midwinter. The novice should not attempt to secure fruits later than Christmas time, for the growing of melons should be undertaken cautiously at first.

The market for forced muskmelons will always be

limited. These fruits are in every sense luxuries. I doubt if one could grow them in winter for less than $1 each, unless he did it upon a large scale. Good muskmelons in midwinter would bring almost any price, if placed before the right kind of consumers.

Insects and diseases.—There have been three serious insect enemies to our winter melons—black aphis, mites (*Tetranychus bimaculatus*), and mealy-bug. The best method of dealing with these pests is to keep them off. It is a poor gardener who is always looking for some easy means of killing insects. If the plants are carefully watched and every difficulty met at its beginning, there will be no occasion for worrying about bugs. A fumigation with tobacco smoke, or with the extract, twice a week will keep away the aphis; but if the fumigation is delayed until after the lice have curled up the leaves, the gardener will likely have a serious task in overcoming the pests, and the plants may be irreparably injured in the meantime.

For mites, keep the house and plants as moist as possible. At all events, do not allow the plants to become so dry that they wilt, for this neglect will sap the vitality out of any plant, and it falls an easy prey to enemies. When the mites first appear upon the foliage,—if the gardener should be so unfortunate as to have them, —knock the pests off with a hard stream of water from the hose, or pick the affected leaves and burn them. If the plants become seriously involved, so that all the leaves are speckled-grey from the work of the minute pests on the under side, then destroy the plants. Melon plants which have become seriously checked from the attacks of insects or fungi are of no further use, and they may as well be destroyed first as last.

Mealy-bugs are easily kept off by directing a fine, hard stream against them, when watering the house. When these bugs first appear, they usually congregate in the axils of the leaves, and a strong stream of water greatly disturbs their domestic arrangements. In one of our melon experiments, when the mealy-bug got a foothold, we picked them off with pincers. We went over the vines three times, at intervals, and eradicated the pests; and the labor of it — the vines were small — was much less than one would suppose.

There are two troublesome fungous disorders of frame melons. One is the mildew (*Erysiphe Cichoracearum*, or *Oidium* of earlier writers), which appears as whitish mold-like patches on the upper surface of the leaves. It also attacks cucumbers. It may be kept in check by evaporating sulphur in the house, as described on pages 91 and 92. It is imperative that the sulphur do not take fire, for burning sulphur is fatal to plants.

The second fungus is canker, or damping-off (see page 84). This usually attacks the plants after they have attained some size in the benches, sometimes even when they are in fruit. The vine stops growing, turns yellow, and finally begins to wilt. If the plant is examined at the surface of the ground and just beneath the soil, the stem will be found to be brown, and perhaps somewhat decayed, the bark sloughs off, and sometimes deep ulcers are eaten into the tissue. In this stage of the disease nothing can be done to save the plant. The treatment must be a preventive one. Keep the soil dry about the stem. Do not apply water directly at the root. In order to keep the soil dry, it is an excellent plan to hill up the plant slightly. It is also well to strew clean, white sand about the plant to keep the surface of the soil and the stem dry. If a little sulphur is mixed with the soil about the plant, the spread of the fungus will be checked. Some persons sprinkle lime about the plant to check the fungus.

A most serious difficulty once appeared upon our melons, and which we have called the house-blight (Fig. 79, page 223). The first visible injury to the leaves was the appearing of yellowish fungous-like spots or patches on the leaves. These patches soon become dead, dry and translucent, and are often very numerous, as seen on the upper leaf in the picture. Finally the leaf wilts and

79. *House-blight of melon. The upper leaf just showing the attack (in the spots), the lower one dead as it hangs on the vine.*

droops, and then shrivels and hangs on the stem, as seen in the lower leaf in Fig. 79. So far as our botanists have been able to determine, this disorder is not due to any fungus or parasite. It is a physiological disease. Fortunately, the cause of this attack was not far to seek. The melons were in a perfect state of health and vigor when, early in October, the gardener and myself went away for a few days. The house was left in charge of an attendant. The weather came off cloudy and damp. The house was over-watered, the plants syringed, and the foliage went through the night dripping wet. The next day the house did not dry off. The second day, when I returned, I had fears that dire results would follow, although the foliage looked well. I had the temperature raised and the house dried off. In two or three days the spots began to appear on the foliage, and in spite of all our efforts a third or more of the leaves were ruined and the plants seriously checked. What promised to be the best crop of melons which we had ever raised turned out to be almost a failure.

CHAPTER XII.

MISCELLANEOUS WARM PLANTS.

There are various crops of secondary importance which thrive at temperatures which are acceptable to tomatoes, cucumbers and melons. The details of the management of the leading ones of these crops are here set forth.

It is probable that okra may be forced with profit, for there is a good demand for the product in the New York market. I do not know that any one has had any practical experience with it as a forcing crop, but it is now being experimented upon at Cornell.

Squashes and their kin can be grown under glass, but it is not probable that they can be made a commercial success (see page 6).

Green corn has been tried in a desultory way at Cornell, but nothing has yet been made of it.

BEAN.

Bush beans are easily forced, and they constitute one of the best secondary winter crops. We ordinarily grow them upon cucumber, melon, or other benches while waiting for the cucumbers or melons to attain sufficient size in the pots for transplanting. We also grow them in 8-inch pots or in boxes, placing them here and there in the houses, wherever there is sufficient room and light. Beans will be ready for picking in six or eight weeks after sowing, in midwinter. Their demands are simple, yet exacting. They must have a rich, moist soil, strong bottom heat, and the more light the better. We cover our benches with about 8 inches of soil, the lower third of which is a layer of old sods. The top soil we make by adding about one part of well-rotted manure to two parts of rich garden loam. The soil must never be allowed to become dry, and especial care must be taken to apply enough water to keep the bottom of the soil moist, and yet not enough to make the surface muddy. With the strong bottom heat which we use for beans, the soil is apt to become dry beneath.

80. *A bench of Sion House winter beans.*

We once had a good illustration in our houses of the accelerating influence of bottom heat. One bench, to which no bottom heat was applied for the first three weeks, gave beans fit for picking on December 27. On another bench in the same house, to which heat was applied from the first, and upon which the same variety was sown at the same time, the second sowing of beans had been up for nearly two weeks at that date. The lack of bottom heat delayed the crop fully four weeks. The house should be light, and the benches should be near the glass. A good bench of beans is seen in Fig. 80.

If the benches are unoccupied, the beans may be planted on them directly, but if another crop is on them, the beans should be started in pots. We like to plant two or three beans in a 3-inch rose pot, and transplant to the benches just as soon as the roots fill the pot.

The night temperature of a bean house ought not to fall below 60°. After the blossoms appear, give a liberal application of liquid manure every five or six days. The growth of beans should be continuous and rapid from the first, in order to secure a large crop of tender pods. The bean is self-fertile, and therefore no pains is necessary to ensure pollination, as in the case of tomatoes, and some other indoor crops. The house may be kept moist by sprinkling the walks on bright days.

The essentials of a forcing bean are compact and rapid growth, earliness, productiveness, and long, straight and symmetrical pods. The Sion House answers these requirements the best of any variety which we have yet tried. It has green pods and party-colored beans. The cut (Fig. 80, page 226) shows with exactness an average bench of Sion House. English growers recommend the Green Flageolet, and we have had good success with it; but it is about a week later than Sion House, and it possesses no points of superiority. German Wax (*Dwarf German Black Wax*) forces well, but the pods are too short and too crooked. It is also particularly liable to the attacks of the pod fungus. Newtown (*Pride of Newtown*) is too large and straggling in growth.

For market, the beans are sorted and tied in bunches of 50 pods, as shown in Fig. 81 (page 228). These bunches bring varying prices, but from 25 to 50 cents may be considered an average. At these figures, with a good demand, forced beans pay well. Only two or three pickings of beans can be made profitable from one crop; and in some cases all the marketable crop is gathered at one time. Much of the success of bean forcing, as of all other winter gardening, consists in having new plants ready to take the place of the old ones. As soon as the old plants are removed, fork up the beds, add a liberal quantity of strong, short manure, and replant immediately.

The enemies are few, red spider and mite being the worst, and these are kept in check by maintaining a moist atmosphere.

87. Winter beans ready for market.

EGGPLANT.*

The possibility of forcing eggplants successfully was suggested by a crop which was grown under glass in one of the market gardens near Boston, in the spring of 1891. These plants were not grown with the intention of forcing them; but as the greenhouse was vacant at the time the main crop of eggplants was set out of doors, it was filled with plants taken from the same lot as those set in the open. The beds in which they were planted were solid; that is, the prepared soil rested upon the natural surface of the ground, forming a layer from 12 to 15 inches in depth. During the preceding winter these beds had served for growing lettuce, and they had consequently been well enriched with stable manure, a fertilizer which is especially effective in the production of

* E. G. Lodeman, Bulletin 65, Cornell Exp. Sta. Bulletin 26 of this Station is an account of the cultivation of eggplants in the field.

rapid growth. In July, when the plants grown under glass were compared with those planted in the open ground, an astonishing difference could be observed. Those set in the house were fully twice as large as the others; the leaves were larger and the stems thicker than those generally found in the gardens of this latitude, and the abundance of healthy foliage was ample proof that the plants were subjected to conditions extremely favorable to their growth.

Another interesting point was soon noticed. Although the plants were blossoming very freely, still comparatively little fruit had set, and it appeared as if the entire energies of the plants had been directed towards the production of foliage at the expense of the fruit. This condition may perhaps be ascribed to two causes. Extreme activity of the vegetative functions of plants is frequently carried on at the expense of fruit production; this fact is commonly illustrated by young fruit trees which blossom sometimes several years before they set fruit. The growth of the eggplant mentioned above was sufficiently luxuriant to suggest the possibility of its having some effect upon the fruiting powers of the plants. The second and perhaps most probable cause of this unsatisfactory fruiting may have been imperfect pollination. Insects, and especially bees, were not working so freely in the house as outside, and later experience has shown very clearly that in order to get a satisfactory crop from eggplants grown under glass thorough pollination must be practiced. The foliage was so dense that the flowers were for the most part hidden. In such a position they were necessarily surrounded by a comparatively damp atmosphere, especially when borne upon branches that were near the surface of the ground, and this would still further tend to interfere with the free transfer of pollen by any natural agencies. Under such conditions a profitable yield could scarcely be expected; yet when carefully observed, the plants proved to be so full of suggestions regarding the proper methods of treating them that they should have repaid the time given to their cultivation by a plentiful harvest of ideas, if not of fruits. The eggplant will generally set fruit without the assistance of pollen, but the fruit never attains its normal size. Fig. 82 shows a non-pollinated fruit which has reached the limit of its size. The reader will be able to measure its size by noticing that the calyx covers almost half of it. The fruit from which this picture was made was about 4 inches long.

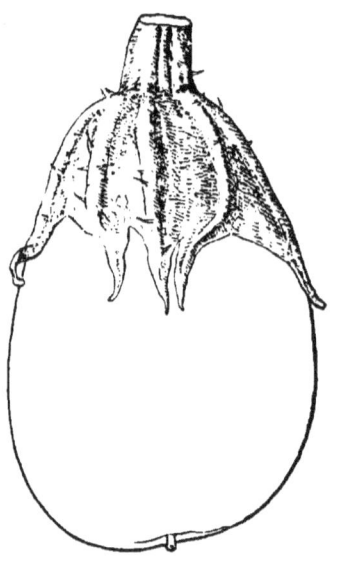

82. *Non-pollinated fruit.*

Acting on the above hints, several attempts have been made to grow eggplants in our forcing-houses, with the object, however, of fruiting them out of season. The first lot of seed was sown August 30, 1893. It embraced the following varieties: Black Pekin, New York Improved, Early Dwarf Purple, Round Purple, and Long White. The seed was sown about ⅜ of an inch deep in rich potting soil. The flats, or shallow boxes, which contained the seed were placed in a warm house, and the after-treatment was very similar to that commonly followed in the growing of tomatoes.

The seedlings required pricking out about four weeks after the seed was sown. They were set in 2½-inch pots, where they remained until November 14, when they were shifted into 4-inch pots. On December 17, or nearly 16 weeks from the time of seed sowing, the plants had filled these pots with roots, and they were again shifted, but this time into benches. They were set 2 feet apart each way. The soil was about 6 inches deep, and different in character in each of the two benches used. One bench had been filled with a mixture of equal parts of potting soil and manure from a spent mushroom bed. This formed a very open and rich soil, which appeared to be capable of producing a strong growth. The second bench received a rich, sandy loam, which had previously been composted with about one-fourth its bulk of stable manure. The temperature of the house was that usually maintained in growing plants requiring a considerable amount of heat; during the night the mercury fell to 65° or 60°, and in the day time it stood at 70°-75°. In bright weather the house was still warmer.

Considerable care was exercised in watering the plants, the soil being kept somewhat dry; when grown out of doors, eggplants withstand drought so well that such a course seemed advisable when growing them under glass. As the plants increased in size the leaves shaded the soil, and an occasional thorough watering maintained an excellent condition of moisture in the bed filled with the loam. In addition, the soil was stirred with a hand weeder when necessary.

For some time all the varieties in each bench appeared to be doing uniformly well, but the plants set in the sandy loam made a stronger growth and appeared to be more vigorous. This was especially noticeable in Early Dwarf Purple and New York Improved. The first bloom appeared on the former during the last week in December, and on the 3d of January, 1894, several plants showed flowers that were well opened. These were hand pollinated, and they set fruit freely. On February 15 some of these fruits were $2\frac{1}{2}$ inches long, the plants still growing well and producing many blossoms. It was at this time that the first flowers of Black Pekin appeared, but New York Improved had not yet produced any, although it was making a strong growth.

Round Purple and Long White were making a very slow and weak growth.

A plant of Early Dwarf Purple that was photographed May 29 is shown in Fig. 83. It was bearing at this time 21 fruits of varying sizes, and appeared to be strong enough to mature fruits from buds that were still forming. The larger fruits were fully 4 inches in diameter, and nearly 6 inches long. They were not removed as soon as grown, as should be done in order to get as

83. *Early Dwarf Purple eggplant in winter.*

large a yield as possible, and for this reason the product of the plant is the more remarkable. All the fruits did not attain the size mentioned above, for the crop was too heavy for the plant to mature it properly; neither were all the plants of this variety equally prolific, although their yield in many cases closely approached that shown in the illustration. This variety proved to be by far the most promising of those grown for forcing purposes, and it appears to be capable of producing crops which rival those grown out of doors. It is also the earliest variety tested, a point which is of the greatest importance. The eggplant is slow in coming to maturity, even under the most favorable circumstances. The above photograph was taken nine months from the time of sowing the seed, but a cutting of fruit might have been made fully six weeks earlier. This set fruit more freely than any other variety, and in nearly every desirable respect was superior to them. This Early

84 *Sprays of Early Dwarf Purple eggplant.*

Dwarf Purple, as grown in the field, is shown in Fig. 84.

New York Improved was a very strong grower, and produced large, handsome fruits. Unfortunately, but few could be obtained from a plant, and the total yield was, therefore, comparatively small, only four or five maturing on the best plants. It is also considerably later than the Early Dwarf Purple. The New York Improved, as grown out of doors, is seen in Fig. 85. In the house the plant may be expected to be taller in proportion to its breadth.

Black Pekin on the whole closely resembled the preceding, especially in the manner of its growth. But it set scarcely any fruit, and that was so late that none was matured before 10 months from the time of seed-sowing.

85. *Field-grown plant of New York Improved eggplant.*

Long White proved to be a weak grower of very slender habit. It was also very late, the fruits being scarcely over 2 inches in length May 29. The plants of this variety were slightly checked when young, and this may have had a certain influence in delaying the maturity of the crop, although the effect was probably not very great. One desirable feature of this variety is its smooth foliage, which appeared to be unfavorable for the development and persistence of some of the insects that attack greenhouse plants. But the lateness of the variety and the few fruits produced by it will prevent it from being profitably grown under glass.

Round Purple proved to be the most unsatisfactory grower. All the plants showed symptoms of being in unfavorable quarters, and the test with this variety resulted in almost total failure.

Later attempts to force eggplants have been made, although no duplicate of the above experiment has been planned. The crops were started later in the season, when more sunlight and heat were present. These trials have thrown light upon some of the doubtful points of former experiments, and have shown that it is possible to force eggplants in winter. New York Improved eggplants are seen on the side in Fig. 71 (page 206). The seeds for these were sown July 20, the young plants shifted to 3-inch pots on August 28, and planted in the bench September 13. When the picture was taken (October 3) flower buds were just beginning to show. The plants are standing 18 inches apart each way in alternate rows, which is too close.

One of the results obtained is of special interest in this connection. Some Early Dwarf Purple plants were started early in August, and some of the seedlings were grown in houses in which different degrees of temperature were maintained. The plants grown in an intermediate or moderately warm house made but little growth, and were soon stunted and worthless. This showed conclusively that eggplants require a high temperature for their rapid and vigorous development. Other plants were placed in each of two warm houses, one of which was shaded by means of a thin coat of whitewash upon the glass. The plants in the other house were exposed to direct sunlight, and they were also subjected to a bottom heat of scarcely 5 degrees. Although the air temperature of the two houses was practically identical, the plants receiving the sunlight grew fully twice as fast as the others, and had open blossoms before those in the shaded house showed any buds. When some of the latter were removed into the same favored position, they very soon showed a benefit from the change. In this way the plants themselves emphasized the necessity of plenty of sunshine for their development in winter quarters; and a certain amount of bottom heat, from 4 to 6 degrees, is also very beneficial, the air temperature at the same time being that of a warm house.

Eggplants designed for forcing should never be stunted. An important aid to prevent this condition is a soil which is open and still rich in available nitrogen. A rich, sandy loam, in which all the ingredients are well rotted, is preferable to one having the manure in an undecayed condition. The latter is too open, and is more difficult to maintain in a proper supply of moisture. The soil should be sufficiently open to afford good drainage, but not so coarse that it dries out very rapidly. The bench mentioned at the beginning of the article as containing manure from a spent mushroom bed did not prove so satisfactory as the one containing the sandy loam, largely because it was more difficult to manage.

Another point which should not be overlooked in forcing eggplants is the pollination of the flowers. This is most satisfactorily done by hand, the small number of insects found in greenhouses during the colder months being of very little use in this respect. The work can be done rapidly by means of a small, flat piece of metal, such as can be made by flattening the point of a pin with a hammer, and then inserting the other end into a small stick, which will serve as a handle. Such a spatula is also very convenient in nearly all kinds of pollination made by hand, as it is so readily kept clean of foreign pollen. In the center of the flower will be seen the stigma, which projects beyond the tips of the ring of anthers or pollen-bearing organs which surround it. If an anther is separated and closely examined, it will be seen that there are two small openings at the tip; it is through these that the pollen normally escapes. But this escape does not take place freely until the flower has matured to such an extent that the tips of the anthers stand erect and recede from the stigma, leaving the latter standing unsupported. The pollen can be most rapidly gathered upon the spatula by inserting the point of the metal into the side of the anther and opening it by an upward movement of the instrument. In this manner a large quantity of pollen may be gathered very rapidly, and it is the work of but an instant to press it upon the end of the stigma. One such treatment, if performed when the surface of the stigma is adhesive, is sufficient for each blossom.

Eggplants are subject to the attacks of all the common greenhouse pests, but if care is exercised from the beginning, no serious damage need be feared. Greenfly is easily overcome by tobacco smoke, or the fumes of tobacco extract, while mealy-bug can be overcome by well-directed streams of water. The foliage of eggplants is not easily injured by such applications of water, and the insects may be dislodged with impunity as often as they appear. The worst pests of eggplant foliage are the red spider and his near relative, the mite. The latter is especially difficult to treat, as it is not so much affected by moisture as the red spider is, and for this reason it cannot be so readily overcome. The rough foliage of the eggplant is especially well adapted to the lodgment of these mites, and when they have once become established, their extermination is practically impossible. Too much care, therefore, cannot be taken in watching for the first appearance of these scourges, and in destroying them as soon as discovered. It is well to apply water freely to the foliage, even before the insects appear, for the leaves do not immediately show their presence, and such applications will do no harm. The

Long White does not suffer from these insects so much as the other varieties, since it has comparatively smooth leaves, which do not afford a very secure retreat. Nevertheless, it will bear watching as well as the others. The water that is applied should be directed mainly toward the under surface of the leaves, as the mites are here found in the greatest abundance, and these parts are also most difficult to reach.

The returns to be derived from eggplants grown in greenhouses cannot yet be estimated, since to my knowledge no such products have ever been placed upon the market. The first fruits from the south command a good price, but whether the home-grown article will meet with such favor that it will repay the cost of the long period of growth cannot be told. The Dwarf Purple variety may be depended upon to give the earliest and surest results, but if bigger fruits are desired, the New York Improved promises to be the best. The fruits ought to sell in midwinter for 50 cents each, and if they are very large and fine, for more than this. The experiment of eggplant forcing from a commercial standpoint is well worth trying.

PEPPER, OR CAPSICUM.

Red peppers are a most satisfactory crop for winter, so far as the growing of them is concerned. They force readily, yield abundantly, and are nearly free of insects and fungous injuries. The large, puffy fruits are in demand, just as they reach their full size and while yet green, for the making of stuffed peppers, a delicacy which is much esteemed in restaurants and hotels. The so-called "sweet peppers" are the kinds sought, such as Sweet Mountain (which we consider to be the best for forcing), Procopp, Bell, Golden Dawn, and the like. If the fruits sell for 5 cents each (and this is a common

87. *A good type of pepper for winter forcing*

price), the grower ought to be able to make his expenses; and if he secures more, as he often can, the growing of them should be fairly remunerative; but he will likely find that the peppers which are shipped in from the south nearly all winter are most unwelcome competitors in the general market. A plant should bear half a dozen good fruits, which it can do if well grown and if the fruits are picked just as soon as they are fit for market.

In winter, about three and a half months are required from the seed to the first saleable fruit, but the plants need not be on the benches more than half or two-thirds of that time. They are usually started in flats, pricked off into 3-inch pots and turned out of these pots (when in the condition shown in Fig. 86) directly into the bench. In one of our experiments, seeds of the Sweet Mountain were sown July 20, plants put into pots August 28, set in the bench September 14, and gave the first picking (one fruit to the plant) on October 21. They require a longer time than this later in the season. A bench 3 feet wide will grow two rows of peppers, the plants standing a foot apart in the row. Earlier results can be secured by growing the plants in 6-inch pots, but the crop will generally be less and the fruits smaller. We think that peppers like an intermediate temperature,— a little cooler than for melons,—although we have had good results in growing them along the edge of a bench

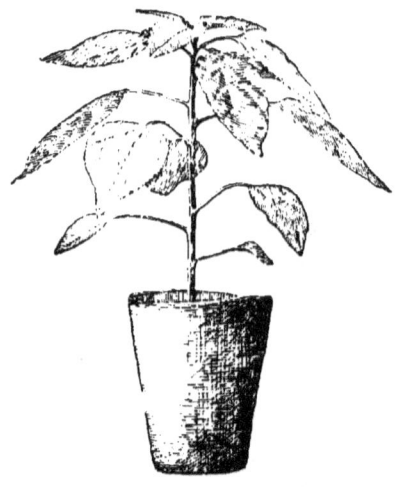

86. *Pepper plant ready to transplant.*

in which melons were growing at the same time. The flowers do not need pollinating. The fruits set of themselves, and are more or less seedless.

CYPHOMANDRA.

In 1886 Peter Henderson & Co. advertised seeds of the Tree Tomato of Jamaica. I procured seeds and grew the plants. The results of the effort, as published at the time,* were as follows: "The so-called Tree Tomato of Jamaica was reared from seeds last year, and two plants were carried over winter in the greenhouse. They were potted out in the spring. They grew well, attaining a height of 8 feet. They blossomed profusely during the fall, but did not set fruit. We shall carry them over another year. This curious plant is a native of tropical America, a member of the Solanum family, though not a tomato. It is *Cyphomandra betacea*. It has been widely distributed through the tropics of late years. The fruit more nearly resembles an eggplant fruit than a tomato. We have also grown it this year from seeds from Peru, which were sent us as the 'Chileno Tomato.' Of course the plant is valueless in this climate."

I lost the plant until three years ago, when I secured seed again from southern California, and as this book goes to the printer two tree-like plants growing together, 7 feet high, and with a spread of 4 feet, bear their crop of 46 curious, egg-like fruits (shown two-thirds natural size in Fig. 88, page 242). The plants are three years old, and were once cut back to stumps. The plants — and we had others — bloomed profusely the second year from seed, but no amount of hand pollination would make the flowers set fruit. The present crop was not hand-pollinated, but the fruits are full of seeds.

---

* Bulletin 31, Michigan Agric. College, 10 (1887).

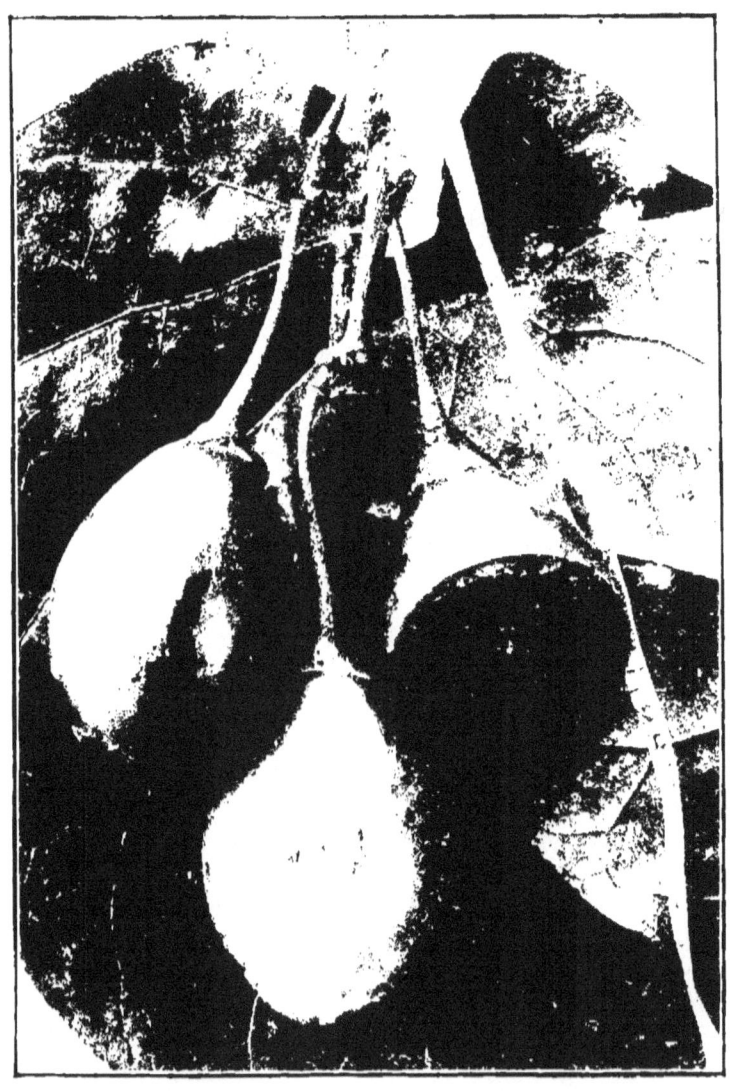

88. Fruit and foliage of cyphomandra. Two-thirds natural size.

They set in the summer when the house was thrown open, but I suspect that the flowers are self-fertile. The fruits measure almost uniformly 2 inches long and 1½ inches wide. The color when ripe is a light, clear, reddish brown, shading into dull olive-green towards the stem, and sparingly streaked with olive-green. In external features the fruits strongly resemble small specimens of pepino. The fruit is two-celled, like a small tomato, and has numerous tomato-like seeds on central placentæ. The flavor is a musky acidity, not very unlike that of some tomatoes. Theodosia B. Shepherd, of southern California, writes in *American Gardening* for July 11, 1896 (and gives a picture), as follows, of the quality of the fruit, which, she says, is sometimes called Brazilian Melon Fruit: "When fully ripe, it is delicious. When the outer rind is taken off, and it is sliced, it can be served as a salad, with dressing, or eaten with sugar and cream. It makes a fine jelly or jam, with the flavor of apricots, but more delicate. The ripe fruit does not bruise easily, because of the thick outer rind, so that it keeps a long time, and can be shipped long distances."

The leaves of this cyphomandra are large and heavy, heart-shaped, and perfectly entire. The plant has a tropical look, and a well-grown plant is always sure to attract attention. The plant is much loved of the mealy-bug, but we have found no fungi attacking it. We do not know what forcing temperature best suits this plant, but I imagine that it likes a cooler place than tomatoes do.

The cyphomandra fruit is sometimes seen in the New York markets, coming from Jamaica, and is often called Grenadilla. In the tropics, the fruit is eaten either raw or cooked, after the manner of tomatoes. The plant there attains a height of 10 or 12 feet. In Spanish America it is said to be known as *tomato de la Paz*. The plant is a native of South America, it having been introduced into British gardens from southern Brazil by Tweedie, who sent it to the Botanical Garden at Glasgow. It was figured, without fruit, in 1839 in *Botanical Magazine* (t. 3684), with a description by Sir W. J. Hooker. At that time it was known as *Solanum fragrans*. The genus Cyphomandra was separated from Solanum by Martius in 1845. The latest account of the genus Cyphomandra admits 38 species, all South American.

CHAPTER XIII.

SUMMARIES OF THE MANAGEMENT OF THE VARIOUS CROPS.

ASPARAGUS.

ASPARAGUS is customarily forced from roots which have been allowed to reach the age of four years or more in the field. These roots are removed to the forcing-house, and after being forced once are thrown away (pages 127, 130).

The roots are dug late in fall, and are stored in a cold cellar or a shed until they are wanted for forcing. They are usually covered with straw, but freezing is not injurious if they remain moist (page 130).

The clumps are generally forced under benches, in a temperature suited to lettuce or cauliflower. High temperatures give quick results, but the shoots are generally more slender and spindling (page 131).

The clumps are packed close together upon 2 or 3 inches of earth and covered with about 3 or 4 inches of loose earth. In two to three weeks, edible shoots will appear, and the cutting may continue for five to eight weeks. The amount and value of the crop will depend largely upon the strength of the clumps (pages 131, 132).

BEAN.

Beans are very easily forced for the green pods ("string beans"). They may be grown to maturity in pots or boxes which are set in vacant places about the house, or they may occupy benches either as a leading crop or as a catch crop with cucumbers, melons, or tomatoes (page 225).

The soil for beans should be rich and "quick." We use 6 to 8 inches of soil placed upon benches, making it of garden loam and nearly or quite one-quarter of very thoroughly rotted manure (page 225).

The temperature for beans should be approximately that for cucumbers,—60° to 65° at night, and 10 to 15 degrees higher during the day. The plants should have strong bottom heat (pages 226, 227).

A good forcing bean is one which is early and productive, compact in habit, and which bears long, straight and symmetrical pods. We prefer the Sion House bean, a green-podded variety (page 227).

Six or eight weeks are required from the sowing of the seeds to the first picking (page 225).

Beans are self-fertile, and hand pollination is, therefore, unnecessary (page 227).

House beans are usually marketed in neat bunches (Fig. 81), containing 50 pods. In special and personal markets, the pods should bring from ½ cent to 1 cent each (page 227).

Not more than three good pickings can be expected from any crop, and very often it is not profitable to retain the plants after a single picking (page 227).

The leading enemies of beans are red spider and mites. Keep the foliage moist if attack is feared (page 228).

BEET, CARROT.

Beets require such a long season, and yield so little profit, that they are rarely grown as a main crop in forcing-houses. They are commonly grown between late cucumbers or tomatoes. Seeds are generally sown in flats, and the young plants are 'pricked out into rows between the other crops. If grown by themselves, beets require a lettuce-house temperature (page 145). Carrot is treated in the same way, but is rarely forced for market.

CAULIFLOWER.

Cauliflower demands a low temperature (about 50° at night and 10 to 15 degrees higher in the day), and a solid bed (page 111).

Four to five months from the seed are required in which to get marketable heads. The plants should be transplanted at least once before they are set in their permanent quarters. They should be planted about 16 inches apart each way (pages 111, 112).

The plants must be kept growing uniformly, else the heads will "button" (pages 109, 112, 113).

The Snowball and Early Erfurt strains are good for forcing (pages 112, 113, 114).

The cauliflower may be troubled with aphis or greenfly, but it has developed no other serious diseases or difficulties under glass, unless possibly, in common with all plants, a facility for damping-off (page 111).

CELERY.

Celery may be forced by starting the seed in fall or very early winter, and holding the plants back until spring. Early in March (or in February), the plants are put in solid beds (in a lettuce or carnation house) 8 to 10 inches apart, and they are then set into rapid growth. The plants are bleached by tying them up in stiff, hard paper (page 139).

CRESS.

Water-cress grows readily on moist ground underneath benches in a cool or intermediate house (page 141).

Garden-cress may be grown in beds or on benches which are suited to the raising of lettuce. The seeds are commonly sown where the plants are to stand (page 142).

CUCUMBER.

Forcing cucumbers are of two types, the English or frame kinds, and the White Spine kinds. The former are characterized by very large size, partial or complete absence of spines, more or less seedlessness, very rampant growth of vine, tardiness in coming into fruit, and a long-continuing period of bearing. The White Spine type is more commonly forced for market in this country (pages 184, 194).

The English cucumbers like a temperature of about 60° or 65° at night, and of 70° to 75° at day (page 186).

It is exceedingly important that the vines should be kept in a uniform and vigorous condition of growth from the start, but avoid pushing them very much in dull weather. English cucumbers are gross feeders, and must have a rich soil (page 186).

From 80 to 100 days are required, in winter, from the sowing of the seed of English cucumbers to the securing of the fruit. The plants must have good bottom heat (page 189).

The plants are started in pots (3-inch rose pots being excellent), which are at first only a third or half full of earth. From these pots the plants are turned directly into the benches, where they should stand about 2½ by 3 ft. apart. When in the pots, the plants must never be allowed to become checked, and they must be kept free of aphis (page 187).

The plants are trained upon a wire trellis, or sometimes on the roof. Usually two or three strong branches or leaders are allowed to each plant, and a few strong side shoots are taken out of each leader. All weak growths are pinched out (page 188).

Leading varieties of English cucumbers are Sion House, Telegraph, Edinburgh, and Blue Gown (page 190).

It is generally necessary, to insure a crop, to hand-pollinate English cucumbers, although fruits will often set without this labor and will be, therefore, wholly seedless (page 195).

White Spine cucumbers are forced in essentially the same way as the English sorts, but they are oftener grown as a spring crop (following lettuce or plant stock) than the others are. They come into bearing sooner, ripen their fruits more simultaneously, demand full sunlight, and may be planted rather closer together than the others (page 201).

The White Spine types should mature the entire crop in about three months after the plants are set in the benches. A plant will yield from 20 to 90 fruits, depending upon the management of the house, the strength of the soil, the distance apart of the plants, and the thoroughness with which the fruits are picked when fit for market (page 202).

Cucumber enemies are the mite, aphis, root-gall, and mildew. For the mite, syringe the plants and pick off the infested leaves; for aphis, use tobacco fumigation and pick infested leaves; for root-gall, use soil which has been thoroughly frozen; for mildew, improve the sanitary conditions, and then use sulphur (page 200).

DANDELION.

Dandelion is sometimes forced from roots which are lifted in the fall, the seeds having been sown in the spring. The plant requires about the same temperature and treatment as lettuce does (page 143).

EGGPLANT.

Eggplants are not forced for market, but the plants can be grown under glass without especial difficulty. Their season is long (5 to 9 months), and eggplant fruits come in from the south in winter (pages 228, 233, 235).

The plants should be started in flats or pots, and

transplanted two or three times before going into permanent quarters. The temperature, soil and general treatment should be essentially the same as for tomatoes. They must have bottom heat and full sunlight (pages 230, 235).

Eggplants should stand about 2 feet apart each way if the coarse-growing varieties are grown, and 20 inches if the Early Dwarf Purple is grown (pages 230, 235).

Fruits will set without hand-pollination (Fig. 82), but they will not grow to marketable size. Instructions for pollination are given on pages 236 and 237.

Early Dwarf Purple is the earliest and most productive variety for forcing, but the fruits are small. Our second choice is New York Improved (pages 232 to 235).

Eggplant is loved of the green-fly, mealy-bug, red spider, and mite. The spider and mite are its most ardent admirers, and they must be freely baptized if it is desired to keep them off (page 237).

LETTUCE.

There are two general kinds or types of forcing lettuce, that which forms more or less solid heads (Fig. 34), and that which remains open and leafy (Figs. 32, 33). The former is more prized in New England and other eastern markets. It is more difficult to grow to perfection than the leafy type is, and is particularly subject to influence by the soil.

Lettuce demands a night temperature of about 45°, and never higher than 50°, and a day temperature of about 55° to 65° (page 94).

Solid or ground beds are most satisfactory for the growing of lettuce. Upon benches, more care is required in growing the crop, and the difficulties are aggravated if the bench has bottom heat (page 94).

Good lettuce may also be grown in pots, and thereby be marketed with a good ball of earth attached. This method is little used, however (Fig. 33, page 99).

The character of the soil has very much to do with the ease of growing lettuce, and also with the quality of the crop. Good lettuce soils should be very open and porous (made so by the presence of sand and the absence of clay), with a capacity to hold much water, but an ability, nevertheless, to remain comparatively dry on top (page 96).

The electric light has a marked effect in hastening the maturity of lettuce (pages 80, 101).

A lettuce crop matures in seven to ten weeks if the seed is sown in September. In the winter months, two to four weeks longer may be required (page 101).

The first sowing (in early September) may be made in the open, but subsequent ones are made in flats or in vacant places in the beds (or possibly in hotbeds). Best results are obtained if the plants are transplanted twice, once into other flats or into temporary beds (about 4 inches apart each way), and again into their permanent quarters, where they should stand about 8 inches apart each way (pages 101, 102).

Leading varieties are the Boston Market (or White-seeded Tennis Ball) and Grand Rapids. The former is a heading lettuce (Fig. 34), and the latter non-heading (Fig. 32). There are several other good varieties (page 104).

Aphis or green-fly is held in check by keeping the plants in a uniform condition of vigorous and healthy growth, and then by fumigating with tobacco or by strewing tobacco stems amongst the plants (page 104).

The rot is worst in soils which remain wet on top and which contain much manure or decaying matter. Keeping the temperature high and the house very wet also favors it (page 105, Fig. 35).

The mildew is worst in houses which are kept very close and warm and wet. It is most frequent when draughts are allowed to strike the plants. When it appears, evaporate sulphur (first, however, improving the sanitary conditions), taking care not to let the sulphur catch fire (page 106).

Leaf-burn or top-burn is the result of bad sanitary conditions, being especially favored by a soil which holds too much water; also by insufficient care in ventilating and watering in dull weather. It is most harmful in the heading varieties (page 106).

MINTS.

Sage and spearmint may be forced from plants transplanted to the house in the fall; or, better, established beds may be covered. They require a lettuce-house temperature (page 143).

MUSKMELON.

Melons, when raised under glass, are generally grown for a late fall or early spring crop. For midwinter use, they are practically unknown, because the quality is generally poor (page 204).

Muskmelons may be ripened in full normal quality in midwinter, however, if given much heat (65° to 70° at night, and 80° to 85° at midday), if the soil is strong (particularly in mineral fertilizer), if the plants are never allowed to become checked, and if the soil is kept dry when the fruits are ripening (page 205).

Houses which are adapted to winter cucumbers and tomatoes are also adapted to melons. The plants are grown only on benches, at least for the winter crops, and are given ample bottom heat. They need unshaded roofs (page 207).

The soil for melons may be well-rotted sods from an old pasture, with some thoroughly composted manure, worked into it. If the soil is naturally rich in nitrogen (tending to make plants run to vine), stable manure should be used very sparingly, or not at all. The soil on the bench may be from 5 to 7 inches deep (page 207).

MUSKMELON.

Melon seeds are started in 2-inch or 3-inch pots, only one plant being allowed to grow in each pot. The plants are transferred to 4-inch pots, and then to the benches. If the plants become stunted, they are worthless (page 210).

In benches 4 feet wide, the plants may be set 2½ feet apart in two rows; or they may be set 18 inches apart in a single row. When only a single row is used, the row may be set near one side of the bench and a part of the wide side left unfilled; in this unfilled portion the soil is added at intervals, thus affording new forage as it may be needed. It is always well to set twice as many plants in the bed as will be needed, in order to insure against losses from accidents, damping-off, and the like (page 209).

The plants are headed-in as soon as they are established in their permanent quarters, in order to make them branch and to set them into fruit-bearing. Three or four main arms are trained out fan-shaped on a wire trellis, and each one is headed-in when 4 or 5 feet high. All blind and fine shoots must be kept off. Some growers allow the main stem to grow straight up, and take out side branches from it (page 211).

The fruits hang free, and are supported in slings of soft broad cord, or in swings (Figs. 73, 77, page 211).

Melon flowers must be pollinated by hand. The first two or three pistillate flowers are not pollinated, for if one fruit is set much in advance of the other flowers it will absorb the attention of the vine, and it will be found to be very difficult to set other fruits (page 214).

We have found good forcing varieties to be Blenheim Orange, Hero of Lockinge, Masterpiece, Sutton A 1, Imperial, and Emerald Gem. There are numerous other acceptable varieties (page 215).

An average of two good melons to a plant is a good crop in midwinter. In fall and spring, four and five fruits may be obtained (page 220).

Insects troubling melons are aphis and mealy-bug, especially the latter. Fumigate with tobacco for the aphis, and knock off the mealy-bug with a hard stream of water. Mites are also serious on house melons. For these, keep the foliage well syringed (page 221).

Diseases of house melons are mildew and damping-off. For the former, improve the sanitary conditions, and then use sulphur. For damping-off, or canker, keep the earth dry about the crown of the plant, and use soils which do not remain wet and pasty on top. House-blight is a name which we have given to a physiological trouble (Fig. 79), which arises when the plants are allowed to go through the night wet, especially when other sanitary conditions are bad (page 222).

PARSLEY.

Parsley is forced from roots taken to the house in the fall, and which are raised from spring-sown seeds. Treat essentially the same as for lettuce (page 142).

PEA.

Both dwarf and tall peas may be forced. The former give earlier results, but the larger and better yields are obtained from the half-tall varieties. Varieties like Rural New-Yorker will mature in 70 to 80 days from the seed in winter. The temperature should be as low as for lettuce. Peas may be grown in solid beds or in boxes placed amongst other plants. Peas yield little, and they are rarely forced for market (page 135).

PEPINO.

The pepino is a solanum, something like eggplant, which may be forced in a cool house. It is a sub-shrub, and is propagated by cuttings. Cuttings taken in March may be expected to bear the next January or February.

It is best to grow the plants in pots or boxes. The plant is little known in this country, but it is no doubt worthy of considerable attention (page 146).

PEPPER.

Red peppers are very easily forced, and if one can get 5 cents or more apiece for the fruits he should be able to grow them for the winter market. The southern-grown product is cheaper, however, and scarcely inferior (page 238).

Peppers need bottom heat, a little cooler temperature than melons, but hand-pollination seems to be unnecessary (pages 240, 241).

The plants are handled like tomato plants, and about 3½ months are required, from the seed-sowing, in which to get the first fruits. The plants may stand a foot apart in the row, and 2 rows can go on a 3-ft. bench (page 240).

We like the Sweet Mountain best for forcing. Only the large and puffy, or "sweet," peppers are forced (page 238).

RADISH.

Radishes require to be grown quickly, else they are worthless. About 35 to 40 days is required to mature the crop, from the time of sowing the seed (pages 115, 123).

The proper temperature for radishes is 45° to 50° at night, and 55° to 65° at day (pages 118, 125).

Radish seed is commonly sown where the plants are to stand. The smaller varieties may be grown in drills which are only 3 inches apart, but most varieties need 4 or 5 inches between the rows. The plants should be thinned to nearly or quite 2 inches apart in the row. Uniformly large seeds give the surest and most uniform results (pages 115, 117, 122).

Solid beds should be used for radishes, and the house should be light and airy. If benches are used, they should have no bottom heat (pages 116, 119, 122).

The soil should be warm and quick, with an ordinary amount of sand, and no coarse manure. It should be made rich by working old manure thoroughly into it. The short radishes will thrive in 4 inches of soil, but better results with most kinds will be obtained in 6 to 8 inches (pages 116, 122).

The varieties are many. Amongst those which may be commended are Ne Plus Ultra, Roman Carmine, Prussian Globe, New Rapid Forcing, French Breakfast, New Crystal Forcing, and Long Scarlet Short-top. The turnip-shaped kinds are usually preferable (pages 120, 124).

RHUBARB.

Rhubarb or pie-plant is forced in essentially the same manner as asparagus (which see). The roots of mature plants are dug in the fall, and they are bedded in hotbeds or underneath benches in a cool or intermediate house, being covered with 2 to 6 inches of soil (page 134).

SPINACH.

Spinach is now rarely forced under glass, because the crop can be more cheaply grown in the south. It is handled in essentially the same manner that lettuce is (page 142).

TOMATO.

The tomato is rapidly assuming great importance as a commercial forcing crop. It is often profitable even in the face of the competition of the early crop from the south (page 153).

For winter crops, the best results are obtained in houses which are used primarily for tomato growing, but spring crops may be advantageously grown following carnations or winter lettuce. The house should be warm and very bright, with at least 5 or 6 feet of head room above each bench (pages 153, 8).

The temperature for tomatoes should be about 60° to 65° at night, and about 75° at day (page 154).

The soil should be rich, but the manure which is used in the earth should be well rotted and broken down. Rich, rather loose garden loam, to which a fourth or fifth of the bulk of fine manure is added, makes an ideal soil. Liquid manure may need to be applied when the plants come into bearing (pages 154, 53).

Tomatoes should always have bottom heat, unless, perhaps, for the late spring or early summer crop. They are grown in both benches and boxes, nearly all commercial growers preferring the former because of their cheapness. The benches contain from 6 to 8 inches of soil (page 157).

House tomatoes are grown both from seeds and cuttings, and both methods are in common use. When made from strong, healthy shoots the cuttings are probably in every way as good as seedlings, and they usually bear sooner; but cuttings are likely to perpetuate a weakness of a plant, and they are apt to give only indifferent results when taken from old and partially exhausted plants. On the whole, seedlings are probably preferable (page 155).

The second crop of the season (coming on in late winter) may be obtained either from new seedling plants, from cuttings, from a shoot trained out from the old stump, or by burying the old stem and allowing the tip to continue to grow. Seedlings are usually preferable, as indicated in the last paragraph (page 166).

From four to five months are required, after seed-sowing, to secure ripe fruit. Seeds are usually sown in flats, and the young plants should be handled at least twice (preferably into pots) before they are put into permanent quarters (page 155).

The plants may be trained either to a single perpendicular stem (being tied to a vertical cord), or two or three stems or branches may be taken out and trained in a fan-shaped fashion (either on diverging cords or on wire trellises). For single-stem training (which is generally considered to be best), the plants may be set about 20 x 24 inches; in the fan system, they are set from 2 to 3 feet each way (pages 160, 158).

The heavy clusters of fruit are held up in slings of raffia or soft cord. The plants must be kept open, and free from all stray and blind growths (page 161).

Especial care must be taken not to water too freely in heavy soils, and particularly in dull weather. Overwatered plants may develop dropsy, and they are liable to many ills (pages 161, 177).

Tomato flowers must be hand-pollinated. This operation is done in midday, when the sun is bright and the house dry. The best method is to collect the pollen in a spoon or ladle (Fig. 53) and to touch the end of the stigma with the dust (page 162).

The tomato fruit seems to be increased in size by a very liberal application of pollen (Fig. 55), and it develops more symmetrically if care is taken to apply the pollen equally over the entire stigmatic surface (page 163).

In winter, single-stem tomatoes should average about 2 lbs. of good fruit to the plant, and in spring and early summer twice that much (page 169).

The most popular forcing tomato in this country is Lorillard. Other good ones are Ignotum, Chemin Market, Golden Queen, Volunteer. Almost any of the free-growing varieties force well (page 172).

House tomatoes are generally sent to market in neat splint baskets (like the Climax) holding from 4 to 10 lbs. of fruit. Each fruit should be wrapped in soft paper (page 174).

Animal parasites of the tomato are the aleyrodes scale (kept in check by tobacco fumigation), mite (held at bay by syringing the plants and picking off infested leaves), and the root-gall (prevented by using only soil which has been thoroughly frozen since a crop has been grown upon it) illustrated in Fig. 29, and discussed on pages 84 and 85 (page 175).

Diseases of house tomatoes are fruit-rot (pick off the injured fruits), blight or rust (spray with fungicide), dropsy (caused by too much wet and too little light), and winter blight (destroy the plants), this last being very little understood (page 177).

INDEX.

	Page		Page
Accidents	2	Beet, account of	145
Adsched, on melon	205	— electric light on	80
"Agricultural Science," quoted.	96	— mentioned	5, 6
Aiton, on pepino	150	— summary of	246
Aleyrodes	89, 175	— temperature for	5
Alga	67	Beets and sub-irrigation	77
Alternation of crops	7	Benches	40
"American Garden," quoted	85, 151	Benson, Martin, and pepino	151
"American Gardening," quoted, 102, 121, 243		Bermuda, cucumbers in	185, 196
		Bisulphide of carbon	90
"American Naturalist," quoted, 192, 194		Blight of tomato	180
		Bordeaux mixture	84, 177, 182
"Annales des Sciences," quoted.	194	"Botanical Magazine," quoted	244
Aphis	104, 111, 125, 200	Botrytis vulgaris	105
— destroying	84, 86, 89	Brazilian melon fruit	243
Apples, pollination of	165	Britton, W. E., quoted	53
Artotrogus Debaryanus	85, 86	Bubbles in glass	207
Ashes for forcing-house soil	55	Building forcing-houses	16
Asparagus, account of	127, 130	Busch, Fred., mentioned	48
— mentioned	4, 5, 7	Butted glass	37
— summary of	245	Cabbage-worm	111
— temperature for	5, 49, 50	California, cyphomandra in,	241, 243
Atkinson, on damping-off	84	— pepino in	151
— on œdema	178	"Canadian Horticulturist," quoted	175
Bailey, on damping-off	85		
— on electric light	80	Canker	84, 222
Barkham, James, on melon	209, 212, 215	Capsicum. See Pepper.	
		Carnations and vegetables	8
Bauhin, quoted	192	Carrot, account of	145
Bean, account of	225	— electric light on	80
— mentioned	6, 7	— mentioned	5, 6
— prices of	4	— summary of	246
— summary of	245, 246	— temperature for	5
— temperature for	5	Category of forcing crops	4
Beds	40	Cauliflower, account of	108
Bees in forcing-houses	81	— electric light on	80

INDEX.

	Page
Cauliflower, mentioned, 6, 17, 43,	140
— summary of	247
— temperature for	5, 49
Celery, account of	139
— mentioned	5, 6, 7
— summary of	247
— temperature for	5, 49
Cellars, use of	4
Cement for gutters	33
— for walls	35
Central America, pepino in	150
Charcoal and damping-off	84
Chester Co., carnations in	8
Chicory	4
Chileno tomato	241
Chrysanthemums, mentioned	140
Cladosporium fulvum	177
Clay and lettuce-growing	8
Climate and forcing	8
Coal, cost of	9–15
Coates, Leonard, quoted	2
Compost heaps	64
Connecticut experiments in fertilizing lettuce	61
— — on manures	63
— — on tomatoes	53
Construction of houses	16
Cool plants	4, 49
Corbett, L. C., mentioned	92
Corn	225
Cornell experiments, quoted 42, 54, 80, 82, 84, 135, 146, 177, 178, 180 225, 228	
— experience with radishes	121
Cornell, sub-irrigation at	68
Cos lettuce	4
Cost of forcing-houses	46
Cow manure	52
Cresses	141, 142
Cress, mentioned	5
— summary of	247
— temperature for	5
Crops for forcing, category of	4
Crosses of cucumbers	199
Cucumber, account of	184

	Page
Cucumber, mentioned 2, 5, 7, 43, 51, 52, 80, 83	
— prices of	4
— summary of	248
— temperature for	5, 50
Cucumis longus	192
— sativus var. Sikkimensis	194
Cut-flowers and vegetable growing	1
Cut-worms	52
Cyanide of potassium	90
Cyphomandra, account of	241
— temperature for	5
Daintiness of product	3
Damping-off	67, 84, 222
Dandelion	143
— summary of	249
Denitrification	62
Diseases, account of	83
Distance from market	8
Drip	29, 30, 38
Dreer's "Vegetables under Glass," mentioned	16, 118
Dropsy	84, 177
Duke of Northumberland cucumber	193
Eggplant, account of	228
— mentioned	5, 6
— summary of	249, 250
— temperature for	5, 50
Eisen, Gustav, on pepino 149, 150, 151	
Electric light for forcing-houses	80, 94, 101
England, melon in	204
Erysiphe	200, 222
Escarolle	4
Even-span	18
Failures, cause of	3
Fertilizers	52
Fire, risk of	2
Fir-tree oil	176
Flanagan, Patrick, and the cucumber	193
"Flora Peruviana," quoted	149

INDEX.

Florida, pepino in 151
— tomatoes from 7
Flowers and vegetables 7
Flues 46
Forcing crops, category of . . 4
Forrest on cucumbers 194
Framework 24
Frost, risk of 2
Fruit-rot of tomato 177
Fuel, cost of 9, 15
Fumigation 86
Fungi, account of 83
— mentioned . . . 23, 51, 59, 66, 67
Galloway, B. T., on lettuce soils 96
— on radishes 121
"Garden and Forest," quoted. 132, 146, 151, 180
Garden-cress 142
"Gardeners' Magazine," quoted 193
"Gardeners' Monthly," quoted, 149, 151, 152
Gardner, John, on asparagus . 132
— on damping-off 85
Gas pipe and sub-irrigation. 71, 72
Glasgow Botanical Garden, cyphomandra in 244
Glass 36, 207
Glazing 36
Green-fly, 84, 86, 89, 104, 111, 125, 200
Green corn 225
"Greenhouse Construction," mentioned 16
Green, W. J., on lettuce soils . 97
— on sub-irrigation 68, 77
Grelck, J., and pepino 150
Grenadilla 243
Grubs 52
Guatemala, pepino in 149
Gulf states, eggplant in 6
Gutters 24, 33
Hare, Thomas, and the cucumber 193
Hastings, Gen. Russell, on cucumber 196

Heating, account of 40
— cost of 9-15
— item 2
Help, cost of 9-15
Henderson, Peter & Co., on cyphomandra 241
Heterodera radicicola 177
Hooker, Sir J. D., on cucumber 194
Hooker, Sir W. J., on cyphomandra 244
Horse dung 63
Horticultural Soc., Royal, quoted 209
"Hortus Kewensis," quoted . 150
Hotbeds, asparagus in 132
Hot-water heating 40
House-blight of melons 222
Hughes' fir-tree oil 176
Humphrey on damping-off . . . 85
Hydrant water 65
Hydrocyanic gas 90
Illinois, heat and labor in . . . 13
Importance of forcing industry 7
Indiana, heat and labor in . . 13
Indian corn 225
Insects, account of 83
— mentioned 23, 51
Irrigation in forcing-houses . . 68
Ithaca, climate of 113, 211
Jamaica, Tree Tomato of . . . 241
Jenkins, E. H., quoted 53
"Journal Obs. Phys.," quoted . 149
Journal Royal Hort. Soc. quoted 209
Kentucky, heat and labor in . . 15
Kerman, John, on tomato . . . 175
Kerosene, to clean houses . . 84, 85
Kinney pump 68
"Kitchen and Market-Garden," quoted 196
Knight, Thomas Andrew, on melon 204
Kühn on manure 63
Labor, cost of 9-15
— item 2

	Page
Lapped glass	38
Leaf-burn of lettuce	106
Leaf-mold	51
Lean-to	18
Lepidium sativum	142
Lettuce, account of	93
— and sub-irrigation	72, 77
— Cos	4
— electric light on	80
— fertilizing	61
— mentioned	5, 7, 8, 43, 46, 68, 83, 140, 146, 153
— prices of	4
— summary of	250, 251, 252
— temperature for	5, 49
Lima bean	6
Lime whitewash	80
Liquid manure	52
Locations for vegetable forcing	8
Lodeman, quoted	82, 86, 115, 135, 180, 228
London Horticultural Society, mentioned	193
Lonsdale, on damping-off	85
Lye to clean houses	85
Maine Experiment Station, quoted	159, 164, 173
Maize	225
Management of forcing-houses	49
Manure	50, 52, 62
Marketing	3, 8
Marrows	6
Martius, on cyphomandra	244
Massachusetts bulletins, quoted	35, 42, 53, 85
— heat and labor in	11
Massey, on damping-off	85
Maynard, on damping-off	85
— on heating	42
Mealy-bugs	84, 221, 237, 243
Meehan, on damping-off	85
Melon, account of	204
— mentioned	2, 3, 5, 6, 7, 17, 43, 51, 52, 53, 65, 67

	Page
Melon fruit, Brazilian	243
— pear	147
— shrub	147
Melongena laurifolia	149
Mentha viridis	143
Michigan bulletins, quoted	42, 165, 241
— heat and labor in	12
Micrococcus in winter blight	182
Mildew of lettuce	106
— mentioned	10, 83, 84
Mills, George, on melon	209
Minnesota bulletins, quoted	35
— heat and labor in	13
Mints, account of	141, 143
Mint, temperature for	5
Mites	84, 90, 176, 200, 221, 228, 237
Mold, leaf	51
Mortises	33
Moss	67
M'Phail, quoted	192
Munson, W. M., experiments with tomatoes	159, 164, 173
— — on pepino	146, 152
Muskmelon, account of	204
— summary of	252, 253, 254
— temperature for	5, 50
— see also Melon	
Mustard	143
— temperature for	5
Naphtha, in whitewash	80
Naudin, on cucumbers	194
Nematode	84, 177
New Hampshire bulletin, quoted	69
New Jersey, heat and labor in	14
— — pepino in	152
— — Station, quoted	54
New York Exp. Station, quoted	99
— — heat and labor in	11
"Nicholson's Dictionary of Gardening," quoted	196
Night man	10
Nitrogen and forcing crops	54
— availability of	62

INDEX.

	Page
Nitrogen, loss of	62
Œdema	177
Ohio bulletins, quoted	53, 69, 72, 97, 104
— Station, sub-irrigation at	68
Oidium	200, 222
Okra	225
Onion, account of	144
— temperature for	5
Ontario, heat and labor in	11
— tomatoes in	157
"Orchard and Garden," quoted	149, 151, 152
Packing	3
Parsley, account of	142
— and sub-irrigation	77
— summary of	254
— temperature for	5
Pea, account of	135
— electric light on	80
— mentioned	5, 6
— summary of	254
— temperature for	5
Peat	51
Pennock, C. J., on tomato growing	163, 167, 169
Pennsylvania, heat and labor in	13
Pepino, account of	146
— de la tierra	150
— mentioned	6
— summary of	254
— temperature for	5
Pepo	149
Pepper, account of	238
— mentioned	5, 6
— prices of	5
— summary of	255
— temperature for	5, 50
Peronospora gangliformis	106
Peru, pepino in	149
Pie-plant	134
Piping	16, 41, 43
"Plantes Potagères," quoted	192, 194

	Page
Plants and vegetables	7
Plate	30
Pollination	81, 162, 195, 214, 236
Potato	146
Pot-herbs, account of	141
Prices of hothouse vegetables	4
Purlines	26
Putty, recipe for	37
Radish, account of	115
— electric light on	80
— mentioned	5, 6
— summary of	255, 256
— temperature for	5, 49
Radishes and sub-irrigation	77
Rafters	26
Rain water	68
Rane, F. W., on electric light	80
— — on sub-irrigation, 69, 71, 77, 78	
Rawson, W. W., on electric light	80
— — on lettuce growing	102, 104
Red pepper: See Pepper.	
Red spiders (see Mites)	84, 228, 237
"Revue Horticole," quoted	189
Rhubarb, account of	127, 134
— mentioned	7
— summary of	256
— temperature for	5, 49, 50
Ridge-pole	33
Risks in forcing business	2
Romain salad	4
Roofs	17, 18, 24
Root crops	145
Root-galls	79, 84, 87, 177
Rose-leaf extract of tobacco	89
Rotation of crops	7
Rot of lettuce	105
— of tomato	177
Rousignon, on pepino	151
Royal Hort. Soc., quoted	209
Ruiz and Pavon, on pepino	149
"Rural New-Yorker," quoted	144
Rust of tomato	52, 177
Sage	143
Salads, account of	141

INDEX.

	Page
Salad, Romain	4
Sash-bars	27, 29, 37
Sash-bar roofs	26
Sash for ventilating	35
Scott, William, on asparagus	132
Sea-kale	4, 128
Sewer pipe and sub-irrigation	70
Seymour, on damping-off	85
Shading, account of	78
Shed roofs	17, 18
Shepherd, Theodosia B., on cyphomandra	243
Shipping	3, 8
Short-span-to-the-south	23
Side-hill houses	24
Sikkim cucumber	194
Sion House, cucumber	193
Soil and forcing	8
Soils, account of	50, 66, 96
Solanum fragrans	244
— Guatemalense	147
— Melongena	151
— muricatum	150
South America, cyphomandra in	243
Spearmint	143
Spiders, red	84, 228, 237
Spinach	142
— and sub-irrigation	77
— electric light on	80
— mentioned	6
— summary of	256
— temperature for	5
Spraying for insects and diseases	84
— roofs	80
Squashes	6, 225
Stable manure	50, 52, 62
Staple crops	5
Steam heating	40
Stoves	46
String beans	6, 225
Sturtevant, quoted	192, 194
Sub-irrigation	68
Sulphur, evaporating	84, 91, 106
Sulphuric acid	90
Sun-scald	79
Sun-scorching	79
Taft, on cost of houses	46
— on heating	42
Taft's "Greenhouse Construction," mentioned	16
Tear-drops in glass	207
Temperatures for various crops	5, 49
Tenons	33
Tetranychus bimaculatus	90, 176, 221
Thoreau, on melon	205
Thouin, on pepino	150
Tiles and sub-irrigation	70
Tobacco extract	89
— for fumigation	87, 104, 111
Tomato, account of	153
— de la Paz	243
— fertilizers for	53
— mentioned	2, 3, 5, 7, 8, 17, 43, 44, 52, 53, 67, 184
— prices of	4
— summary of	256, 257, 258, 259
— temperature for	5, 50
Tomatoes and sub-irrigation	77
Top burn of lettuce	106
Transportation facilities	8
Tree tomato of Jamaica	241
Turnip, account of	145
Tweedie, and the cyphomandra	243
Uneven-span	18, 36
Van Fleet, W., on onions	144
"Vegetable Forcing," mentioned	16, 92
"Vegetables under Glass," mentioned	16, 118
Ventilating, account of	78
Ventilators	35
Vilmorin, quoted	192, 194
Violets, fumigating	90
Wagner on manure	62, 63
Walker, C. D., on electric currents	80

	Page
Walks	16, 17, 24
Walls	16, 33
Warm plants	4, 50
Washington experience with radishes	121
— heat and labor in	15
Water-cress	141
Water heating	40
Watering, account of	65
— mentioned	9, 50
Watermelon	205

	Page
Watson, on damping-off	85
West Virginia Station and sub-irrigation	69, 71
— — — electric light at	80
White Spine cucumbers	201
Whitewash	80
Winkler's "Vegetable Forcing," mentioned	16, 93
Winter blight	180
Wire-worms	52

The Garden-Craft Series.
Edited by Prof. L. H. Bailey.

THE HORTICULTURIST'S RULE-BOOK.
A COMPENDIUM OF USEFUL INFORMATION FOR FRUIT-GROWERS, TRUCK-GARDENERS, FLORISTS, AND OTHERS.

By L. H. BAILEY,
Professor of Horticulture in Cornell University.

Third Edition, Thoroughly Revised and Recast, with Many Additions.
16mo. 302 pages. Cloth, Limp, 75 Cents.

This volume is the only attempt ever made in this country to codify and condense all the scattered rules, practices, recipes, figures and histories relating to horticultural practice in its broadest sense. All the approved methods of fighting insects and plant diseases used and discovered by all the experiment stations are set forth in shape for instant reference.

Among the additions to the volume in the present edition are: A chapter upon "Greenhouse and Window-garden Work and Estimates;" a chapter on "Literature," giving classified lists of the leading current writings on American horticulture; lists of self-fertile and self-sterile fruits; a full account of the method of predicting frosts and of averting their injuries; a discussion of the aims and methods of phenology; the rules of nomenclature adopted by botanists and horticultural societies; score-cards and scales of points for judging various fruits, vegetables and flowers; a full statement of the metric system, and tables of foreign money.

PLANT-BREEDING.
By L. H. BAILEY.
16mo. 293 pages. Cloth, Limp, $1.00.
Uniform with "The Horticulturist's Rule-Book."

CONTENTS.

The Fact and Philosophy of Variation.
The Philosophy of the Crossing of Plants.
Specific Means by which Garden Varieties originate.
Borrowed Opinions, of B. Verlot, E. A. Carrière, and W. O. Focke, on Plant-Breeding.
Detailed Directions for the Crossing of Plants.

COMMENTS.

"I have read the work on 'Plant Breeding' by Prof. L. H. Bailey with keen interest, and find it just what I expected from such a source; viz., a most satisfactory treatise on a subject of most pressing horticultural importance. I shall earnestly commend the work to my horticultural classes."
E. J. WICKSON,
Agricultural Experiment Station, Berkeley, Cal.

"The treatment is both scientific and practical, and will enable gardeners and horticulturists to experiment intelligently in cross-breeding. The subject is fully elaborated, and made clear for every intelligent reader. Professor Bailey's reputation, founded upon careful labor and observations in original investigations, is still further enhanced by the presentation of this excellent manual."—*Vick's Monthly.*

THE MACMILLAN COMPANY,
66 Fifth Avenue, NEW YORK.

The Garden-Craft Series.
Edited by Prof. L. H. BAILEY.

THE NURSERY-BOOK.

By L. H. BAILEY.

New Edition. Thoroughly recast and revised.

16 mo. Cloth, $1.00.

This little manual has been one of the most popular of all current horticultural books. It contains no discussions of the theory or physiology of the propagation of plants, but it is a simple and practical account of all the ways in which plants are multiplied. It has found a wide circulation, both amongst nurserymen and amateurs. Many new illustrations have been made for this edition, bringing the number of cuts up to over 150. In its revised form, the Nursery Book is the most complete propagating manual in the language.

IN PREPARATION.

THE PRUNING-BOOK.

By L. H. BAILEY.

It is strange that the one subject upon which horticulturists have always asked the most questions should be wholly without a treatise. The subject of pruning is so vitally connected with every horticultural occupation, and the questions which it presents are so numerous and so difficult of answer, that nothing less than an entire volume can ever set people right in respect to it. Professor Bailey has been making definite experiments and observations upon the subject for a number of years, and the results of these labors are now approaching readiness for publication. The work will comprise the entire range of the theory and practice of pruning, both of fruit and ornamental trees and bushes, and it is expected to be on sale early in 1897.

THE FORCING-BOOK.

By L. H. BAILEY.

THE MACMILLAN COMPANY.
66 Fifth Avenue, NEW YORK.

The Rural Science Series.
Edited by PROF. L. H. BAILEY.

THE SOIL.

ITS NATURE, RELATIONS, AND FUNDAMENTAL PRINCIPLES OF MANAGEMENT.

By FRANKLIN H. KING,

Professor of Agricultural Physics, University of Wisconsin.

16mo. Cloth. 303 pages. Price, 75 cts.

CONTENTS: Introduction.—Sunshine and its Work, The Atmosphere and its Work, Water and its Work, Living Forms and their Work, Over and Over Again; The Nature, Functions, Origin, and Wasting of Soils; Texture, Composition, and Kinds of Soil; Nitrogen of the Soil; Capillarity, Solution, Diffusion, and Osmosis; Soil Water; Conservation of Soil Moisture; Distribution of Roots in the Soil; Soil Temperature; Relation of Air to Soil; Farm Drainage; Irrigation; Physical Effects of Tillage and Fertilizers.

COMMENTS.

"I consider it a most desirable addition to our agricultural literature, and a distinct advance over previous treatises on the same subject, not only for popular use, but also for students and specialists, who will find many new and useful suggestions therein." E. W. HILGARD,
Director of Agricultural Experiment Station, Berkeley, Cal.

THE SPRAYING OF PLANTS.

By E. G. LODEMAN,

Instructor in Horticulture in Cornell University.

16mo. Cloth. 399 pages. Price, $1.00.

CONTENTS.

PART I. *The History and Principles of the Spraying of Plants.*
PART II. *Specific Directions for the Spraying of Cultivated Plants.*

COMMENTS.

"This volume of the Rural Science Series not only gives a complete history of this comparatively new and important subject, but is a valuable manual as well, which should be in the hands of every farmer, gardener and fruit-grower. I shall take pleasure in recommending it to my students and others."
B. C. BUFFUM,
The University of Wyoming Agricultural College, Laramie, Wyo.

"This is a book for every gardener and every one who has a garden, for every fruit-grower and every farmer. The necessity of spraying for a great variety of garden, field, and fruit crops is now so generally recognized that a manual on the subject has become a necessity. The destruction of injurious insects and fungi occupies an important place in the operations of gardeners, farmers, and fruit-growers, and the very careful and elaborate manner in which the subject is treated in this volume is highly creditable to the author, and commends it to the attention of every cultivator."—*Vick's Monthly.*

THE MACMILLAN COMPANY.
66 Fifth Avenue, NEW YORK.

The Rural Science Series.
Edited by PROF. L. H. BAILEY.

IN THE PRESS.

THE APPLE.
By L. H. BAILEY.

The work is to comprise two parts—the first treating of all the practical matters of apple-growing, and the second of such scientific matters as the botany of the apple, its history and evolution, production of new varieties, and the like. It is expected that the work will be completed and ready for publication in the fall.

MILK AND ITS PRODUCTS.
By H. H. WING.

THE FERTILITY OF THE LAND.
By I. P. ROBERTS.

Other volumes in the series to follow are:

Physiology of Plants. By J. C. ARTHUR, of Purdue University.

Grasses. By W. H. BREWER, of Yale University.

Bush Fruits. By F. W. CARD, of University of Nebraska.

Plant Diseases. By B. T. GALLOWAY, E. F. SMITH, and A. F. WOODS, of the United States Department of Agriculture.

Seeds and Seed Growing. By G. H. HICKS, of the United States Department of Agriculture.

Leguminous Plants. By E. W. HILGARD, of the University of California.

Feeding of Animals. By W. H. JORDAN, of Maine Experiment Station.

Irrigation. By F. H. KING, of the University of Wisconsin.

IN PREPARATION.

EVOLUTION OF OUR NATIVE FRUITS.
By L. H. BAILEY.

THE MACMILLAN COMPANY.
66 Fifth Avenue, NEW YORK.

www.ingramcontent.com/pod-product-compliance
Lightning Source LLC
Chambersburg PA
CBHW032112230426
43672CB00009B/1706